What Ever Happened to the Faculty?

What Ever Happened to the Faculty?

Drift and Decision in Higher Education

Mary Burgan

The Johns Hopkins University Press
Baltimore

© 2006 The Johns Hopkins University Press
All rights reserved. Published 2006
Printed in the United States of America on acid-free paper
9 8 7 6 5 4 3 2

The Johns Hopkins University Press
2715 North Charles Street
Baltimore, Maryland 21218-4363
www.press.jhu.edu

Library of Congress Cataloging-in-Publication Data

Burgan, Mary.
   What ever happened to the faculty? : drift and decision in higher
education / Mary Burgan.
      p.   cm.
   Includes bibliographical references and index.
   ISBN 0-8018-8461-6 (hardcover : alk. paper)
   1. Universities and colleges—United States—Faculty. 2. Universities and
colleges—United States—Administration. I. Title.
LB2331.72.B87 2006
378.1'94—dc22   2006009630

A catalog record for this book is available from the British Library.

For Bill

Contents

Acknowledgments

This book owes much to the many students and colleagues with whom I have worked throughout my years in higher education. To try to name them one by one would obscure the ways in which they have helped me by burying them in a litany of praise. I therefore mention only a few names from places in the academy where I have found advice, help, and a practice of the ideals I've tried to explicate here. My most significant and continuing debt is acknowledged in the dedication of this book.

I must mention, first, my colleagues from Indiana University–Bloomington. In my first major administrative assignment there, I benefited from the example of Jack Shiner, dean of the College of Arts and Sciences, whose leadership derived from his stature as a chemist as well as his instinct for the valuable connection between teaching and research. Among my colleagues in the Department of English and in the American Association of University Professors (AAUP) at Indiana, I should single out Don Gray, who read a bit of the present manuscript, and Paul Strohm, who not only led faculty governance on the campus but encouraged my writing about educational topics when he was editor of *Academe*. I have only recently discovered that the subtitle for the issue of *Academe* in which Paul Strohm published my essay on "the superstar syndrome" was "Whatever Happened to the Faculty?" Carol Bastian, one of many who began as my student and remained as a colleague, gave me specific and thoughtful advice on the manuscript from her viewpoint as a retired professor of English at Centre College.

Many colleagues from elsewhere have made direct contributions to my thinking about higher education. The faculty of the Lilly Endowment Workshop on the Liberal Arts, with whom I worked from 1987 to 1994, introduced me to ideas from outside English departments: among them, I single out here the late Frank Newman—with whom I engaged in friendly skirmishes through the years. David Noble introduced me to the issues involved in "digital diploma mills" at the important conference he convened under that title on the Harvey

Mudd campus at Claremont in 1998. More recently, Professor William O. Pruitt, of the University of Manitoba, has read and commented on my chapter on science. The scholars at the Center for Studies in Higher Education at the University of California, Berkeley, gave me an office and an opportunity to discuss much of what I was writing about during the spring term of 2004–5. I also owe a debt to many colleagues from the Modern Language Association and the Association of Departments of English. Cary Nelson was one member of MLA who made a difference in my thinking there, and at the AAUP as well, both in his writing and in his activism.

My debts to colleagues in the AAUP are to be found everywhere in this book. In my ten years as director of the Association I worked with three elected presidents—Jim Perley, Jim Richardson, and Jane Buck—and with many other faculty leaders who freely shared their expertise. Among the gifted and dedicated national AAUP staff, I should thank, specifically, John Curtis, who read an early draft of my chapter on distance learning, and Mark Smith, who tutored me on lobbying in higher education. I also mention Mike Mauer and Ernie Benjamin, with whom I collaborated in launching a forthcoming joint MLA/AAUP book on academic collective bargaining. I have learned about the law in higher education from David Rabban and Michael Olivas, AAUP general counsels, as well as from the superb lawyers on the AAUP staff. During my time as general secretary, Robert M. O'Neil and Joan Wallach Scott, chairs of the AAUP Committee on Academic Freedom, have been models of thoughtful activism on behalf of the professoriate. And I have also learned from AAUP stalwarts who are leading scholars in the field of higher education—especially Bill Tierney, Sheila Slaughter, and Jack Schuster. In the early stages of my research, AAUP gave me the help of a fine student intern—Mary McIlhenny from the University of Alaska. She reminded me at the outset of the interests and energy of undergraduate students.

I hope that any critical comments I have made about the higher education "establishment" in Washington will not obscure my debts to colleagues in the Washington Higher Education Secretariat. Even when resisting some of their views, I have never doubted that we were working together for the benefit of the academy as a whole. I have also made use of the American Council on Education library at One Dupont Circle and thank Jill Bogard for her help there. She led me to search the *New Yorker* cover archives for a dust jacket illustration. Charles E. Martin's 1973 frieze of a graduation ceremony seemed to suit the book's themes—with one important omission, its depiction of an all-male, all-white academy. Affirmative action has changed that pattern during the past forty years—and enabled my own career in higher education.

My work at AAUP put me in touch with colleagues abroad. I have benefited greatly from interactions with faculty in the Canadian Association of University Teachers and La Fédération québécoise des professeures et professeurs d'université. Jim Turk, the director of CAUT, read and commented on a prospectus for this book. My sense of the faculty stake in globalization was established through conversations at meetings of Education International, especially with colleagues from faculty associations in Australia, New Zealand, Ireland, and Denmark. These interchanges convinced me that what I have described about American higher education applies in many other parts of the world.

Much of the thinking in this book was done amid the bustle of the AAUP office in Washington. Its beginnings and conclusion were encouraged by Jacqueline Wehmueller, the extraordinary executive editor for higher education at the Johns Hopkins University Press. Alice Falk, a peerless friend and critic, had the task of making the text correct and clear; her editing has clarified the logic of some arguments and cleared up some patches of tangled prose. The concentrated writing started in September 2004, at the Rockefeller Study and Conference Center in Bellagio, Italy, in the company of an especially sympathetic group of colleagues. My month's residency there reassured me that despite all my misgivings about the academy, it is still a place where the life of the mind and spirit can flourish.

In asking "What ever happened to the faculty?" I mean to give notice that their *presence* has always been a gift for me.

Introduction

The concerns in this book began to take shape when I was leading a task force on teaching for the Faculty Council at Indiana University–Bloomington in the spring of 1990. After a seven-year stint as chair of the Department of English, I had just moved from administration back to the faculty. I had made a similar move in 1981 when I joined the Faculty Council after being an associate dean in the College of Arts and Sciences for half a dozen years. Indeed, throughout my academic life at Indiana, I regularly shifted between administrative and faculty work. Early on, I became director of the freshman programs in English and thenceforth served the university happily as a hybrid—departmental administrator, associate dean, member and chair of the Faculty Council. I was asked to bring to the task force, then, the perspectives I had gained over the years as a faculty member involved in administration.

During my term as chair of a large humanities department in the 1980s, however, I had already begun to have the uneasy feelings that permeate the arguments of this book. Those feelings crystallized during my year on the Task Force on Teaching as I discussed the connections between teaching and research with my colleagues. Our committee had been formed as a result of a request that the Faculty Council respond to a proposal to accept a new "clinical" rank designated for teaching faculty who would not have access to tenure. Many members of the council were disturbed by the prospect of inserting such an official demarcation between the "real" faculty and the merely "teaching" faculty, and wanted the task force to study the issues. It became clear that we needed to articulate our ideas about the status of teaching on our campus, its relationship to research, and the changes that should be made to keep a reasonable balance between the two.

The task force enlisted the membership of respected colleagues from across the campus. There were professors of business, education, and fine arts as well as biology, chemistry, economics, French, and telecommunications. There was also an advanced teaching assistant (TA) from sociology and the current undergraduate student body president. The group got along well and finally agreed on almost every detail. Its report strongly supported tenure for all faculty and, in doing so, recommended that a concept of "the balanced case" be added to the *Faculty Handbook*'s criteria for tenure. The balanced case was intended to enforce the notion that a worthy career might combine solid, if not nationally prominent, research with unusual talents in teaching and service; it was a balance of the three that could warrant the institution's commitment of tenure. Of course, Indiana tenure committees had found such cases to be legitimate in the past, even though they were likely to fiddle with definitions to accentuate the research component. But the Task Force on Teaching believed that the emphasis on research had by now begun to overshadow other considerations in a candidate's tenure dossier. Especially troubling was a newly emphatic dependence on letters of recommendation from authorities outside the institution. Clearly, such a dependence privileged research; evaluators from the outside could hardly be competent to comment on a candidate's local teaching or service.[1] The task force also reasoned that sensible decisions based on talents other than research would be negated if a non-tenure "clinical" rank were instituted. Why give tenure to good teachers when they could be retained off the tenure track?

The task force's proposal on the balanced case seemed sensible and modest to me, but I was struck by the institutional anxieties that it inspired. Some members of the administration worried that such an acknowledgment of teaching and service would suggest that the institution had been slack in the past. And some of the science faculty and members of the medical school were equally concerned that any official articulation of the balanced case might undermine their aspirations to the kind of national prominence gained only through research. Overall among the critics of the report, there was a fear that we might lose our competitive edge, despite our institution's fine reputation and its obvious emphasis on the discovery and promulgation of knowledge. When the balanced case provision passed the Faculty Council, one dean vowed that he would never permit it to be invoked for tenure or promotion in his school.

The task force report also suggested reforms in other campus activities that impinged on undergraduate student welfare—faculty teaching loads, for example, course scheduling, and faculty involvement in student activities. Our proposal for variable course loads for professors whose research had lapsed was suspect among some faculty as being punitive—even though research failures were already "punished" by low salaries, with little chance given to catch up.

We wanted faculty whose research was "in hiatus" to be able to negotiate added teaching to compensate—with a per-course stipend to increase their income and perhaps free them from summer teaching so that they could return to their research projects. Moreover, our notion that the university teaching awards should entail a continuing effect on annual salaries rather than a once-only cash award was rejected as too costly—even though the research-based designation *distinguished professor* carried such an arrangement. And the expectation that every faculty member be involved in teaching at the introductory or under-graduate levels seemed impractical in those departments where advanced TAs were already teaching upper-level courses. I was bemused by the controversy, even though the report was well received among most faculty and among alumni and other university supporters. Indeed, it was a great hit when I presented it to Indiana supporters and alums in the Bloomington North Rotary Club; there I heard comments of delighted surprise that the faculty would actually criticize itself and commit to reasonable adjustments. But I was shocked when the only nontenured faculty member of our task force announced later at an AAUP meeting that her work on the task force had "politicized" her because it had revealed how perilous her love of teaching might be for her career. I was struck by her passion, for she had been a "safe" assistant professor; the chair of her department had permitted me to draft her for the committee because her book was under contract at an esteemed university press. She got tenure the following year.

And I must now confess that my work with the Task Force on Teaching politicized me, as well. The feelings of unease I had during our investigations helped influence my decision to leave my own teaching and research to take on the directorship of the American Association of University Professors as its general secretary. That decision was not a rejection of my institution, which I continue to admire as a humane and progressive school. But even in this excellent university, I could see shifts away from faculty teaching and service that were symptomatic of major problems appearing in higher education everywhere. As state support for higher education was waning, for example, I had already begun to feel the effects of a new emphasis on finding "outside" sponsorship for my department. I was acutely uncomfortable with the notion that we could turn every faculty administrator into an entrepreneur through a new system of "responsibility-centered management." And as chair, I had been regularly harried by my dean to think about raising our department's already very good national rankings.

As classes expanded and more and more teaching was handed over to TAs, I also worried about the experience of ordinary Hoosiers who were coming to Bloomington for an education. I verified their problems when I volunteered to become a "faculty friend" to the fourth floor, east, of a women's dorm on campus, for there I found passels of cheerful young women who had barely a clue about what was going on in their introductory psych or poli-sci or math classes. One was from Milan (pronounced *Mylun*, with the accent on the first syllable), that one-horse Indiana town with the famous basketball team that won the state championship in 1954. She mentioned that there were special sessions for honors students in her poli-sci lecture class. "But what about me?" she said. "I'm not an A student, so I need help more than they do!" I worried over her experience. That's why I criticized programs for honors students when they seemed to be offered as a substitute for faculty encounters with ordinary students. I thought that setting up faculty-taught seminars for a small percentage of the incoming class could not hide the fact that introductory courses were becoming larger and the students in them more anonymous. And besides, this Indiana undergraduate had a father in the state legislature; what would happen if we lost his support and that of his fellow legislators—not to mention the public in general?

The concerns that drove the report of the Task Force on Teaching became even more imperative during my ensuing ten years as general secretary of the American Association of University Professors. I experienced them afresh as I plunged into the swirl of representing the faculty within the higher education establishment in Washington. After absorbing the shock of trying to find my way in a world of association acronyms, Department of Education initiatives, and educational reforms coming from various quarters, I began to observe that the faculty themselves were hardly ever present in the imaginations of the policy makers. I had long held the provincial notion that "the faculty *are* the university," but I soon realized that only a few of those who officially represent higher education appreciated being reminded of that formulation. After all, it derived from a Columbia University professor's correcting President Dwight D. Eisenhower when he addressed them as "employees of the university."

Perhaps the most significant discovery I made in my initiation to the national scene was that faculty members actually *were* seen as "employees" who require to be suffered, led, negotiated with, cajoled, and kept out of trouble. While my colleagues back in Indiana, and in AAUP everywhere, clung to that traditional claim of faculty centrality in higher education, some of my new friends in higher education circles found it merely annoying. If the faculty *were* the university, why were they so ignorant about some of its realities and so unable to compromise on them? About tenure, for example, one of the main faculty concerns, my new association colleagues could barely summon a pretense of interest. Most of them seemed to believe that tenure was a hindrance, and, anyhow, it had become so rare that fussing about it was a waste of time. Some of them had matching sentiments against shared governance as well as a pronounced animus against faculty collective bargaining. The higher education establishment was wise and active on matters that pertained to many of the interests of higher education, to be sure, but they considered the faculty as merely one among many stakeholder groups in that vast enterprise.

I found that my Washington colleagues in the higher education association world, gathered in and around One Dupont Circle (the address of the National Center for Higher Education), served educational stakeholders very well on the whole. They worried about costs, access, federal grants and loans, and the uses of technology in teaching. They could be counted on to defend affirmative action, women's equity, and the new "service" or "civic" learning programs designed to make students aware of the responsibilities of citizenship. They were enchanted with distance learning but at the same time apprehensive about the growth of proprietary schools. Although they drew sustenance from the hefty dues paid by member institutions to their associations, they showed significant wariness about the political and managerial activities of boards of trustees—advocating seasoned leadership from that quarter but warning against meddling. They seemed to me both smart and effective in lobbying for the interests of colleges and universities, making sure to maintain a bipartisan stance at all times. In their practical cast of mind, and because of their backgrounds (many of them had been college or university presidents), they tended both to trust academic CEOs—using that term in increasing preference to "president"—and to sympathize with them. Given these preoccupations, they tended not to worry about faculty fortunes, for they rightly considered that if the institutions of American higher education survived, so would the faculty.

All politics is local, and so even as I noted the absence of some specific faculty interests in our nation's capital, I found them in plenty as I visited colleges across the country. Although I was impressed by the good faith and commitment of faculty in the trenches, I also perceived that they were so overwhelmed by the demands of their positions that they had to struggle to keep themselves together as effective and continuing activists for their profession. Indeed, although they shared the concerns of Washington's higher education establishment, they needed more immediate solutions than those offered by the necessarily general statements emanating from One Dupont Circle. Many of them felt that their specific interests were muffled by administrative pep talks couched in the current managerial jargon. And their sense that the immediacy of their problems was alien to their leaders, local and national, could lead to antagonism toward all academic administration.

For example, professors around the country, and in their disciplinary societies, were alarmed about the rise of what they called "contingent" faculty. But their administrative leaders seemed mainly relieved to have such a reservoir of cheap and flexible instruction at hand. While many faculty sought to raise the alarm over the growth of these exploited colleagues, deans and provosts appeared to find such efforts unrealistic and wondered why term contracts were not satisfactory. The faculty also seemed extra cranky about administrative efforts to install information technology as the solution to all the problems in their labors. I observed, however, that faculty resistance often derived from their frustration at already working overtime to keep abreast of technology. No one seemed to notice that they were beset by floods of e-mail from their students, the prevalence of Internet plagiarism, class sizes that were ballooning, and service responsibilities made the more onerous by the absence of tenured colleagues to share the load.

Nevertheless, in multifarious areas throughout higher education, I found generous and impassioned faculty members seeking to act cooperatively on the crises of the day. The faculty in religiously affiliated schools continued their historic efforts to thread a way between belief and academic freedom amid the growth of doctrinal rigidity. Physician professors in medical schools fretted over the massive changes in teaching and research triggered by the always looming crisis of funding for medical education and care. Every campus I visited featured committees of women faculty who were engaged in building access, equity, and status for themselves and their graduate students. It was these women faculty who joined other "minority" faculty to maintain an emphasis on diversity in a decade when that term was being loaded with negative implications. The courage of faculty activists in seeking to loosen the hierarchical bindings of control in historically black colleges and universities was a revelation. Moreover, a considerable segment of faculty leaders at schools with big-time sports were continuing the age-old effort of academics to control the excesses of intercollegiate competition. Though the standing of faculty senates has fallen in some institutions, there were still diehards ready to ramp up faculty governance to meet one campus crisis or another. And, after 9/11, every faculty member I met was profoundly concerned about the maintenance of academic freedom in our time of crisis.

In talking about these faculty efforts in Washington, however, I also came to recognize an entirely new phenomenon—the rising resentment of the faculty by some reformers within the establishment who seemed inclined to locate the causes of all our problems in professorial intransigence or carelessness. It also became clear that this resentment found a fertile field for growth in a society that was becoming unsteady in its values. In an age of technology, why insist on the expensive, labor-intensive work of individual teachers with individual students? In an age of universal job insecurity, why give faculty special claims to employment protections? In an age of total politics, why accept any judgment about public policy or American history or even science as disinterested? As for research, it should be limited to presenting data without conclusions; those could be made by the various think tanks that had sprung up to spin out theories satisfying to their patrons on everything from economics to evolution.

This book brings together the misgivings and insights of such observations of faculty, students, and administrators in order to consider higher education from a faculty member's point of view. Although many of the points made here were first articulated at AAUP meetings or in the pages of *Academe*, this book does not represent official AAUP policy, and indeed some of my AAUP friends will strongly disagree with parts of it. Nevertheless, our work together has provided some of the happiest times of my career. And my view of American higher education has benefited from conversations with the wise administrators I worked with at Indiana and met with in Washington as well. Those academic leaders—the chairs, deans, program directors, and presidents who still consider themselves members of the faculty—are among the most dedicated and effective people I know in higher education. I have argued with them on some occasions, but I continue to respect and learn from their views and believe that faculty should do the same.

With all the debts I owe to colleagues, however, it may be that the most important influence in preparing this study has been the opportunity to return to campus life once again as a visitor in the Center for the Study of Higher Education at the University of California, Berkeley. There, from an office in the South Hall Annex, in the center of a marvelous campus and next door to the library, I have had the chance to renew my sense of the vitality of a campus community. The most rewarding features of my life as a faculty member were refreshed for me as I mingled with students at the Free Speech Café in the undergraduate library, rediscovering the exhilaration of finding the exact right book there on its shelf in the stacks. I also noticed the wholly new phenomenon of the wired campus—the student walking down a campus slope with white iPod lines dangling from his ears or a cell phone cupping her face. I was jolted from my ten years of work in Washington back into a world of quiet writing broken by the shuffles of sneakers at change of class times, the rhythms of exam anxiety and post-exam euphoria, and then the sublime quietude of a campus on break.

Behind these familiar sights and sounds, I've sensed that hordes of scruffy young people from every race and background imaginable are seeking education as never before. Driven by economic insecurity, dreams of greater affluence and status, or both, they are now pursuing knowledge, relationships, and the solace of some kind of community through new style electronics—and old-fashioned beer. I've also sensed their idealism at work. The first rumble of student activism I heard outside my window at Berkeley turned out to be an ROTC drill squad running up the hill in formation. But I also saw a phalanx of students marching in the spirit and raggedy dress of the old Berkeley; they were demonstrating against the decline in minority enrollment on the campus. And then at the lunch hour on Fridays, I would stop at Sproul Plaza to listen in when a group of well-rehearsed young women performed very spiffy versions of pop standards for no obvious cause other than their delight in their own mastery.

I've wondered how well I or their teachers can know such students these days, for in the digital age, their pursuits have become highly internalized, seemingly shared mainly through their wires. Are their bewildering, muted choices as deafening as they seem to me? Is there any way to unhook the mechanics—take out the wires, turn off the laptops, and shut down the messaging—to find out what they aspire to? Can the faculty I've observed stepping from one class to another have the kinds of rich exchange with such students that I valued throughout my own teaching life? Can they serve as admired mentors and models for the promise of the examined life that Socrates mandated? Do faculty understand their own role, or stake, in the institutional changes that threaten this vital, mutual exploration?

The urgency of these questions informs this book as deeply as it did when I was a "real" faculty member a decade ago, writing a report on teaching in higher education at my own institution.

❧ ❧ ❧

There are many books about higher education these days—critiques marked by varying degrees of polemical fervor from the right and left, sociological and statistical analyses by scholars of higher education, and memoirs by retired presidents and assorted administrators. My aim is to write less as a social scientist or retrospective administrator than as a faculty member in the humanities. It will be no surprise that driving my account is a belief that the slow but steady acceptance of the market model of competition now being applied to American education is a colossal blunder that threatens its very identity. I assume that education is one of our most precious services to one another, but that under market pressures, colleges and universities are in danger of losing their ability to provide human answers to the very human problems that are evolving in this twenty-first century. To those who are familiar with recent critiques of higher education, my conviction will be familiar. Over the past ten years, analyses of academic "corporatization" have multiplied—some for, some against, and some resigned at its inevitability. As a faculty member, I am not resigned at all. Despite my solidarity with antimarket colleagues, however, I want also to challenge them to consider what to do about the absence of faculty power. Given the economic facts of academic life, where choices seem inexorably determined by the market, what can faculty do to resist?

Thus my critique is directed not only at the managerial establishment but at the faculty establishment as well. I believe that my colleagues have at times ignored the rising tide of academic competition, responding more passively than they would care to admit. Sometimes they have actually joined the flow. One of my motives, then, is to describe where the faculty itself has been complicit in forces that drive the market model of higher education as a business— a market that requires it to break even without public support, or indeed to show a profit. On the one hand, I certainly agree that colleges and universities must be both efficient and effective (and that they cannot be one without the other). But because I also believe that our colleges and universities are more than the sum of their statistics, on the other hand I call on American faculty to become more active in defending the immeasurable value of what they do. In the current environment ruled by the dismal science, faculty must defend their vocations as scholar-teachers not only in rhetorical flourishes but in daily institutional decisions. And so my title asks, "What ever happened to the faculty?"

The question itself presupposes a former time when faculty were a more decisive presence in the governance of higher education. Thus it is true that my book is conservative; it often looks back to abandoned faculty practices as possible solutions for present problems. It is also conservative in its suspicion of the universal invocation of "change" as the solution to the root problems in education, for this emphasis often veils an irrational fear of being caught behind the leading market edge. I became aware of how powerfully this fear drove policy in some academic circles during the dot-com bubble. It remains potent, even though institutions that didn't buy into "change" in those days are now relieved that they had been so wise. Finally, there are traces of intellectual conservatism in my opposition to the faculty taking refuge in their disciplines—and especially the esoterica of their specializations. Although I honor philosophical efforts to probe more deeply into the ways in which commonly accepted values have been shaped by social preferences and economic determinants, I believe that we have now come to a point of necessary return to some common ideals. Our students need more from us than sophisticated uncertainties about things that matter.

In order to recapture their authority, I am convinced, faculty will first need to shed the blinders that have been provided by their own tolerance for the status game both in their institutions and in their personal careers. The universal criticism by friends and foes alike is that faculty members have become so specialized that they cannot act for the benefit of the whole. Neither have they shown much aptitude for organizing themselves for fights beyond the issues of salaries and workload and parking. Having led a powerful faculty organization, I must acknowledge the validity of this criticism. Despite my years observing passionately caring colleagues from a wide variety of schools and disciplines, I have to admit that they are a minority among the faculty in understanding that the crisis in the academy mandates intense and continuous attention. Once they have received tenure, too many professors seem content to let well enough alone beyond their disciplinary enclaves. They may be very sophisticated about theoretical politics—gender, race, class, and ethnicity. They may even be registered liberal Democrats, as critics on the right contend. But in practice they too often give up on their power to act effectively and efficiently. I remember one nontenured colleague calling such faculty the "Nieman-Marxists." Although the bon mot always brings a chuckle of recognition from academics, I find that recognition too easy for comfort.

Speaking as a faculty member, then, I will in this study call on my colleagues to do more than complacently unveil the ironies in current managerial and political attempts to define and control higher education. Those ironies are, after all, relatively easy to spot. We must not let them undercut our necessary commitment to propositions about freedom, truth, and responsibility to students. In such a spirit, I suggest, over and over again in each of the chapters that follow and again in the conclusion of this book, an emergence of faculty from classrooms and studies and labs into a newly conscious determination to participate in institutional decisions.

Finally, my differences with some colleagues include the belief that faculty must cooperate with their administrations wherever they can. That means that members of the administration will need to have more open minds about the faculty as well. The routes of interchange between faculty and administrators should be opened for regular traffic: administrative leaders should not devolve into a separate species in the academy, but should remain colleagues and peers even as they make difficult decisions. Although I abhor the increasingly obscene distance between faculty and administrative compensation, I also know that good academic managers are hard to find and should earn reasonable salaries. In doing my share of administration, I've discovered how difficult it is, and I've also participated in the administrator's leading psychic disorder—self-pity. But faculty who mainly want to be left alone with their research and teaching must realize the extreme irrationality of that ambition within a collective structure of such complexity as a modern college or university. Their access to choices about their professional lives must, after all, reside in their engagement with all those who work with them for the welfare of life on their campuses.

🐝 🐝 🐝

This study starts by mapping the campuses of higher education, for they present the most visible manifestations of the ascendancy of the market in the American academy. Panning from the center to the peripheries of "bricks and mortar," the survey in chapter 1 both celebrates the varieties and traditions of American colleges and universities and points to topographical dislocations that indicate a skewing of priorities. Often the arrival of the bulldozers and cranes signifies some sign of progress to faculty, and so they go about their business waiting for things to return to normal, though grumbling a bit about the contrast between their narrow cells and the fabulous offices in the new building. But facts on the ground are powerful embodiments of institutional identity, and only now are professors beginning to understand the distortions that unquestioned expansion can bring. In looking at such outlying campus enclaves as the athletics complex, the medical center, and brand-name business conference centers, the chapter suggests that when these additions are welcoming to students and faculty, and when they advance central programs in the campus mission of teaching and research, they serve campus life. But when they are isolated, out of bounds for all but a narrow range of privilege, and inhospitable to faculty oversight—then they denote detours from the world of education into the world of commerce.

What happens to the outsides of campus structures is not as significant as what happens inside them, of course. Chapters 2 and 3 therefore investigate controversies about what goes on in the nation's classrooms: chapter 2 tries to unpack trends in current pedagogical reforms, and chapter 3 takes on debates about curriculum. In doing so, each of these chapters identifies some of the presiding criticisms leveled at the faculty. The discussions in these chapters thus gather around perennial questions of method and content: what is the core learning that should mark advanced education, and how is it best transmitted? In trying to untangle recent arguments on these questions, each chapter identifies the political implications of current reform movements as well as their cogency for actual conditions in classrooms.

Chapter 2, "The Myth of the Bloviating Professor," singles out a key term in the pedagogical reforms fostered by constructionist activists who aim to decenter classroom activity away from the instructor. While such reforms rightly emphasize student motivation and engagement, they underestimate the complexities of both motivation and cognition and discount the valuable forensic skills of many effective college instructors. Further, the mantras of the true believers in "learning" over "teaching" not only alienate practicing faculty members but tend to justify some untenable educational practices—a normalization of massive lecture courses, for example, and an undue reliance on technology to "fill the gaps" through student self-instruction. There is no doubt that pedagogy in higher education requires thoughtful consideration by all faculty members, but this chapter maintains that no theoretical approach can suit all teachers in all circumstances and for all subjects.

Chapter 3, "Getting the 'Liberal' Out of Education," engages the question of the curriculum by recounting the history of the conservative castigations of higher education for abandoning the traditional core texts in introductory humanities programs. The chapter's analysis of the canon wars sympathizes with the curricular problems identified in these skirmishes, but notes that such engagements have been transformed by some critics into accusations that faculties who reject canonical texts are in some sense anti-American. Acknowledging the danger in any blind adoption of any set of sacred scriptures, this chapter nevertheless asks faculty curriculum committees to be more sympathetic to some of the opportunities of a standard core. These include the ease of articulation between high schools and colleges through shared understandings about the nature and progression of study in particular fields, the creation of a community of common study of texts in students' introduction to college work, and the articulation of coordinated rationales in introductory courses to help entering students who are all too often confused about the value of what they're doing. Although I accept that traditional canons tend to foster structures of political power and social status, and that trying to construct a canon with "better" texts would not only take an unimaginable consensus but would simply install one set of interests over another, I also believe that some kind of structure is necessary. This chapter suggests that academics surrender to the inevitability of curricular choices, but with the awareness that any set of courses must be explained, criticized, and changed as part of normal curricular review.

Chapter 4 moves from physical classrooms onto one of the most contested sites of pedagogy in the past decade—the Ethernet. Massive commercial investments in distance learning have reinforced some of the pedagogical reformers' idea that learning can do without teaching, to which is added the notion that it doesn't need campuses either. Even though many of the early ventures in distance education have failed, they have made way for the proliferation of proprietary schools. And although some of these vocational schools perform an essential service in training, especially for returning students, they have also managed to undermine the concept of liberal education by selling a notion of education as a matter of "deliverables" that can be packaged and priced by the bundle. In the process, they have infiltrated the mainstream of undergraduate education—redefining the terms and powers of our accrediting system and tapping into the very federal support that some of them originally disdained in favor of profit. Chapter 4's title, "Distance Makes the Heart Grow Colder," suggests that my focus will be on teaching as a necessarily personal, and present, interaction between ongoing communities of faculty and students. Yet faculty cannot take refuge in a Luddite reaction to IT resources; rather they must engage technology, make sure on-site students receive full social value from their educational experience, and work with regional accreditation bodies to ensure appropriate standards for measuring distance and proprietary education.

Having laid out questions about campuses and their landscape in its first four chapters, the book turns in chapter 5 to the question of campus governance. I have titled this chapter "A More Perfect Union" in part to indicate its sympathy with collective bargaining and, more broadly, to signal the need for faculty to come together effectively in making choices about their institutions. Governance is the key to whatever influence the faculty might have in responding to present challenges, for if professors are to have any influence on the growth and development of higher education, they must engage themselves in its planning and regulation. Once again remembering their lost power, I try to imagine ways for faculty to regain a significant share in the governance of their institutions. It is in this regard that I consider not only managerial and traditional governance but also the option of unionization as a tool for faculty choice. In some ways, the presence of a faculty union requires more intentional faculty activity in governance and provides a set of practices that have been proven over time. Becoming alert to the need for concerted action is one important step; being organized to take on the difficulties of mutual effort is another. Faculty are likely to attend to the first and neglect the latter.

The three final chapters of the book investigate the most significant areas in which many faculty members have complied with market forces in their professional work. Chapter 6, "Superstars and Rookies of the Year," turns to a fixation on research acclaim that is deeply embedded within the academic psyche. This fixation tends to be aroused by the rituals of recruitment and retention that take place on all campuses. Hiring new colleagues is a matter that engages individual faculty members intensely, for peer control of admission to the professoriate has been a highly successful source of academic quality. But when recruitment becomes an exercise in what some economists have called "the-winner-take-all" mentality of contemporary American culture, departments and programs can become unhealthy environments. When a department's faculty assents to the extremely volatile criteria of early promise or current fame in choosing their colleagues, their efforts to build a community of scholarship can become an exercise in professional pathology. The antidote is a wise consideration of the total identity and mission of their disciplines and programs.

Although it is clear that the survey of higher education in this book derives from my identity as a professor of humanities, the problems it raises are not confined to English or history departments. Chapter 7 therefore approaches questions about academic science, and it begins by describing an episode at the University of Alaska in the mid-1950s. There a handful of untenured researchers helped to put the brakes on plans by "firecracker boys" from the federal government to experiment with "atoms for peace" nuclear explosions in the Arctic. Elements in the dismissals of those researchers lead to pressing questions about past and present influences on university research by business and government. In raising these questions, the chapter takes a measure of the extent to which academic scientists have lost their sense of community with their colleagues, their students, and the public. Thus they are now praised (and paid) for their discoveries, but they are also contradicted and edited when their conclusions do not conform to the desires of one or another interest group. Although there has been some encroachment on academic freedom by conservative critics of the canon, efforts by political and commercial interests to undermine the public's traditional trust in science are probably more damaging, for in applying an ideological litmus test to all disciplines, they attack the nation's basic reliance on secular education as a reliable guide in forming public policy.

Chapter 8, "The Disposable Faculty," picks up the issue of the politically defined "public epistemology" that now besets the entire academy by discussing the status of the professoriate in terms of its reliance on tenure to protect academic freedom. While academic freedom is universally invoked with reverence by critics of the academy, it is now defined as "presenting both sides" when only one of them is sound. Thus although there is always lip service to free speech for faculty, it seems that enemies, and even friends, of the academy fail to understand how dependent academic freedom is on the security of a stable profession from which individual scholars can speak. In a society in which credibility itself has become a commodity, there is little use for academic claims of a singular dispensation. Thus frontal attacks on tenure from such initiatives as the "New Pathways" project of the now defunct American Association of Higher Education are consonant with public suspicions about the intellectual life that goes on within the academy. This chapter summarizes the New Pathways arguments, indicating ways in which some insiders in the higher education establishment have helped undermine protections for the faculty by giving cover to the "unbundling" of faculty functions and questioning the traditional features of professorial status. Rather than lingering on the defense of tenure, however, the chapter suggests that one of the most significant errors in efforts to undo it is a failure to appreciate that the tenure system has sustained a unified ecology of scholarly development and discipline in the American academy. Finally, I will appropriate the attitude of management by arguing that a tenured professoriate, with all of its flaws and limitations, has been extraordinarily effective in terms of human resource allocation and "quality control." Thus the most significant enemy of tenure is the increasing use of untenured faculty who work as single and dispensable cogs in the educational machine and therefore lack the professional standing or the organizational sanction to teach without fear. This situation poses a threat to the integrity of American higher education, for without an integrated faculty, the advances of a century and a half of excellence can decline into the spiritless mediocrity that derives from standardization and loss of individual autonomy.

In the arid contemporary atmosphere of charge and countercharge, academics need to find ways to bring back cool reason and philosophical calm. In the conclusion to this book, I therefore offer some modest but concrete proposals for the return of faculty to the arenas of choice in their institutions. These proposals will not solve every problem, but they may make a start on some of them. In the main, they derive from effective faculty efforts that I have observed firsthand through the years. They also suggest some promising initiatives in faculty-administration cooperation, for such cooperation will be essential in guiding the inevitable changes of the coming decades. It is clear that since the faculty has gone missing in recent years, it is up to members of the profession—helped by enlightened administrations—to stage a comeback. The faculty's behavior as academic citizens under this new awareness must be informed, inclusive, coordinated, and continuous. In short, the presence of professors in campus decision making should become their automatic exercise of a tradition rather than their transitory response to crisis.

Most books on higher education are better on analysis than remedy. That may be because evidences of failure are always ready at hand while arguments for reform lie in visions of the future. But failures can, after all, clear the field for building anew. This book surveys that field. Its conclusion seeks to offer pointers for further reclamations that are practical and strategic.

What Ever Happened to the Faculty?

CHAPTER ONE

Bricks and Mortar

The American Campus

At the height of the dot-com mania in higher education, faculty were urged to disencumber themselves of their love for the physical campus—their cozy offices, their histrionic lecture halls, and their landscaped walks—because such elitist enclosures would no longer serve the interests of the masses of students who would need access to higher education in a technological and global economy. Just as this new horde would have to be served by part-time faculty and semiprofessional "information workers," they would also have to be served away from standard campuses—most probably in educational storefronts in local malls, office buildings ranged along interstate highways, or the bare ether (though in full color and with animated tours of "trademark" campuses where possible). Sir John S. Daniel, vice chancellor of Britain's Open University, was dismissive of the traditional faculty's resistance to this environmental change in statements he made on an American speaking tour in the mid-1990s and in an essay published in *Change* in 1997: "Who can blame university staff for enjoying the civilized environments of these well-endowed seats of learning?" he asked. "To be reluctant to exchange them for workplaces that are less extravagantly over-engineered is only human nature."[1]

After further experience of the promises and limitations of Internet education, however, Sir John has come to acknowledge the persistence of impulses on the part of students as well as of faculty to come together physically in actual places.[2] His subsequent speeches warn against imagining the demise of the campus. Thus in a 2000 keynote address to an international conference, "Teaching and Learning," he told the audience: "I often argue that university campuses will always be in demand because they create a protected environment where young people can come to terms with life, love, liquor and learning—while sparing the rest of the community the sight of these often unsightly processes."[3]

I cite this change of heart by an early critic of educational bricks and mortar to help introduce my own concerns about the physical and moral state of American higher education in a time of change. I believe that American campuses can—and often do—embody the best ideals of our system, and since I have visited at least 150 of them, I begin this book by giving a panoramic survey of the variety of places in which education is enacted. I must admit, however, that many of the college and university campuses on which I've based my sketch seem to be floating toward a reality that is less benign in terms of its generosity, access, and adherence to some vision of a particular educational mission than the one imagined in their founding. That is why my energy in writing about higher education rises from my sense of what we stand to lose if we do not take care to preserve what we already have.

What we already have, most tangibly, are the physical settings of America's colleges and universities—bricks and mortar. American campuses will endure, but even as we faculty recognize their necessity, we may also neglect to give them the kind of care they deserve. It is true that campuses provide sites for students to experience "life, love, liquor and learning," and while the spectacle is frequently either demoralizing or scandalous, it is a necessary feature of the initiation of our youth into a sanctioned maturity. The importance of this sanctioning is emphasized in Erik Erikson's writings, especially in his descriptions of the ways in which the intergenerational exchanges between adolescents, young adults, and society are mutually instructive and enriching.[4] Under such a view, the physical campus embodies our society's commitment to the passage of its young into maturity by providing a setting that may be seen as "extravagantly over-engineered," but provides both freedom to choose among a number of possible self-identifications and the challenge of mastering the skills of an adult. Erikson maintains that the American system of education "is probably the greatest organized and artificial postponement of adulthood, emotionally speaking, that could be imagined," but he also notes that its artificiality facilitates an escape from the limitations of childhood: it is available when "the young person leaves home and comes to live in a new institution, which only in sentimental allegory can be called a 'home,' or a 'family,' even though it is symbolically situated under the wings of an Alma Mater."[5]

It seems worth pausing to answer those who object to speaking of today's students as if they were all adolescents. It is true that the hiatus of adolescence in delightful surroundings may actually be extravagant when compared to the abrupt shift from childhood to adulthood in less affluent societies,[6] and in the current traffic from the working world to the classroom and back again; traditional campuses may thus seem an indulgence in special privilege. Especially in light of the fact that "upwards of half our college and university students are now of the age group we used to refer to as nontraditional," and that most of those are full-time workers, backers of stripped-down places of study present themselves as spokespersons for "grownup" students.[7] But it is also true that the learning of more than a specific, passing skill at any time in the human life cycle warrants extraordinary space and time; that is why some schools have begun providing "executive" campuses for CEOs or special camps for alumni educational programs. Though early university campuses were constructed partially to signify privilege for those who had the luxury of a moratorium from the world of work, the belated learning of those who have never had such luxury should be equally important. Skeptics about the value of campuses for "nontraditional" students like to invoke the image of the busy mother who needs a campus that she can enter and leave quickly in order to be with her family. My experience with a number of "mother" students is that they've valued their time on a real campus as an orderly refuge from their domestic duties. What they really need is parking.

In any case, American campuses have been less burdened with significations of privilege than those of Europe. Even though there remains a mystique about Harvard Yard, in the past thirty or so years, its pathways have become available to a cross section of gifted American young people—regardless of their origins. Other American campuses have likewise become magnets for the sons and daughters of the Republic, and they have become available in every region of the country. The campuses of American public universities are now as often distinguished for design and repose as are the hallowed halls of private schools.

Despite the manifest plenitude of bricks and mortar in American higher education, however, I worry about the potential of its campuses to become less and less effective as social spaces for our democracy. One source of this anxiety is the increasing competition for entry into the "name" schools that still carry great prestige in the eyes of parents and their children (this kind of competition is discussed further in chapter 6, "Superstars and Rookies of the Year"). The social stratification involved in being admitted to such colleges is intensifying, no matter how ardently they seek to enlist disadvantaged and nontraditional students. There are so many worthy applicants for the limited spots available that the impossibility of admitting all of them turns too many students into academic losers who may then see their own excellent campuses as second-rate. Added to this narrowing of opportunity is the reluctance of state legislators to expand or build campuses for the new seekers from immigrant and minority populations. The online Western Governors University was initially set up in part to forestall the need for additional campus development in the Southwest and West.[8] The failure of legislators to recognize the social significance of our many and various campuses could undermine the impulse toward the maintenance of equality that inspired their foundation in the first place.[9]

But beyond the social and physical survival of our egalitarian system, there is also a threat from within. Perhaps in fear of indulging in Mr. Chips–like sentimentality, some faculty are careless about both the communal and symbolic functions of their campuses. They begrudge every penny spent by the administration on physical plant. And many of them consider any edifice contributed by an alum as some kind of Trojan horse. Narrowing their institutions down to their own offices and classrooms, they are rarely present in student areas, leaving all concern about the extracurricular lives of undergraduates in the hands of the counseling office. Too many faculty absent themselves from the convocations, investitures, graduations, founder's days, and other such collegiate festivities that mark the continuity linking their institutions, students, and themselves.[10]

A more significant absence is marked by the failure of faculty to exert their traditional power of governance oversight to make sure that the core of the campus survives. It is not sentimental to argue that higher education needs an unencumbered local habitation and a name. Even though most current faculty members have spent time as wandering scholars because of the widespread failure of campuses to commit to them, it is incumbent on them to imagine how they might ensure the continuing identity of the places where they work. For education to serve as a socializing enterprise, a critical mass of resources and people must come together. And because the developmental effect of education is a process rather than a product, they must stay together for relatively long periods of time. Students need places to gather, interact, and grow. To keep in touch, the faculty also has a critical need for campuses—grounds, classrooms and lecture halls, libraries and labs, offices, spaces for recreation and public functions. And campuses need faculty. Accordingly, it is important to make sure that the structures on campuses aid this educational cohabitation. The sites of this complicated pedagogical enterprise must be protected from exploitation by agents from the world beyond the campus, agents usually guided by short-term definitions of success. Thus campuses should be places set apart, shaped by long-term conceptions of the need for generational interchange. They should be spots that students will remember as refuges from the daily calculus of getting ahead, and return to when they need a restorative breath of freedom.

Finally, without campuses safeguarded by administrations, faculty, and students through foresight and pride, higher education would actually lose a vital link with the larger community of the outer world. It would forfeit what Robert Putnam calls "social capital."[11] Educational bricks and mortar would be just that—piles of inanimate rubble with little of the human music of community and mutual endeavor. Should life on campus become such an isolated activity for students, campuses themselves may eventually be seen as expensive frills. And then the buildings could indeed become overengineered anachronisms—factories for stamping out vocational automatons, theaters for entertainment, or circuses for games.

❧   ❧   ❧

In American education the bricks and mortar of colleges and universities have had signal national importance. The Morrill Act (1862) establishing land-grant colleges across the country became a source of distinguished architecture as well as of educational opportunity, for it emphasized the fact that American higher education would occupy a real as well as an ideal estate. And so, along with the obligatory domes in pioneer state capitals, American collegiate Gothic, Queen Anne, or Victorian buildings rose up in towns and cities across the continent. These campus structures imaged the solidity of the country's social investment in the future skills and understanding of the citizens of the democracy.

The Morrill Act specified the establishment of "at least one college where the leading object shall be, without excluding other scientific and classical studies and including military tactics, to teach such branches of learning as are related to agriculture and the mechanic arts."[12] And perhaps because these practical expectations were made explicit, American campuses rarely carried the looming mustiness that darkened the university town of Christminster in Thomas Hardy's *Jude the Obscure* (1896): "High against the black sky the flash of a lamp would show crocketed pinnacles and indented battlements. Down obscure alleys, apparently never trodden now by the foot of man, and whose very existence seemed to be forgotten, there would jut into the path porticoes, oriels, doorways of enriched and florid middle-age design, their extinct air being accentuated by the rottenness of the stones. It seemed impossible that modern thought could house itself in such decrepit and superseded chambers."[13] Though often modeling themselves physically on European structures, most American universities and colleges saw themselves as starting afresh, with a new slant on the relationship between advanced study, learning, and the common good. Allan Bloom has captured the spirit of their founding in describing his first impressions of the University of Chicago's fake Gothic buildings: "Those buildings were a bow to the contemplative life by a nation addicted more than any other to the active life. The pseudo-Gothic was much ridiculed, and nobody builds like that anymore. . . . To me it was and remains an expression of what we are."[14]

That so many of the state schools began admitting women by the first decade of the twentieth century was one sign of their novelty. Another was the development of professional schools allied with and embedded in universities. There were vocational departments concerned with teaching, engineering, and agriculture from the start, and soon most state schools added schools of law and medicine. Then other newly included disciplines—business, social work, music—became major components. The aspirations of American universities to combine advanced research, professional training, and undergraduate education within a total system of higher education marked its difference, in many respects, from systems elsewhere. Observing the need for specialized research and study, however, the designers of campuses also premised a core—the library, chapel or auditorium, and student union—where all campus inhabitants would meet. Although the current trend to center much undergraduate training in community colleges has many benefits, its potential has been limited by the failure to provide adequate space for community college campuses.

The college towns fostered by the land-grant provisions after the Civil War were to beckon to young farmers and mechanics as places of light and life and access to the great world beyond. Historical and fictional heroes of the American experience have found the physical presence of the campus less ominous than Hardy's Jude did in England, though many may have found a share of disillusionment there as well. Perhaps Jim Burden of Willa Cather's *My Ántonia* (1918) should stand for many of the young people who left small towns for the state university—to find there a room of their own, a faculty mentor, entry to a new world, and possibly alienation from the old. In any case, the building of new campuses made going away from home feasible for thousands of American young people. Accessibility was fostered by the fact that the building of land-grant universities accompanied the founding of other kinds of colleges in every state and most fledgling communities. So if you couldn't go to, say, the University of Illinois at Urbana (1867), you could go to Illinois State in Normal (1857) or to Illinois Wesleyan (1850) in the twin Illinois cities of Bloomington-Normal. Many developing institutions were teachers' colleges; others were denominational schools with seminaries attached. In most cases, they were centers of community, county, or state networks, and their graduates connected the college with its wider constituency through their work in county extension offices, local schools, or pulpits.

So what are American campuses like now? There are many different versions, but most academics can imagine a standard campus map. Usually there is a core of the old campus, centered by the first building—often called "Old Main"—that is now used as a museum or an administrative building. Other buildings tend to spread out beyond the Old Main core cluster like the rings of a tree trunk, according to age. There are surrounding classroom buildings, the auditorium and sometimes a chapel, the student union, the dormitories, the gym, and the football or other playing fields. What were once residential quads at the center of campus may now house departmental offices or classrooms, while—especially on larger campuses—the residence halls have been moved to the outskirts and are within easy reach of the playing fields. On mega campuses, the medical complex may lie far out, and so may the school of agriculture or the very high-tech science buildings. In many cases, as a matter of fact, the medical school has eventually moved from the founding site to the state's biggest metropolis (Indianapolis, Birmingham, Houston) in search of an indigent population to practice on. Indeed, by now many medical schools have spawned independent campuses, and in some cases these "academic health centers" form the financial base for an entire city. On or near most campuses there is usually some kind of "campus town" or a walkable fringe; such areas can consist of a couple of eateries, a student hangout with beer on tap, and a convenience store. Sometimes they are extensive commercial enclaves used by students, townspeople, and visitors alike.

From afar, most campuses loom on the landscape—even in cities where many of their parts are dispersed. For example, the City College campus still stakes a definite CUNY presence on the Upper West Side of Manhattan. And so also does Low Plaza at Columbia, though there is always controversy about that university's impact on the geography of West Harlem's development.[15] NYU is both a part of and apart from lower Manhattan—helped by its identification with the Washington Square arch in Greenwich Village. On its Web page, NYU explicitly claims Manhattan as its campus, but Columbia and the colleges of CUNY also advertise the learning environment of the city. They are all right to do so, for while keeping their identifiable campus centers, they participate—with many, many smaller New York City institutions—in the character of that metropolis.

In some cases, of course, the campus virtually *is* the town. That is true for many big state schools, for example. Much as it has sprawled throughout its entire surrounding area, the University of Michigan does define the town of Ann Arbor. And the same holds for the University of Wisconsin at Madison, Indiana University at Bloomington, the University of North Carolina at Chapel Hill, and the University of Kansas at Lawrence, not to mention Harvard (and later MIT) at Cambridge. Some towns got their names from their schools—as did State College, Pennsylvania; College Station, Texas; and College Park, Maryland. Indeed, the sense of place is so critical to campus identity that every campus bookstore I've visited features framed views of campus landmarks for sale. If the landmark is not a building, like Frank Gehry's Weisman Art Museum on the Mississippi River running through the University of Minnesota campus, or "Mr. Jefferson's Lawn" at the University of Virginia, it will be a football stadium, such as those dominating the campuses at Ohio State and the University of Nebraska–Lincoln. One of the strongest images of identity of any city campus in America is the University of Pittsburgh's Cathedral of Learning, which towers above and identifies its neighborhood as harboring not only Pitt's campus but an entire complex of museums, a Carnegie library, and both Carlow and Carnegie-Mellon universities as well.

But quieter spaces mark other campuses in their relation to their surroundings. St. Bonaventure's University in Olean, New York, reveres a secluded spot that Thomas Merton used for meditation when he was a young professor there and has expanded his legacy in the founding of a retreat house named after a close friend of his. And the campus at the University of Illinois at Urbana-Champaign has protected a prairie cornfield, the Morrow Plots, since it was first planted in 1876. The preservation of a field in the middle of the Urbana campus has influenced the planning for U of I building projects over time, mandating, for example, the placement of a large part of the nearby undergraduate library underground. True to the heritage of the land-grant college, the Morrow Plots have embodied the notion that practical research should be at the center of the university. Even though they are surrounded by student traffic, the plots have been an open-air lab for experimentation in crop rotation, fertilization, and conservation for more than 100 years.[16]

I have kept an informal inventory of the key campus features that have had a special appeal for me in my travels. Thus I know where to find the ice cream at Cornell and Penn State, and where to have breakfast at Iowa City. Visitors can have a glass of beer in the Wisconsin Union, overlooking Lake Mendota (most state campuses are dry). There are memorable gates, fountains, and statues everywhere. The relatively secluded polished limestone Nittany Lion at Penn State is aesthetically pleasing, for example, but there may be more social appeal in matching male and female lion statues at Hofstra University—a school intent on emphasizing the fact that it serves women as well as men.[17] Several casts of Rodin's *The Thinker* occupy campuses (Columbia, the University of Louisville, and Stanford), but my sense of academic rectitude is better satisfied by the prim statue of Bishop Hamline at Hamline University in St. Paul. There are patron bishops on the campus of Catholic University and saints scattered about Catholic school grounds everywhere. Abstract sculpture is not to be left out, for there are bold, unidentifiable contemporary monuments in front of important new collegiate buildings. I have intimate acquaintance with Lorado Taft's *Alma Mater* on the prairie campus of the University of Illinois at Urbana-Champaign; I had to pass it every day on my way to the English building when I was a graduate student there, and I was always delighted by the latest indignity visited upon it by undergraduate pranksters. I have been at the University of Vermont for the fall colors, and I have been awed by the flowering trees in the quad at the University of Washington in Seattle and at Southern Methodist in Dallas in the spring. The sea-seasoned frame buildings of the University of Rhode Island have seemed wonderfully appropriate to me, as have the monumental, sun-drenched adobe buildings at the University of New Mexico. I have walked through the crowded urban campus of Wayne State as well as the quads of Baylor in small-town Texas and St. Mary's across the hills from Berkeley. In each case I've mentioned, and many others, I have observed that the American campus usually declares a unity and distinctiveness for the kind of education it offers to its students.

This wealth of landmarks can be sampled on the virtual campus tours that nearly every school now offers. These assert that the bricks and mortar of our campuses are not random appropriations of space—or of salvaged municipal buildings. They are, rather, intentionally organized structures designed to set borders between the campus and its surroundings. Such borders define an identity zone for students by marking the campus as an enclosure for the special uses of study and development. Although the borders are permeable, and every institution now announces its relations with the world at its doors, campuses also mark a barrier against unwarranted intrusion by the non-academic realms that surround them.

Each campus has its own distinctive way of dealing with its borderline status vis-à-vis the non-academic worlds around it. Usually this status involves a dynamic interchange—especially on city campuses, where there is much interaction between town and gown. Several of these exemplify the ways in which American campuses have adapted to their environments and also distinguished themselves as places for study that enable an interchange among faculty and students and the world outside. For example, in Milwaukee the presence of two major schools—Marquette University and the University of Wisconsin–Milwaukee—has been a leading factor in the development and redevelopment of urban neighborhoods. The cityscape of downtown Chicago displays the same interchange between school and community—from the University of Chicago's identification with its section of the South Side, to the Illinois Institute of Technology's enclave of modern architecture at McCormack Place, to the Roosevelt University restoration of the J. W. N. Sullivan Auditorium Building on Michigan Avenue, to the new buildings of the University of Illinois–Chicago near downtown, to the northern Lake Michigan shoreline from Loyola to Northwestern in Evansville. All exemplify the campus as both a self-identifying structure and a local resource.

American campuses are relatively private places, but they often serve as community enclaves for a variety of public purposes—lectures and performances, local service club meetings, professional conferences, even presidential debates. Among the most important of these events for local neighbors are graduation ceremonies for surrounding high schools. One June several years ago, I was visiting the spacious campus of the University of Southern California, located near a largely black and Hispanic neighborhood in central Los Angeles. Classes were out for the summer, but still I noticed unusual campus activity one Saturday afternoon. There were neighborhood families strolling through the grounds, dressed in their very best. The explanation for their presence came to me when

I spied several young people in caps and gowns. I realized that this private university, seemingly a bastion of privilege in an underprivileged area, was providing its facilities for a local high school graduation. The students and families who came there had stepped from crowded streets into a world of pleasant trees and plantings and well-kept, orderly buildings. Whether their view of this world was as bitter as Jude Fawley's is difficult to judge, but I believe that it was not. Their occasion was significant as an academic exercise and therefore important enough for a nearby institution of higher education to offer its facilities. I sensed that welcoming these members of the town onto the precincts of the gown was a matter of hospitality rather than the noblesse oblige that signifies exclusion.

Of course, the tuition and fees of a private university like USC would be prohibitive for most of the families I observed on the campus, but the state of California has been wise enough to follow through on the promise of the Morrill Act by building a range of public institutions to ensure that lower-income students have access to a real campus. My most vivid memory of the kind of social synergy inspired by such a campus derives from another visit I paid to Los Angeles—this time to a faculty group at the campus of Cal State–Los Angeles. Once again, I wandered through the maze of Los Angeles in a rented car, trying to find my way to the top of a hill, where CSULA was located. Finally I got the right street, found a visitor's parking spot, and went to the nearby union building to have a rendezvous with a colleague. The "Free Speech" plaza around the union was teeming with the most diverse student body I have ever seen. I became aware of the varieties of Asian faces—from the South Pacific islands, Southeast Asia, the Philippines, Japan, China, and Korea. And then there were native or second-generation Hispanics, African Americans, and Caucasians. Accompanying the racial mix was a mix of ages; most students seemed in their twenties, though others were in their late teens and still others were obviously "mature" adults. At change of class time, the mass became thicker. As my colleague and I wended our way through these students, one young man came up to her with a shine on his face. "Professor Frasier," he announced, "I've been wanting to see you! Do you remember me? I was in your biology class two years ago? I wanted to tell you that I've been on the Dean's List the last two years and that I just got a post-doc to study at Drew University in New Jersey!" My colleague remembered him with obvious pleasure and congratulated him for his success. She told me later that he was a first-generation Hispanic student, whose parents were from Mexico. He had left the barrio nearby for CSULA, and now he was going far away—to the unknown, exotic state of New Jersey.

The encounter has stayed in my mind as a story of mutual confirmation. In running into his professor on campus the student confirmed her work with him even as he was asking her blessing on his own future. This exchange could happen because they shared a place.

Lest my praise seem devoted only to the camaraderies of town and gown on undergraduate campuses, let me add that graduate and "hard" science programs share the same need for places to meet and greet. For example, on the Web page introducing Harvard's Department of Molecular and Cellular Biology, the current chair dwells on "the close proximity to our sister departments of Organismic and Evolutionary Biology Chemistry and Chemical Biology, Physics, The Division of Engineering and Applied Sciences and Psychology" as representing a contrast to the "scientific monoculture" that can result from departmental segregation. The virtual Internet tour pauses to detail the construction in 1931 of the severely modern Biological Laboratories, humanizing the buildings in the process. The hyperlinks show the process of sculpting and unveiling the two stone rhinos ("Victoria" and "Bessie") that flank one of the entrances, and the narrative tells of a student prank that placed a bedpan under each of them to unsettle the dignity of the inaugural ceremony for the building. Fixing on those architectural features to define itself, the Department of Molecular and Cellular Biology calls its volleyball team "The Rhinos."[18]

🙚 🙚 🙚

It may be that scientists have a special relationship with bricks and mortar because so much of their work must take place in labs. But humanists have been equally fervent about their structures—the campus library, for example. And while ordinary faculty members grump and gripe about the waste of money on campus landscaping, they are also fervid in defense of their offices as well as their classrooms. For many faculty members, the campus *is* the office and the classroom.

I will describe campus classrooms in some detail in the next chapter, but it might be useful here to peer inside campus buildings briefly to get a sense of the life there. Faculty offices are usually burrowed into classroom buildings, and these may vary from the cubicle that still shows its original cinderblock structure to more palatial dens in dark walnut and crackled leather. Some have windows, but many do not. The lack of windows in the English department at the University of Kansas at Lawrence—housed in the bowels of a building designed for other uses—has been a cause of great anguish to faculty and TAs. On the other hand, the airy English department chair's office at Yale has its private lavatory. But most faculty offices, even at Yale, are big enough to accommodate only a desk and chair, and perhaps another chair and worktable for students. There will usually be some bookcases, always coveted, and a jerry-built computer setup crowding the desk.

The signage of faculty offices can vary widely from one to another—and from one discipline to another. Going from door to door in a hall of faculty offices can be a fascinating tour. Some doors are, of course, bare. But others will be papered with advertisements for everything from student scholarships to announcements of lectures, the latest tidbit in the field, sly political ironies, anti-gun-law ads, and course grades (the names of the students coded to protect individual privacy). It is true that some faculty air their beliefs—in English, Latin, Farsi, and even mathematical formulae—by using their office doors as personal bulletin boards. Such usage can cause controversy from time to time, and administrators have sometimes attempted to control it by setting up poster codes. In one case a California community college administration attempted to draw up rules for posting all flyers and messages on campus. Under this regime such material could be posted by faculty only *inside* their offices, and then in such a way that it could not be seen through any campus window. The code did not survive the satire it evoked, and so faculty in Orange County continue to act on their beliefs that the campus is a marketplace for ideas, and that ideas deserve whatever billboard space they can get.

Offices are as various as their doors. Some may be so spare and uninviting that their valuable space seems wasted; many times professors prefer to meet students elsewhere, and it must be admitted that some prefer not to meet students at all. But then there are other, lived-in offices that have accreted assorted emblems of the inhabitant's discipline or hobbies. I once visited the office of an archaeologist in a department of Middle Eastern studies that was a wonderland of signification. Everywhere could be seen images or models of every imaginable sarcophagus, including one that extended a hand for a penny when touched in the right way. The walls held pictures of Egyptian queens from Nefertiti to Elizabeth Taylor as Cleopatra, and scattered throughout were photographs of local helpers from the digs that the faculty member had engaged. And there was a handsome threadbare Persian rug upon which lay a big, hairy, affectionate dog. I imagined that a student entering that particular office would experience all at once a total college education. The place invited familiarity and inquiry, for the books seemed always on loan and the teacher always eager to explain.

For students, among the most instructive things in faculty offices are the books themselves. Most students come from homes that do not have libraries, and the mere spectacle of overflowing shelves can be eye-opening. My own students have exclaimed over my books—quizzing me about whether I had actually *read* them all. And I have noticed them spying out the titles to get an idea from my reading of what kind of person I might be. As revelatory as a faculty office is to the student, however, the sacredness of its significance for the faculty member can be more deep and abiding. One of the hardest challenges for retiring faculty members is giving up their offices and labs.

The sketch I have given here represents a relatively comfortable academic world for faculty members, even though most of them are used to complaining about lack of bookcases, lack of tables, lack of lab space. Most full-time faculty members on the campuses I've described are more privileged than they know by the fact that they actually *have* offices. It is now a well-known fact that many of the teachers of introductory undergraduate courses are not "real" faculty and so don't have their own offices. There is no more telling a symbol for the status of part-time and adjunct faculty than the need of many of them to meet students in the library or lunch room or on a park bench. Some even work out of the cars that they drive from one campus to another as they try to cobble together a living as teachers. Or they have office space, but only in a makeshift alcove, frequently shared with several others and hidden away in some obscure part of the campus. I once visited a school where all of the lecturers—PhDs who had not been able to land tenure-track jobs and so were kept on to teach a full load of undergrad courses—were assigned space in the recesses of the football stadium. They were out of sight and out of mind, having little chance to intermix with full-time faculty members who might help them eventually find "real" jobs with real offices and not so many papers to grade. Thus, when we talk about the map of typical campuses, we need to remember invisible as well as visible manifestations of the institution's educational economy.

During my time as a departmental chair, tasked with assigning office space, I became aware of these less visible spaces for less visible teachers on campus—especially the teaching assistant staff, who had offices in a house off campus. Visiting their offices, as well as others throughout the campus, I realized how personal each work space was to colleagues, and how exotic and mysterious to the outside world. The panoramas of favorite posters, icons, secondhand rugs or easy chairs, hordes of paper clips, and sacred paper piles constitute anthropological evidence about the habits of different disciplines on all campuses—large and small. I also discovered that moving from the School of Business to the School of Fine Arts was to experience culture shock. Even the dress is different—from clipped hair, ties, and jackets to flowing locks, blue jeans, and paint-spattered T-shirts. And even within a school, a practiced eye can spot the varying specialties. The singers in the School of Music's opera department may seem always costumed and ready to take the stage, whereas the instrumentalists—poised to disappear into the orchestra pit—seem oblivious to style.

From the informal campus surveys I've made, I've often imagined a freshman student overwhelmed with the bewildering variety of academe's intellectual habitats but then growing more and more accustomed and knowing as the years pass. The variety itself is instructive; it embodies the principle that the campus should be a multiculture rather than a monoculture. Even very small religious colleges, like the one I went to many years ago, attempt to embody this cultural diversity in scheduling on-campus lectures and performances or in providing students with semester abroad programs. Posters for such opportunities paper campus bulletin boards. Such "enrichment" programs may seem frills to some critics, but they are designed as a part of campus life that might unify specialized interests into some common core of experience and let students experience the fact that education is not a simple amassment of skills and facts. The following chapters will expand on the issue of maintaining a liberal core for higher education in an age of specialization and vocationalism; here I want to continue my campus survey by considering some trends that can move institutions farther away from that core.

❧   ❧   ❧

There is one standard motive in online publicity about the bricks and mortar of every college and university in the country. That motive is, of course, the establishment of bragging rights. Glossy booklets draw implicit comparisons with other, lesser schools, in language about the history, beauty, convenience, and newness of buildings and grounds. Virtual tours on campus Web pages subtly assert campus excellence by featuring noble pictures of Old Main or another such landmark in fall colors, narratives of the unique history of the institution, and effusive emphases on the very newest campus structure—often inscribed with the full names and even middle initials of the donors. There may be some interior pictures showing a clutch of students (usually featuring the politically correct mix of genders and races) gazing intently through microscopes or at computer screens, or manipulating experimental apparatus, or contemplating a new sculpture in the fine arts collection; many times donor names are attached to these activities as well. Classrooms themselves are rarely featured, unless they contain the latest in technical innovations; ordinary classrooms may be difficult to photograph, they are usually the least dramatic feature of the campus, and they are rarely endowed. Some virtual tours—especially for big campuses like Ohio State—do explore dormitories or "student residence options." The aim here is to reassure students that dorms are not as crowded and ratty as they are reported to be; in fact, many new dorm buildings are downright luxurious. There are, indeed, studio apartment complexes for juniors and seniors—though some old grads regret the loss of community in such new dorms.[19] Finally, each Web site that I've visited either devotes special space to the athletics center or has a separate page devoted solely to the school teams.

These online celebrations of the campus indicate both the importance of bricks and mortar in contemporary higher education and the equally pervasive impulse to compete for every possible point of distinction. Those who have become concerned about campus balance believe that this impulse has nourished an urge to build that threatens the core of liberal education. I don't want to ignore the budgetary climate of the past two decades, which has forced universities to vie with each other and with other service enterprises for outside funding, struggling as costs rise while state and federal provisions for covering them lag. And I know that the ability to cultivate philanthropic gift-giving has become a primary criterion for selecting college presidents, and that university development offices have grown in importance—and in campus office space. But though the search for donors is understandable, there are some gifts that should not be accepted. The inappropriateness of some kinds of bricks and mortar signals the problems in higher education's current eagerness to meet the demands of the outside world without considering the effects inside the campus.

There are two significant sources for the bricks and mortar competition that now intrude on many campus profiles. One is the urge to upgrade athletic facilities—not only those that are devoted to intramural sports but those that are designed to lure star (or "semiprofessional") athletes to enroll.[20] The other is the hot haste to promise new centers for specialized research, professional development, or vocational training. In both cases, the engine that drives the new construction and hypes its importance is the institution's conviction that it must have bragging rights at every level.

In athletics, especially, this motive has become a self-propelling engine for interested parties—athletic conferences, coaches, star athletes, alumni, and the media—that seem to have forgotten the range of education for which the university or college should stand. The scandals of intercollegiate athletics are well known and well studied.[21] And it has become very clear to educational reformers that the boom in new stadiums and field houses not only distorts the educational institution's mission but drains its budget. Nevertheless, the proponents of competition seem unfazed by criticism, and the new arenas rise on the outskirts of the campus. The faculty, many asleep in their ivory towers, have begun to awaken to the extent to which such competition can corrupt their entire enterprise. The situation at the University of Oregon, where faculty senate members began a serious reform movement several years ago, can provide a prime example. Inspired by the contrast between legislative reductions in the university's budget and grandiose improvements to the football stadium, faculty in the senate began to take notice, and to protest. James W. Earl, the president of the senate and a scholar of Old English by trade, has recounted what happened as well as his perceptions of what matters on a campus, once he became involved in trying to assert some faculty control:

> To some people, the university is a business; to others, it's a state agency; to others, it's an engine for the economy; and for others—many, many others—it's little more than a great team, like the dazzling Ducks. And the university is all these things; but for you and me—for the faculty—the university is obviously something else and something more: it's academic freedom; it's the arts and sciences; it's the library, the all-nighter, the seminar table; it's liberal education, pure research, the sharing of ideas, the love of books, and the Socratic method; it's young people on a steep learning curve; it's Phi Beta Kappa and lifelong learning; and also, to be honest, it's the absent-minded professor—Einstein with his bad hair, Einstein who can't remember his phone number. That's okay with me.[22]

Once embarked on a campaign to put a brake on the distortion of campus values by thoughtless expansion not only in space but in time—the TV networks demanded the rescheduling of a game that intruded into the closely safeguarded study week before final exams—Earl found himself engaging with non-academic fans in their version of academic excellence as an entertainment value: "One of the witty things that sports fans say to me is, Don't you wish you could pack 60,000 people into the stands for a lecture on *Beowulf?* This tiresome question is supposed to remind me that more people care about what happens at the stadium than in my classroom, that classrooms are in fact boring, that literature isn't nearly as exciting or as popular as football. So, who am I to be criticizing athletics? Obviously, I'm just envious."[23]

Despite faculty "envy," and even in a university where faculty relations with the administration have been cordial and productive, the athletic program nevertheless seems to have become self-generating—especially when fueled by commercial interests. As Earl acknowledges in his narrative, because Nike wants to build a $200 million arena in Eugene, it will happen no matter what the faculty think about its necessity or desirability. And in the rhetoric of the athletics Web page of the University of Oregon, the "Nike Arena" will be applauded as the last piece in the athletics pattern. The page at goducks.com presents the facilities at Oregon in the exalted rhetoric usually reserved for moral or philosophical achievement. The banner line is "Second to None," and the text begins: "A vision and a commitment. The two have combined to put the University of Oregon on the 'facilities map' in the world of intercollegiate athletics." As the page continues, however, the agency for Oregon's boasting about its physical plant becomes clear in an emphasis on the fact that its football, basketball, and track facilities are "intimidating."[24] The "finest facilities" in the nation, then, embody a vision of winning through intimidation. A winning team needs facilities that shock and awe its opponents.

There has always been criticism of college athletics programs. The Knight Commission, made up of distinguished administrative leaders in higher education, issued an important call for reform in 1995 and has entered the fray once again in recent years. Professor Earl organized colleagues from the Pac-10 conference, welcomed another group from faculty senates around the country, and has enlisted the help of NCAA president Myles Brand (himself a former university president both at Oregon and at Indiana) to try to bring some measure of balance, and perhaps humility, to an academic enterprise gone completely awry. The interest is high among faculty—especially when they look at the exalted salaries of coaches and athletic entourages—but there is a note of defeat in Earl's account. He worries that the faculty may at last have become so barricaded in their own quarters that they are not willing to look across campus at the looming presence of an athletics empire that asserts its precedence not only on the campus map but in many activities of the institution—its admissions, grading, scheduling, and curricular standards. In a guest editorial for the NCAA newsletter in 2000, John Biaggio, a former member of the Knight Commission, placed the onus on presidents themselves to take control: "In my view, the issues can best be addressed at the institutional level. If we could somehow steel the spines of university and college presidents to confront their athletics departments by insisting that they meet all the standards that apply in all other institutional matters, we would not require any further expansion of NCAA regulations and control."[25]

Meanwhile, as athletic scandals continue and multiply, other campus enterprises also become entrenched outside the control of central administrations or general faculty oversight. These can also be identified by their new, state-of-the-art structures as well as by their determined independence from the rest of the campus in funding and academic control. I am speaking now about some of the professional units—business schools, research institutes, and even academic health centers—that have become domains unto themselves.

Academic health centers are in a special category, perhaps, because medical education absolutely requires a hospital and other such specialized buildings for teaching. The concentration of advanced medical research at the expense of teaching in our universities, however, has impelled many medical schools to build huge hospital/research complexes. In some cases, drug companies have attempted to seal their relationships with universities by building research facilities in the neighborhood. According to Arnold S. Relman and Marcia Angell (both former editors of the *New England Journal of Medicine*), "Merck is now [2002] building a large new research facility on land in Boston immediately adjacent to the Harvard Medical School (the first such facility in an area previously reserved for academic and clinical institutions), and Novartis has leased two research facilities in Cambridge close to MIT, joining several biotechnology companies already there."[26]

In many other cases the academic health centers are found far away from the original home campus—relocated in major cities, where they become essential to the economy and the social services of the surrounding area. The University of Alabama health center in Birmingham is critical in its home city's economy, for example. And so is the massive Texas Medical Center in Houston, combining the Baylor and the University of Texas programs on one site. Once the pride of the founding campus, however, many such centers have become burdens because of the collapse of our health care system. There are many philanthropists eager to put their names on new medical buildings, but there are few willing to endow the training of physicians. With the crisis in funding, and intense competition among private HMOs for Medicare and other government subsidies that once helped support university hospitals, the need to sustain academic health centers has threatened many university budgets. Solutions have been suggested on both a retail and wholesale scale. I will discuss the situation for teaching in medical schools in chapter 7; for now it is sufficient to say that many experts in medical education have come to the conclusion that the crisis in funding for academic medicine is a corrosive problem for universities. Some medical schools have had to divest themselves of their teaching hospitals; schools such as St. Louis University, the University of California–San Francisco, and the University of Vermont have made arrangements either to close their hospitals or to privatize them. Other schools have decided on mergers of teaching hospitals: some worked, but others haven't.[27]

Thus medical schools find themselves bound to expensive physical plants without the means to keep them running. I want to make clear that the medical structures are necessary for some schools in areas where the state university is also the source of advanced medical care for the entire region. But it may be that the glory of the buildings has masked the financial demands of the education that should take place in them. It is clear that the medical centers must emphasize the need for new sources of philanthropic and federal support. A tax on Medicare has been suggested as one course of action. In any case, the moral of this story may be that no matter how significant or worthy the cause, universities must not be carried away by investing in add-ons that receive minimal oversight as to their governance, budget, or relevance to other units in the institution. The motto should be "No buildings without overhead. No narrowly specialized programs without endowments."

While medical schools have been hard-hit by the competitive urgency of the late 1990s, business schools have flourished by capitalizing on a general approval of competition and an accompanying mania to foster "entrepreneurship" among students. Universities have always depended on the kindness of friends to finance ventures in new fields, and there have been many occasions when the expectations of the donor met such resistance on campus that the gift had to be withdrawn, or redrawn. But in an environment where the motto is "Grow or die," the administration is unlikely to reject any gift—especially if it has been cultivated by an ambitious business school dean. There will be a number of such offers that a president can't refuse. And once the dean of a school has her own privately funded domain, she becomes a law unto herself. The dean may have an advisory council of faculty, but many of its members may come from a professional culture that sees faculty governance as meddling. The gift that can command the attachment of a donor's name to a building, or a whole program, usually commands other gifts that attach professorships to other donors' names. Thus the signage for some business schools has become a litany of wealthy patrons to which the campus and the school owe some kind of fidelity.

As David Kirp has detailed in his book on the selling of the American university, the University of Virginia's Darden School of Business has taken the business school fiefdom possibility to a new level—referring to its ties with the university as its purchase of a franchise only.[28] The school acts on its own, has built a bijou resort hotel to accommodate its "Executive MBA" program, and actually bars undergraduate students from its graduate campus. Most business schools nowadays are attached to donors' names—in contrast to the traditional naming of buildings for the university's founder, president, or a notable scholar. A reporter from the *Wall Street Journal* has suggested that only the most traditional business schools and universities—Harvard and Columbia among them—have resisted selling their brand to a corporate benefactor.[29]

The world of these new corporate trademarks on campus buildings is a world of busy commercial enterprise. Similarly, student unions and dining halls that once offered "home-cooked" menus devised by local staffs—of varying culinary skills but often loyal to the university—have been taken over by fast-food franchises. Since the 1980s, the philosophy has been to outsource all possible operations, and thus many campus eating places have become Pizza Hut or Subway venues. Only a few college presidents were wise enough to foresee the kinds of local labor resentments such outsourcing might cause, especially in small communities. And none seems to have consulted nutritionists about the effects of a steady diet of junk food on student health. And so student unions now seem convenient alternatives to the local mall. As such, they add to a developing image of the campus as a market itself rather than a refuge from the marketplace.[30]

The balkanization of contemporary college and university campuses is reflected in a shift of focus from the academic center to peripheries that are less and less dedicated to the balance of teaching and research or to concern for undergraduates' transition to maturity. Such a shift occurs when the football stadium is enlarged, the old field house torn down for a new basketball arena, and a new residence hall built for athletes. It also happens when ornate new professional complexes with only tangential ties to education are opened off campus and off-limits to ordinary students and faculty. It happens when the financial donations of alumni or corporate donors or the government are closed to the inspection of faculty governance because they have been granted exemptions from the ordinary campus budget overview.

The irresistible urge of one institution to imitate and improve upon another has been beneficial in the past, inspiring the rise of the land-grant college, as we have seen. But such initiatives in the history of American higher education were also motivated by a democratic concern that local citizens have the same access to learning as those in neighboring towns, states, or regions. Thus, the tradition of bricks and mortar as a vital aid to the American system of higher education has been rooted in several important principles:

1. Students, especially early and late adolescent students, need and deserve a place apart from "the real world" for their initiation into adult thoughts and concerns.
2. Research should be integrated with teaching.
3. The places where higher learning is pursued should have some distinction and dignity.
4. Because the campus is set within public spaces, it should be available for suitable public occasions but not for commercial manipulation.

The shifting topographies of modern campuses violate these founding principles when structures are built that exclude undergraduate students, encourage the separation of teaching from research, replace the dignity of learning with mindless hoopla, and invite the general public to consider the campus as one more playground to be exploited at will. Reducing the school's name to a logo, proud new temples dedicated to athletic or corporate power threaten to divert the energies of our colleges and universities from public service to corporate ambition.

The faculty is the population on the campus most likely to question such diversions. But faculty critique must be founded on faculty knowledge of the *whole* campus—beyond their own studies, labs, and classrooms. Recent faculty senate efforts to reform college athletics are a hopeful first step. But faculty senates should move beyond athletics. Faculty leaders must reopen dialogue with alumni and boards about the purposes of the campus. In doing so, they will have to resist the temptation to micromanage the physical plant, complain about petty annoyances, or demand special treatment for their own domains. Neither should they resist the growth and change that institutions require. Rather, they should declare that respect for their professional home drives their desire to help in making decisions about its material conditions. Accordingly, they should ask friends of the institution to be thoughtful custodians of campus values rather than cheerleaders for real estate development. Perhaps it is because bricks and mortar are so tangible, their material presence so real to so many members of the campus community, that architectural designs, building blueprints, and landscaping plans can provide a firm grounding for faculty, administrators, students, and alumni working together to decide what campuses are for.

CHAPTER TWO

The Myth of the Bloviating Professor

Sages and Guides

The landmarks and faculty offices are important bricks-and-mortar structures on American campuses, but classrooms are the heart and soul of the educational enterprise there. Although a great deal of learning goes on outside classrooms, the transactions between faculty and students that define the college experience take place within them. Efforts to change classroom practices have preoccupied two groups of reformers in the past decade or so. On one side are the reformers of pedagogy; their concerns can touch curricular matters, but their main emphasis is on the mode in which classes are conducted. On the other side are the reformers of the curriculum; the most contentious of them believe that the ideals of liberal education that once informed the founding of our academic system have been lost and that restoring them has profound philosophical and political implications. I will discuss the pedagogical reform movement in the present chapter and curricular reform in the next. Before analyzing either of these movements, however, I want to say a word about my own sense of where each can be located in terms of the situation of students on our campuses today.

The pedagogical reform group is likely to cite incontrovertible research in psychology as its source of authority, and the curricular group bases its claims on foundational ideas of philosophy and politics. I believe that although each tries to consider the student as the ultimate beneficiary of its views, both give only partial accounts of actual students in actual classrooms. For example, pedagogical reformists tend to be tied to a constructivist view of learning that depends heavily on observations made about children's cognition by Jean Piaget and Lev Vygotsky—observations that point to the roots of human learning in the child's interaction with the environment. By contrast, curricular reformers are likely to be attracted to the schemas for mental and spiritual formation drawn up by thinkers in the past, Plato being a presiding example. Philosophically, then, the two are based on foundations that oppose one another. The pedagogists are actually romanticists, in that they want to unleash students' impulses to learn; the canonists are classicists, in the sense that they view students as blank slates upon which the correct principles must be inscribed. But both share a concern about the impersonality of many contemporary college classes, and so each sponsors thoroughgoing changes in current practice that sometimes seem far removed from the complexities of today's college campuses. One seeks "student-centered learning," the other seeks an induction of students into the rigors of "great ideas." I have some sympathy for both points of view, but I believe that each can state its position in such extreme ways, and so simplistically, that classroom teachers are likely to respond to either with skepticism.

As I hope to make clear in this chapter and the one that follows, I do not believe that matters in pedagogy or curricula should remain as they are; their critics make many valid points about the status quo. But any reform on any campus has to call into play the political will of the entire educational establishment, and such motivation has been undercut by the divisiveness of making faculty the primary targets for blame. Thus both sides have condemned the reluctance of the professoriate to change, whereas many of the critical problems lie in the structure of values within the academy as a whole—including the expectations of administrations, boards, and even students. In some sense, then, the current reforms are distractions from everyday problems in classrooms. Nevertheless, I believe that those faculty and administrators who understand the realities of campus life must come together to make undergraduate teaching better. The main common ground for any reform must be sponsorship of teaching in the reward system in the academy. All the current reform movements eventually arrive at this point in their critiques. It is the one thing we can all agree about.

Perhaps I should declare my own pedagogical allegiances at this point. In my own practice in thirty years of teaching at a large public university, I was guided less by cognitive psychology or moral philosophy (or even literary theory) than by the most practical and reflective form of psychology that I know of. I am referring to the kind of developmental psychology that pays attention to psychosocial growth in adolescence and early adulthood. Those who know the work of Erik H. Erikson will recognize my appropriation of his vocabulary, but I would also add William G. Perry and Carol Gilligan to the list of developmentalists who seem most relevant to college teaching. Tied to clinical practice as well as observational research, their findings have helped me make sense of what I've observed among the students in my own classes. My literary research has been oriented to understanding issues of identity and personal agency in the study of texts. I define education in the humanities as a pursuit of such understanding as well. I believe that without it, students will never be fully liberated from the expectations loaded on them by the vagaries of their environment.

In administration, my experience has been grounded in the practical. I have brokered curricular and other changes both as a "curriculum dean" in a research university's college of arts and sciences and an English department chair. Thus I have threaded my way through thickets of disciplinary interests and budgetary constraints in efforts, not always successful, to satisfy the various concerns while maintaining essential core requirements and some degree of coherence for students. As a result, I have finally been convinced that the exigencies of choice made in the extremities of actual practice drive change more thoroughly than does any single schematic program.

And so I return now to the classrooms housed by the bricks and mortar described in my previous chapter—to the actual rooms where the pedagogical and curricular contests of our day are enacted. In doing so, I will note that controversies may come and go, but classrooms tend to stay the same. There are occasional face-lifts, but the rough service of these rooms to passing generations makes signs of their wear among their enduring graces.

❧ ❧ ❧

Responding to complaints about careless and impersonal teaching at many schools—but especially at large public campuses—some current reformers of pedagogy who emphasize the need for more intimate interaction between faculty and students have sought to redefine the classroom model that places the teacher at the podium and the students in rows before him. In an issue of

Change devoted to campus architecture, Margaret Miller gives a clear description of the reformist view:

> I taught at a campus that projected a splendidly modern profile: Who would have thought that concrete could soar and curve like that? But the assumptions about teaching and learning that were literally built into the classrooms could not have been more old fashioned and (even then I knew it) wrong. Students were seated in miniature amphitheaters at desks fastened to the floor, all facing the stage on which the professor was expected to perform. They too seem bolted to the concrete—only the most venturesome awkwardly swiveled in their seats to address their classmates. The Procrustean message was clear: to teach was to lecture; to learn was to listen to the expert.[1]

Miller's description of a typical classroom emphasizes its theatrical design with the center as a stage for the faculty member—a description that suggests the tiresome rhyme criticizing the teacher for being a "sage on the stage" rather than a "guide by the side."[2] Thus in debates about undergraduate teaching spaces, pedagogical reformers are likely to imagine classrooms that accommodate seating for discussion circles or satellite groupings. Acceding to the pressure of heavy enrollments that demand large classes, however, they persist in resisting the image of the lecturer at the head of the class. Rather, they tend to imagine the teacher as a manager-conductor—orchestrating course exercises, PowerPoint sessions, computer chat rooms, and a host of assistants. They abhor the notion of the teacher as a mistress of fabulous arias, belting out tunes with a harmonic chorus of TAs to provide background accompaniment. In a significant effort to bridge the divide between their ideals and the necessities of mass education, pedagogical reformers turn to technology to make education "student-centered." Thus one convert to student-centered pedagogical reforms states his view of the "new" teacher: "We won't meet the needs for more and better higher education until professors become designers of learning experiences and not teachers." And how is that transformation to be effected? The answer involves "expert-designed learning spaces and experiences, where numerous students can learn on their own, driven at their own pace and guided by their own interests. Using emerging information technologies, such environments can serve many thousands of students at low per-capita costs. The new task for faculty is to form teams to invent and create such learning environments."[3]

The emphasis on the student as the center of the pedagogical structure involves critical questions about the work of the faculty. These questions invoke an inescapable pedagogical polarity: the relationship between "teaching" and "learning." Whose agency is most critical in powering the pedagogical endeavor—the teacher's or the student's? Most experienced faculty agree that these are two sides of the same coin; nevertheless, the most notable general effect of the reformist program for higher education pedagogy has been an emphasis on the word "learning" in all talk about pedagogy. An insistence on this term is so obligatory as to have become politically correct in educational circles, where "teaching" is seldom mentioned without being yoked to "learning." Far from creating a balance in pedagogy, however, such a semantic move radiates a sense that individual faculty are inveterate hams or gasbags, and—more disastrously—that the masses of aspiring students sentenced to their tutelage are actually eager learners who have hitherto been thwarted in their longing to take part in mutual discovery. Under such an extreme critique of college teaching, classroom environments must become spaces for mutual exchange, designed to deemphasize the locus of authority at front and center.

There are some stubborn realities that deserve attention in this teaching/learning debate. Most faculty would agree that these include the condition and size of classrooms as well as the degree of student motivation and development. And most faculty also agree that many of the calls to trust students to manage the pace and interests of their learning ignore multivariate social and economic distractions that beset the student population. In other words, reform notions need to be seasoned with accounts of what individual faculty members actually confront in real places, with real students. Perhaps an inventory is in order.[4]

For example, the classrooms on most campuses tend to contain random samples of styles and furnishings suitable for the *Antiques Roadshow,* or a 1960s-era K-Mart, or the starkest corner of a current Ikea showroom. When students and faculty members are lucky, they get scheduled into some old room with original woodwork and weathered oak desks that have table arms carved with generations of initials. What such classrooms lack in physical comfort, they may make up for in the consolations of solidarity with all the student sufferers who've come before. For example, student opinion about remodeling the old physics lecture hall at Iowa State in 2004 reveals a conflict between wishing to make the room more comfortable and wishing to stay in touch with its history:

Jenny Rixen, senior in health and human performance, has attended classes in the lecture halls and said the chairs in the rooms, which are wooden and have 90-degree angle seat backs, "need some improvement."

Other students see the wooden seating as a piece of history and originality within the classroom.

Aaron Bullington, senior in biology, said the seats are very uncomfortable, but the chairs carry some history with them.

"They're the original seats," Bullington said. "But I think they need to be replaced—they hurt."[5]

Perhaps the physics students at Ames were reflecting on modern alternatives to such traditional sites, for most regular classrooms these days are spare, fluorescent-lit boxes with industrial-strength, tubular student desks that may or may not conform to the student body. And even relatively modern classrooms are likely to have a ratty old instructor's desk—its lectern missing or stolen for use in another classroom. There are also green chalkboards in various shades of dust, a pull-down screen for slides or other media, and—especially near the classics or geography department—pull-down maps of the ancient or modern world. Some classrooms even exhibit the failed technologies of yesteryear: the dangling brackets for TV monitors, the grimy carts for overhead projectors, the empty sockets and tattered speakers for defunct sound systems. There may also be mechanical systems for raising or lowering chalkboards, the intricate paraphernalia of window shades, and heating or cooling systems that defy regulation. By some mysterious mechanism, the simple expedient of raising a window in a classroom often triggers activity by a nearby lawn mower. At the other extreme, and in buildings that are usually off-limits for ordinary classes, there are brand-new classrooms with warm wood paneling, cushioned seats, and the latest in technology for laptop hookups. Such advanced classrooms are most often found in law schools, business schools, and new science halls.

Whatever of inspiration, imagination, or wisdom happens in such classrooms—old or new—must emanate from the teachers and students rather than their ambience. There may be some accommodation of reform notions about active learning, but actual blueprints for the new layouts must await both funding and faculty assent. One campus administration's adjustment to the new pedagogy can be seen in a report issued several years ago for plans to remodel lecture halls at Creighton University in Nebraska. In a campus newsletter, the director of Creighton's campus services commented that "The size of the lecture-halls is not the preferred teaching format." Accordingly, one lecture hall in the business school would be removed altogether: "The greater need . . . would be to create offices in that space."[6] Exchanging lecture space for smaller teaching rooms is rare; in this case, the trade-in serves a growth in administrative space. Some medical schools offer exceptions, however, moving to replace lecture classes with more intimate demonstration theaters. Lecture halls have thus become clinical spaces where hands-on sessions for advanced students answer a public call for better clinical training of doctors. But such reforms seem to have been relegated mainly to professional schools. Most of the classrooms for general undergraduate teaching remain locked into dimensions that can meet enrollment pressures.

Added to the general lack of distinction or comfort in the nation's classrooms is the tendency of student culture to treat them as a cross between a movie theater and the dorm. Students can be unruly, rude, and expressive in body language of their resistance to the obligation to attend classes. Although many instructors find themselves forced to lay out the basic ethos of classroom behavior on course syllabi, minor professorial explosions may erupt at new infractions day by day. Most faculty would agree that student behaviors that impede the mutual flow of learning during a class include (a) flagrantly opening a newspaper to read; (b) carrying on an assignation with a fellow student nearby through whispering, passing notes, or cell messaging; (c) surfing the Web or playing video games on a laptop; (d) failing to remove iPod earphones and spending the hour nodding rhythmically with the beat; and (e) failing to silence cell phones.[7] Syllabi can mandate that students come to class on time, but actual classes can be frayed at either end by individuals arriving late and leaving early. In lecture classes a hundred students closing their notebooks and reaching for jackets makes a noise like the hiss and rattle of a departing train. The clatter can also drown out the professor's concluding remarks. If these include comments on the topic and due date of the next assignment, the professor will be deluged by phone calls or e-mails in days following. Then the naïveté of the student's inquiries can be stunning: "Did I miss anything?"

There are some irritating infractions on the professorial side as well—small agonistic tableaux on display in rooms and corridors across many campuses. The display of disgust by a faculty member waiting with a posse of students outside a classroom door while a colleague rambles overtime inside. A tender-hearted professor standing over the last student in an exam session, valiantly holding back incoming students to let him finish writing out his last thought. Another professor's audible sigh at having to erase a chalkboard covered with notes from an earlier class. The rustling impatience in a lecture class waiting for its professor to track down the microphone that has been carried off by a previous lecturer. The exasperated scuffle when class members must rearrange desks that have been left awry from a previous professor's effort to get everyone to break into small circles. Some instructors feel that the circle should be the "default setting" for classroom seating, while others are adamant about the Platonic beauty of rows (the views of the janitorial staff are rarely sought).[8] Other classroom faculty vices include sheer noise—talking too loud, running a video at high volume, or engaging a class in audible choral speaking or debate. Niceties of faculty behavior in the classroom have never been encoded, but violations of basic care for pedagogical etiquette cause almost as much campus discord as disruptive faculty behavior in that other contested campus site—the parking lot.

I intend this sketch of the material conditions of faculty interactions with students in classrooms to give a fair account of the physical challenges for most faculty in the pedagogical compact. Those challenges frequently call forth extraordinary effort and creativity, and too often the effort is either overwhelmed by circumstances or diverted into the other duties of professorial life. My survey has not, however, mentioned the most daunting feature of campus classrooms. That feature is sheer size.

✻   ✻   ✻

One source of the stereotype of the pompous professoriate is the truth that in the past few decades many introductory courses, especially in research universities, have come to be delivered by lecture to very large classes of students. Most faculty would agree that an institution's dependence on lectures to teach introductory students is not pedagogically sound. Indeed, rationales offered for the increase of lectures have less to do with the professorial penchant for histrionic pedagogy than with the limited resources for instruction. It is much cheaper to double or triple class enrollments than to hire a new professor.

The current dependence on mega classes in many universities and some baccalaureate colleges derives from the sheer numbers of students who have come into higher education since the end of World War II. This population grew almost geometrically with the baby boomers in the 1960s and threatens to do so again with the grandchildren of that first demographic group, plus the many new aspirants for postsecondary education. This onslaught in enrollments is now known as "Tidal Wave II." Its entering students may be from immigrant parentage, from families that do not have a tradition of higher education, and frequently from single-parent families that struggle to support them. Resources are not always to be found by raising tuition and fees—both kept in check by institutional concern about preserving access and by public revolt against higher tuition. One recent study of the use of technology in a science lecture course at UC Berkeley summarizes revealing numbers not only for California but for the whole country: "Public and private colleges and universities nationwide expect to enroll more than two million new full-time students by 2010. . . . The University of California 10-campus system faces an increased enrollment of . . . 43%."[9] Coping with such growth, in the context of inadequate levels of state or tuition support, has required refinements in classroom strategy, especially in introductory courses.[10] It should be noted that the pedagogical crisis of enrollments growth is not limited to research institutions. Community colleges, liberal arts colleges, comprehensive urban institutions, and the regional campuses of public universities find themselves having to compromise on the luxury of small classes, especially in the sciences. The crunch is especially severe in these schools because tech support is often out of reach and because the absence of graduate programs means that there are no TAs to help in coping with small discussion sections or individual tutorials—especially in writing courses.

But the crush of enrollments is not sufficient to explain the ever-increasing dependence on lecture classes in higher education. The reputation of many schools is built on the productivity and fame of their faculty, and so the need to keep up with the competition in research has furnished an important additional rationale for large lectures in many universities. This rationale will be invoked time and again in the chapters that follow, for it is one of the major features of higher education today. In fact, though the turn to lecture classes from smaller classes at most schools was at first inspired by enrollment pressures, large lectures eventually were normalized when it became clear that these classes could also be handy for creating economies of time for faculty. Once lecture classes of more than a hundred students each became a rule rather than an exception for introductory courses, multiplication of such classes presented an opportunity to consolidate enrollments in some of the foundational courses for majors as well as upper-level "service" courses offered to nonmajors. One argument for this expansion of lectures has been that it could free up faculty to teach the specialized courses that required smaller enrollments. Perhaps more significant, the ambition of four-year schools to establish graduate programs plus the increased enrollments in established graduate programs siphoned faculty off from undergraduate teaching and at the same time provided opportunities for graduate students to support themselves by teaching some advanced courses as well as freshman sections.

As the rationale for large classes shifted in this way, the imperative for faculty to do research intensified. Although undergraduate teaching requires currency in the field, graduate teaching requires the degree of scholarly recognition that attracts the best graduate students to the program. Thus the competition for the status of offering graduate degrees began to deflect institutional emphasis away from the classroom to the study and the lab. The American Association of University Professors issued its first statement on course loads in the late 1960s, seeking to protect those faculty who were expected to do advanced research from unreasonable burdens: "It must be recognized that achievement of nine- or six-hour teaching loads may not be possible at present for many institutions. The Association believes, nevertheless, that the nine- or six-hour loads achieved by our leading colleges and universities, in some instances many years ago, provide as reliable a guide as may be found for teaching loads in any institution intending to achieve and maintain excellence in faculty performance."[11] That the Association returned to the statement in the 1990s indicates not only continuing enrollment pressures but an increase in faculty research expectations.

Thus course load has become one of the most important considerations for faculty everywhere. As the chair of a Spanish department in a Big Ten school noted in a 1991 essay on faculty recruitment, the first question asked by most candidates for jobs is about the number of course assignments and the possibilities for reduction. He commented on the mismatch between such concerns and the university's teaching mission: "Perhaps it is ironic that absence of teaching is considered a measure of faculty and institutional quality."[12] But by the 1990s, course assignment practices had become markers of status as well as responses to student pressures.

The situation of faculty in foreign language departments highlights the imbalance in course assignments, for many language courses must be small enough to encourage recitation and response, and recitation and response are extremely labor-intensive. Thus basic language courses usually meet more frequently than do other introductory courses. So do composition classes, and for similar reasons. In either case, it would be impossible for full-time faculty to handle all the students enrolled in small classes—some of which are essentially remedial. And so English and foreign language departments began to employ large numbers of TAs or nontenured faculty to teach double the number of courses, if not the number of students, being taught by tenured faculty. As I have already noted, such ghettoization of teaching is often reflected in the structure and location of campus offices and classrooms. And so the increase in class size, accompanied by the shrinkage in course load, has helped create a perverse work imbalance in the academy. That imbalance denies status and tenure to those who do the most difficult teaching, often one-on-one, with the least-prepared but most needy students.

When I became a professor of English at Indiana in the early 1960s, the standard number of courses taught per semester by faculty was three (with no more than two preparations), and the classes usually had no more than thirty students apiece. Given that English courses usually require papers, this assignment was demanding, but most of my colleagues found it doable. Although we were expected to conduct a viable research program, we could receive tenure for teaching or service when published writing of distinction and promise was also present. Many of us were granted tenure on the basis of a growing body of significant articles, the prospect of a good scholarly monograph in the near future, and successful teaching. By the 1970s, the requirements for research in the tenure process had tightened—in my field, a book was the only sure way to guarantee tenure—and so the standard faculty load in English became two courses per semester, or four per year. Of these four, one must be a large lecture with TA graders. Although the paper grading of faculty might be relieved by those graders in this scheme, additional time would be required to organize the TAs, the sections of the courses, and the ever more plagiarizable exams or paper assignments.

Meanwhile, the driving motive of our academic lives had become the effort to keep abreast with disciplinary developments that themselves were mushrooming both in theoretical elaboration and in primary texts new to the traditional canon. Bright new faculty were arriving, and the challenge of senior teaching faculty was to keep even with them in publication and mastery of the latest developments and so escape the indignity of finding their own salaries lagging behind the pay of the new kids on the block. I will analyze in detail the deleterious effects of this competition in chapter 7; for now it is sufficient to acknowledge that competition also drove the turn to lectures as a prime pedagogical mode for general undergraduate classes. As the system has gradually worked to open upper-level undergraduate major courses to TAs, indeed, the enrollment-size rationale for lecture courses has all but disappeared. Just give the TA two or three sections of twenty-five students in any undergraduate course and get over it. The TAs like teaching classes of their own, and the experience could help them in their interviews for teaching positions. And so the hydraulics involved in the shift to large courses and TA teaching in them has been self-perpetuating, even though the TAs who were once dependable allies in the change now seem ready to rebel against it—there being so few jobs to interview for.

The formula of normalizing the workload for faculty to fewer courses with larger enrollments has been accompanied by deflations in course assignments in other ways. Any type of administrative assignment now carries course release. So does reception of a research grant. Administrators actually budget for such grants so that they can yield part of the recipient's salary back to the personnel budget for other things. This gain can be achieved by appointing cheaper substitute instructors—or by enlarging the small course vacated by the grantee to lecture size. The entrepreneurial figure of Morris Zapp in David Lodge's academic novel *Small World* articulates some faculty members' "omega" for such release—total freedom from teaching:

> That was the beauty of the academic life. . . . To them that had had, more would be given. All you needed to do was to write one really damned good book—which admittedly wasn't easy when you were a young college teacher just beginning your career, struggling with a heavy teaching load on unfamiliar material, and probably with the demands of a wife and young growing family as well. But on the strength of that one damned good book you could get a grant to write a second book in more favourable circumstances; with two books you got promotion, a lighter teaching load, and courses of your own devising; you could then use your teaching as a way of doing research for your next book. . . . In theory, it was possible to wind up being full professor while doing nothing except to be permanently absent on some kind of grant or fellowship.[13]

To be sure, Morris Zapp's theory about privileging research over teaching is a reductio ad absurdum, but the history of course reductions awarded for research has had plenty of such absurdities. One happened in my own department in the 1950s when it moved from a four- to a three-course load. Then the women faculty members were asked to keep the heavier load on account of their being "better" teachers than the men were. They were promised pay raises based on their classroom work. The record soon showed, however, that they were actually teaching more for less—and performing research at a level that equaled or surpassed that of some of their male colleagues. I have not researched this kind of arrangement at other schools, but I suspect that it was not uncommon before affirmative action came to campuses. Perhaps it is because of the evident unfairness of such old deals that current reform programs urging the calculation of course loads variably, according to faculty research activity, rarely gain traction. Nevertheless, among the ranks of part-time and adjunct faculty who teach the bulk of service courses on our campuses, 46.4 percent are women[14]—still overloaded and underpaid.

Institutional or departmental strategies to reduce teaching loads by consolidating introductory students into large classes have proved to be contagious. What happened to course loads in humanities departments like my own happened in the hard sciences with a vengeance. There the standard two-course load was reduced to one, and even that minimal assignment could eventually be reduced to periodic lectures on special topics as part of "team teaching" in a large class rather than responsibility for an entire course. Since new science faculty were expected to spend probationary years getting a lab funded and running, they were conscientiously removed from the design and execution of introductory courses. Without such training, then, teaching faculty in the sciences became an endangered species. Moreover, the social sciences, aspiring to the status of hard science but classified with the humanities in terms of course load, began to reduce their course assignments as well. And so at the present time, the sizes of science and social science courses have exploded: lectures of 500 or more students per section have become routine on large campuses.[15]

As the size of courses increased throughout most of higher education, lecture classrooms became coveted physical assets. Departments scrambled to schedule their classes in every available lecture hall across campus. As a lecturing faculty member, for example, I have taught in a chemistry demonstration hall, where I was always tempted to see what happened if I fiddled with the mysterious jets in the podium sink; in the fine arts auditorium, where I imagined delivering the course in a soft-shoe routine from my stage far above the students; in the business school amphitheater, where I could neither see nor hear students in the back row; and in one strangely narrow lecture room, where students could neither see nor hear me. This last was divided by an elaborate entrance intersecting the rows of desks halfway down. I later figured out that the classroom had been the dining hall in this former campus residence hall, and that the entrance, which cut my class into north and south segments, was its original broad portal. On my campus, as on many others, not only were the lecture rooms jobbed up from previous uses, but they tended to be so far afield from faculty and students that pedestrian traffic jams were chronic when classes changed. One immediate result of the growth and dispersion of classes on my campus was the shortening of the standard fifty-minute sessions to forty-five so that students and teachers could make it from one class locale to another in time. On other campuses, like the University of Minnesota in Minneapolis, there are overpasses and tunnels to handle traffic and keep students from freezing during their treks in winter.

Meanwhile, new building and renovations have afforded faculty scattered opportunities to try to influence the design of new classrooms either to fend against lectures or make them more workable, both for the lecturers and their students. Faculty members may be lazy about governance over general campus development, as I have suggested, but their resistance to large lectures can goad them into collective strategizing against a dean or provost. The long-term chair of a big English department in the Midwest once boasted to me that when the English building was built in the 1960s, he and his colleagues gained enough control over the blueprints to make sure that no classroom would hold more than thirty-five students. More recently, bitter faculty members at a metropolitan business school told me that they felt themselves outmaneuvered by an entrepreneurial administration when it abolished medium-sized classrooms in a lavish renovation of the old building, providing mainly state-of-the-art lecture spaces and an occasional seminar room. A colleague from a small liberal arts college has commented, however, that although earlier faculty influence on the design on her campus had led to most classrooms having tables for no more than fifteen students, the actual classes have now grown so large that students have to crowd in, sitting in tiers behind the fortunate students at the conference table.

Hard-pressed administrations are not, I think, unaware of the pedagogical imperatives that would dictate smaller classes for introductory courses, but their budgets now force them to overlook the evident drawbacks to controlling enrollments. One solution to the problem would be to increase teaching loads. While administrations might welcome such a shift, faculty themselves would be alarmed. And even though the idea of increasing faculty teaching loads has been deemed too hot to handle, increasing the loads of present faculty would hardly cope with all the students who now need small classes. In times when the public mood is to cut rather than add employees, administrations tend to be more willing to pump scarce resources into dubious technology fixes than into the obvious remedy of hiring more faculty.

Meanwhile, in recent years, the student preference for smaller classes has become a significant issue in college choice. Since most students value small classes, one of the points of appeal emphasized by many smaller schools is their ability to offer intimate classrooms. An online claim by Central Oregon Community College is typical of recruitment efforts that promise emotional safety to prospective students who fear getting lost in big classes:

> COCC is a mid-sized school. With just over 7,000 credit students taking classes each year, the numbers may seem daunting. But guess what? They're not! With an average of just 24 students per class, students get some of the best instruction around.
>
> Having small class sizes taught by top-notch faculty means you'll be treated like a somebody instead of just an anybody. No huge lecture halls. No overwhelming campus. Just us and just you.
>
> What could be better?[16]

Given such competition, even large universities have responded to the growing conviction that huge classes are repellant to entering students. Both Harvard and the University of California, for example, boast about carving out a number of "freshman seminars," taught by faculty members, in an effort both to appeal to freshmen and to undercut the impression that all their first-year classes will be enormous. These claims may be offered in good faith, but in truth the small number of such courses usually limits them to a small percentage of entering classes. One strategy in staffing them has been to rehire retired faculty at a modest honorarium. That seems to me a fruitful approach, even though it threatens the case for making smaller classes something more permanent than window dressing. There is no escaping that even if schools could alter the system that rewards research more than teaching, the critics of higher education have consistently refused to support hiring enough faculty to offer reasonably sized classes to all students.

The size of a class does not necessarily determine the teaching mode, of course. Many a lecture is mounted in an average classroom (or even in a seminar room), and some classes designed as lectures manage to evoke a surprising amount of discussion with students. In point of fact, there is nothing more demoralizing than a small class when students come either unprepared or unready to speak up. That's another reason why I tend to be somewhat skeptical of the emphasis on seminars for freshmen, finding capstone courses for seniors more logical. Most undergraduate students need to gain experience in how to participate in discussion, to present ideas, and to formulate useful questions. They have more success in all these endeavors if they have attained a level of comfort with being in college as well as some grounding in the subject. Being clueless in a small class is much more embarrassing and destructive of a student's self-confidence than struggling to understand in the anonymity of a lecture.

❧ ❧ ❧

Reformist notions can build on theoretical preoccupations that ignore some of the everyday facts of pedagogical life sketched above. But I believe these everyday facts give evidence that most college teachers are devoted to teaching no matter how forbidding the environment. Most are genuinely engaged in making each class better than the last. And most find meeting with students an essential factor in their enjoyment of their jobs. In thirty years as a professor, I have met only a few colleagues who are genuinely impervious to the flop sweat that comes when a class is not connecting or when an examination shows that students just haven't gotten it. In fact, discussions of what students ought to know and what works in classrooms are always matters that bring out the most impassioned speeches in faculty meetings. Nevertheless, I agree with reformers that teaching is in trouble in many colleges and universities today. But reform efforts that undermine the didactic transmission of information also call for critical scrutiny.

Among the most important influences in the turn to teaching/learning have been the imperatives, as well as the mantras, issued from the world of work. Peter Drucker's predictions about the coming of "the knowledge society" have directed intense concentration to the collaborative model of discovery as preparation for entry into the job market.[17] The success of such early computer developers as Bill Hewlett and David Packard, who led businesses that emphasized discovery through collaboration, has also led management orthodoxy to mandate "learning communities" everywhere.[18] The dicta of this orthodoxy are frequently cited by pedagogical reformers alongside the mandates of constructivist cognitive psychology; indeed, high-powered management gurus are now as likely to address teaching reform audiences (usually in large lectures) as business audiences. Management gurus such as Peter Senge and Tom Peters have traveled the higher ed conference circuit, and although Drucker tends to be more private, his name is invoked with reverence everywhere educational managers meet. Knowledge is the key to an entrepreneurial future; its generation should therefore follow the patterns of the entrepreneurial past. (Chapter 5, on governance, will discuss Drucker's work and management fads more thoroughly.)

Under the entrepreneurial dispensation, it is no wonder that the teacher becomes a "manager." Whether intentional or not, the preference for such a designation deprives the teacher's activity of its agency, placing that energy elsewhere—in the student's frequently unpredictable motives and capabilities, the classroom interchanges with peers, or the technological choices in instruction. Meanwhile, the term *professor* is taken to imply the prideful claim to superior information, the assumption that there are things to know as well as ways of knowing. Assertions of the priority of expertise may be viewed as overreaching by teaching/learning reformers who believe they know better, as they draw on theories of childhood language acquisition, communications, and management. Unpersuaded that many, many faculty devote a great deal of time and ingenuity to devising ways to communicate and even to "sell" their knowledge to students, many reformers in their discourses about teaching and learning indict, more or less openly, the professoriate as a power center that can be stubborn, demanding, and indifferent to change.

The discourses of these pedagogical reformers gathered impetus in the early 1990s, and although there were many versions, the most fervent advocacy occurred within the American Association of Higher Education at its conferences and in its magazine, *Change*.[19] In an important 1995 issue of *Change* two enthusiasts who advocated shifting the "paradigm" from "instruction" to "learning" drew up a chart of opposing pedagogies—contrasting the old "50-minute lecture" with new "learning environments." These columns also set up the cognitive goals of the "new paradigm" as they cast recognizing the need to "Elicit student discovery and construction of knowledge" against working for "Transfer of knowledge from faculty to students."[20] Other sets of oppositions in the chart suggested an array of assumptions about the nature of cognitive development and how it impinges on the instructor's approach to arranging his classroom. Thus course designations of class periods and their scheduling would open up, as would markers of success and the status of instructors—

"'Active' learner required, but not 'live' teacher." Presiding over this "learning paradigm" was the presumption that "Knowledge exists in each person's mind and is shaped by individual experience."[21]

The tone announcing the learning paradigm was by turns ecstatic about the future and disdainful of the past. The authors believe that the new regime promises a true transformation—"The Learning Paradigm also opens up the truly inspiring goal that each graduating class learns more than the previous graduating class. In other words, the Learning Paradigm envisions the institution itself as a learner—over time, it continuously learns how to produce more learning with each graduating class, each entering student." And they dismissively assess the total failure of traditional faculty practices: "the primary learning environment for undergraduate students, the fairly passive lecture-discussion format where faculty talk and most students listen, is contrary to almost every principle of optimal settings for student learning."[22]

With assaults like this one, contentions about the nature of what happens in campus classrooms became the manifestations of an ongoing guerrilla conflict that has only slowly come to public notice, sometimes in the guise of the "whole language debates" or the "math wars." The battles are still engaged at national conferences, in journals and bulletins published by higher education associations, at administratively sponsored on-campus colloquia, and in teaching resource centers that continue on many campuses as remnants of the teaching reforms of the early 1970s.

There are also many national conferences on teaching/learning for faculty, but it is my impression that pedagogical conferences are more likely to be peopled by administrators than by rank-and-file faculty members. In the always tight budgets of academic departments, faculty must decide whether to use their travel money to attend such conferences or to go to disciplinary meetings, and they usually opt for the latter. This absence may account for an animus against the faculty that I and other faculty colleagues have felt at such gatherings. It may explain as well the faculty's sense that teaching/learning reforms usually come down upon them from the top. It is also true that pedagogical reform programs have been slighted by many faculty, preoccupied as they are with the demands of their disciplines and the heavy daily tasks of making their courses work. Their seeming indifference has generated much of the frustration that some reformers feel with the faculty. One such critic of the faculty once asked me whether academic freedom should be construed as protecting a faculty member's refusal to comply with new pedagogical mandates. He had been warned off by more than one unreceptive professor for infringing on professorial autonomy in the classroom.

When pedagogical reform mandates do penetrate to the teaching faculty, the reaction can be irritation. For example, in a 2005 *Academe* essay titled "The Managed University," Kevin Mattson warns colleagues to "beware" of the mandates of "active" or "engaged" learning because they "portend trouble for the future of higher education and the American professoriate." Mattson is mainly concerned about the transformation of teaching into frantic entertainment under the urgency to engage all the students all the time. He sees reformist hype as a substitute for actually funding higher education in ways that might alleviate the problems of massive lectures.[23] This irritation is shared by some leaders in higher education disciplinary associations as well. The late Phyllis Franklin, executive director of the Modern Language Association, once told me that educational foundations "don't want to help us. They only want to *change* us!"

The teaching/learning debate is not only a matter of faculty individualists against reformers, however; it is also a matter of contending notions about the nature of knowledge and its mastery. Each side tends to dismiss the other's stance on these more philosophical issues as well as on the practical ones. Critics of the learning/teaching movement often assert, for example, that the insistence on the "construction" of knowledge by student learners overvalues the half-truth that deeply effective learning is achieved only through the internalization of problems that have been solved from scratch and then mastered by each individual in his or her own way. They find themselves frustrated by reform proponents who do not comprehend the spectrum of variables at work in the learning of late adolescents as compared with that of young children. They also worry about the inefficiencies of taking the long way around on every learning item.

Students in the modern university or college classroom not only are in multiple stages of development but have multiple tasks to master. Thus their cognitive development is frequently distracted by the stage-specific social challenge of exploring relationships and establishing a somewhat stable identity. The very fact that many of them are away from home or on their own for the first time can inspire behaviors that disrupt their learning far more than course design can. By the same token, because of their need for intellectual models and adult approval, students may be more engaged by particular qualities of teaching than by intense grappling with first principles. Indeed, many research surveys have shown that the two features of an individual instructor's pedagogy that most engage undergraduates are her control of the material and her concern with students' understanding of it.[24] Students may never achieve total control of the material itself, but their fascination with observing a master handling it can give them "good enough" learning in fields that they may not need to know in great detail.[25]

Sometimes this kind of learning happens best in the lecture format, for lecturing has a long and distinguished history. Lecture halls seem to have been a feature of higher education from the very beginning, perhaps setting off advanced learning in a metropolis from the more informal tutelage of the home or village. Indeed, at the site of the library at Alexandria in Egypt, archaeologists have recently discovered thirteen classrooms—all with rows of limestone seats surrounding an elevated area that must have served as a podium. These date from about 30 B.C.E. and are situated beside a main lecture hall that seems to have had a capacity of 5,000 students![26] It is difficult to imagine how such a lecture hall would work; in our own time it would require a sound system, projection facilities, and more comfortable seats.

Contemporary lecture halls are less massive than the main one at Alexandria, but they may hold as many as 500 or 1,000 students. Although I am concerned about the reliance on large lectures for introductory science classes, I must admit here that equipping chemistry or other science classrooms is very expensive, as they require demonstration equipment and high-tech projection. Furthermore, the dependence on lecture classes by the sciences may involve cognitive issues as well. Although most science reform programs from within the disciplines call for efforts to find ways to apply principles so that students can see their relevance, many scientists still worry over the question of whether the foundational knowledge in fields of hard science can really be learned effectively through group discussion.

One contemporary enthusiast of "communities of learning" sees the new paradigm as forcing the redesign of science classrooms to provide "ongoing opportunities for 'hands-on,' laboratory-intensive science, from the introductory level for all students through capstone courses for majors," suggesting that we should speak of "sciencing" rather than teaching science.[27] Steven Pinker has argued, however, that basic knowledge, not only in math but in other science fields, cannot really be learned except through more direct exposition. Thus he criticizes the constructivists: "The ascendant philosophy of mathematical education in the United States is constructivism, a mixture of Piaget's psychology with counterculture and postmodernist ideology. Children must actively construct mathematical knowledge for themselves in a social enterprise driven by disagreements about the meanings of concepts. The teacher provides the materials and the social milieu but does not lecture or guide the discussion. Drill and practice, the routes to automaticity, are called 'mechanistic' and seen as detrimental to understanding."[28] Pinker believes that concepts have to be laid out, explained, and expounded. And even so, their final mastery must be based on the student's control of fundamental information that can be learned only through memorization and drill.

Yet it is true that despite an almost punitive longing for its return by some pedagogical reformers on the right, sheer rote memorization, associated often with lecture classes but also more generally with rigorous instruction throughout the curriculum, is inadequate as the main instructional mode for college students. It can be incredibly boring, for one thing, and it is ineffective without the reinforcement of application. But I agree with Pinker in believing that reformers on both sides of the memorization controversy dismiss the value of some such repetitive exercises too easily when they identify them either as damaging souls or as building mental muscles. The fact is that math educators spend a great deal of time trying to find ways to explain problems in ways that can motivate "reluctant learners." The fact is also that somewhere along the way, as a colleague who has worked in math education has commented to me, "they must learn the arithmetic."[29]

When exercises in learning the basics of any field are lightened by social competition, mnemonic cues, and, in early childhood especially, the rhythmic chants of nursery tunes or jingles, they create paths in the brain that will endure for many years. Some scientists feel that their strength can penetrate the fog of sleeping sickness and other neurological afflictions or even Alzheimer's.[30] Thus the much-maligned memorization of poetry may be more healthy than harmful in the long run. In my own freshman classes, where recitation by heart of one of the notable speeches from Shakespeare was a course requirement, I found students willing to try and later proud of their achievement. After all, there is a "natural" memorization of popular song lyrics and tunes—which many students achieve by hearing them over and over through their earphones. Although such repetition and memorization are normal, as is the conscientious mastery of baseball statistics by young fans, their pervasiveness does not seem to influence the arguments of those pedagogical reformers who abide by a sense that learning by rote is somehow coercive.

In short, although both learning and teaching are social endeavors, they cannot always be personal transactions. No faculty member can "guide" an ordinary student into familiarity with the periodic table. It takes an extraordinary mind like that of Primo Levi or Oliver Sacks to spontaneously find the drama in chemicals and the poetry in their symbols fascinating.[31] Some theoretical physicists, like Richard Feynman, are born with an instinct for mathematics, but for most students mastery comes from the mental labor of learning foundational information so thoroughly that it comes spontaneously to their aid in solving problems. As a matter of fact, Feynman's three-volume set of lectures, drawn from his introductory classes in the early 1960s, became indispensable for students of quantum mechanics, even though his undergraduate students at Caltech are said to have abandoned their seats in his lecture hall—to be replaced by graduate students and his colleagues.[32]

And, of course, there are faculty whose gifts are forensic and dramatic as well as intellectual. They thrive in lecture halls and their classes are oversubscribed and overflowing. Such teachers exist on every campus, and attending one of their lectures can be as exciting as hearing a great violinist play the Beethoven concerto. Rarely do students have the chance to observe intellectual mastery and excitement in their daily world. When they find it on a campus, it validates the life—the liveliness—of the mind. And that undergraduates seek not only performance but the shared appreciation of it can be gauged by their willingness to hand over large fees to attend mass concerts in which the star is a distant speck bathed in a spotlight. Universities need faculty with such daring expertise, and they need rooms big enough to accommodate them. In one of the best accounts of teaching that I know of, Barry Kroll describes his discovery of the power of the lecture for undergraduates in a course on Vietnam that attempted to engage their "hearts and minds": "That fall I went into the freshman course aware of the pitfalls of lecturing and prepared to try some alternatives for large-group instruction. But because I was new at it, I had to learn about the special opportunities afforded by a lecture hall filled to capacity. At the beginning of the semester, I did not suspect that a large audience could generate such a degree of emotional intensity. There were days when the energy crackled through the air, as though someone had wired all the students and plugged them into the main current."[33]

Ordinarily good teaching finds ways to lay out material in an orderly way, making a shortcut for the student through the thicket of detail and argument that experts already know by heart. The diagrammatic presentation of material may be one positive feature of such a teaching mode. Another may be the student's relief at having an expert rescue him from mistakes a novice might make along the way—and also save him the irritation of having to spend his precious time listening to the opinions of classmates rather than a clear exposition of the known facts and issues. Many students have complained to me about the palaver in a class that insists on collecting every opinion and never comes down on the side of any. Others have told me that they find the breaking up into small groups a bore, and that the group's discussions are frequently off the point. Study groups may be sites for some forms of student predation as well. An honors student in business once told me that in all her group projects, the women ended up keeping the team on task. They wrote the reports while the guys joked and flirted. Such complaints about slackers may betoken adolescent intolerance, but they also point to the need to qualify some features of current pedagogical orthodoxy with classroom reality.

It is just common sense that college classes need to be scenes of the systematic transfer of information, and the desire for information is by no means an appetite for "just the facts" on the part of students alone. In making this point, I cannot forbear mentioning a press release I saw on a Web site for farriers and horse trainers announcing, "International Hoof-Care Summit Succeeds with Innovative Format." The success was obvious from the first sentence: "More than 500 farriers, equine veterinarians and other hoof-care professionals filled the lecture halls and meeting rooms of the first annual International Hoof-Care Summit." The story ascribes the triumph of the Cincinnati meeting, held in February 2004, to the event's "heavy emphasis on education." The publicist notes that the meeting eliminated "hands-on horseshoeing demonstrations, contests and organizational meetings" in favor of what one attending farrier called "pure information"; he added, "It was really a fascinating 4 days."[34]

🐎 🐎 🐎

The mutual distrust that has grown up between educational reformers and their faculty colleagues not only obscures the fact that we've done quite well but also impedes the very real possibility that we could do better. Having engaged in some of the pedagogical reforms that swept many campuses during the early 1970s, I myself became convinced that successful college teaching does not come naturally; it requires training, discussion, and openness to criticism. The reforms of those days made major changes in the classrooms on many campuses. I can remember a time in my own undergraduate education when syllabi were not published until the last minute and when exams were given on the spur of the moment and returned at leisure. There were never teaching evaluations then; indeed, faculty members had no systematic way to find out about the effectiveness of their teaching. I believe that faculty need such feedback from students. And they need conversations with one another about what works and what doesn't in the classroom.

But pedagogical reform works best when it earns the support of teachers themselves. I submit that more than criticism and exhortation, college teachers in today's overflowing classrooms need support for working together on their pedagogy. They also need more determined administrative efforts to decrease the number of students they must teach and to reward their efforts at reaching each one. Professional reformers can help more by advocating reasonable class sizes and the hiring of permanent faculty than by peddling room design, hardware, or their favorite methodology as solutions to the problems of scale in mega classes. And since it is clear that cutting-edge discoveries in research must be taught if they are to alter or refine the public understandings of science, I think that research faculty must also pay their dues in undergraduate classrooms. Course assignments, and even course loads, may vary, but universities and colleges are not research institutes, and the faculty who work there must therefore be involved in teaching.[35]

Finally, also, the narrow view of student learning as mainly self-generated and invariably effective neglects the fact that the vitality of the educational exchange derives in large part from the engagement of the professor in a lifetime of discovery. In an eloquent essay on the "teaching/learning" nexus, Robert Scholes, former president of the Modern Language Association, makes this point. We "teach in order to learn," he says. "Organizing a course, preparing a lesson, we become acutely aware of what we need to know to do that job properly—and of the gap between that blessed state of perfect knowledge and our actual situations. Teaching drives us to learning—and to the learned who can help us join their company."[36] I suspect that Scholes's definition of college teaching best matches the understanding that drives many of the good teachers in American higher education. They believe that it takes a knowledgeable, trained, passionate professional who has committed to a career in real classrooms to instigate and direct what students do there.

In discussing the settings for such instigations, those who insist on small classrooms and personal interactions are apt to appropriate James A. Garfield's observation that "The ideal college is Mark Hopkins on one end of a log and a student on the other."[37] Loyal to his alma mater and its president, Garfield thus invoked the charisma of one of the greatest educators and orators of his time to define the best that higher education can offer. But it is clear that the power of Mark Hopkins's pedagogy was not tutorial alone. His gifts also flourished on the pulpit and in the lecture hall. Most important, their authority derived from a lifelong commitment to the academy. I think, then, that we can take him to have enacted at once the two models of the teacher that are often invoked as opposed to one another. Hopkins was both a "sage on the stage" *and* a "guide by the side." Under such an interpretation, the "log" in Garfield's aphorism stands for the quality of the pedagogical transaction rather than the choice of one mode, or site, of teaching over the other. Colleges and universities need both lecture halls and seminar rooms with teachers in them. And so do students.

CHAPTER THREE

Getting the "Liberal" Out of Education

The Curriculum

Since the founding of universities in the Middle Ages, there has been debate about what should be taught in classrooms, and since Plato there have been competing notions about the best mode of instruction. Likewise, in the past two decades an array of reformers have turned their attention to teaching and the curriculum. On one side are the pedagogical reformers discussed in chapter 2, who seek to open up teaching so as to provide a more hospitable environment to the wide variety of students now encountering higher education. On the other are curricular reformers, who eye with skepticism the effort to accommodate this growing student diversity through the dispersion of "core" content in the curriculum. These critics see the loss of foundational subject requirements and texts as a source of incoherence for introductory students, a retreat from rigor in challenging them to achieve, a failure in transmitting the best traditions that underlie American democracy, and a symptom of the lack of commitment to undergraduate education among the faculty. Like the pedagogical reformers discussed in the previous chapter, advocates of curricular discipline view the professoriate with suspicion; they see the faculty—especially the humanities faculty—as a privileged group who have lost track of their educational vocations by arguing about epistemological niceties while bewildered students wander off to the business school. These attitudes toward choices and requirements are the subject of this chapter.

In analyzing them, I want to describe the historical course of the present wars over the curriculum, the forces that have come into conflict across its boundaries, and the political fireworks that have been activated by such academic friction. In actual fact, I believe that many college teachers are attached to ideals held by critics of the state of the curriculum and that a substantial number wish that they could accommodate some of them. On the other hand, they know that curricular reform is extremely complicated—especially at large universities, where scheduling is a nightmare, many students do not follow traditional four-year patterns, and new disciplines simply have to be opened for undergraduates. Most professors are also sensitive to the rigidity of the old "great books" model, its exclusiveness, and its frequent blindness to new ideas and new talents. Despite faculty worries about these matters, however, proponents of a return to the classics have tended to depict the practicing faculty as careless and deaf to their criticism. Thus, powerful advocates for cultural conservation in higher education have become embattled against the professoriate, and faculty members who try to conduct their classes in good faith, day by day, find themselves suspected not only of educational faddism but of a lack of respect for the nation's past.

Given the atmosphere of accusation and recrimination that debates about the canon have created, it is no surprise that the faculty in the center have assented to a moratorium on sweeping curricular revision, under the rubric of "a pox on both your houses." A recent survey of curricular changes among leading universities has shown that out of twenty-five major public and private universities canvassed, eight had no record of substantial curricular evaluation in the past fifteen years. Nine had "reviewed" general education requirements in the past five years; of these, most had issued reports that simply reemphasized sweeping statements about the need for liberal learning informed by courses that acknowledge cultural differences. But few had made fundamental changes in their requirement structures.[1]

One notable exception is Harvard University, which began a major review when Lawrence Summers became president in 2001. A preliminary report with a set of guidelines for specific changes was issued in 2004, with interesting commentary from some of Harvard's leading professors. Thereafter, faculty committees took over. The preliminary report was extremely ambitious, calling for more concentrated and accessible courses in the sciences, more integration between introductory and advanced courses (including a "faculty-taught" freshman seminar and capstone courses for advanced students), postponement of the deadline for declaring a major, a change in the calendar to permit coordination among all programs plus a special January term for "experimental" study, and a new emphasis on study of a foreign culture, with a strong language requirement and a directive for a semester of study abroad. The dean's 2004 progress report indicates that the implementation of these recommendations is taking place, albeit slowly. It lists a number of promising interdisciplinary themes that have already been prepared, though it does not detail particular undergraduate courses in these areas. The leading university in the country apparently will not be getting into the canon controversy but will concentrate on broad general goals by modifying existing regulations. Significant intentions have been carried through, especially in new hiring at the junior level. And in a departure for Harvard, assistant professors will be deemed tenurable.[2] The resignation of President Summers in February 2006 followed that of the dean of the college in January 2006, but it seems to have had little relation to the curricular reforms listed in the report of 2004. Progress on these reforms was praised by Dean William C. Kirby in his letter to the Faculty of Arts and Sciences of March 1, 2006, in which he expressed his intention of seeing them carried through during the time remaining to him in office.[3] By all accounts, the major source of Summers's problems seems to have been his managerial conduct rather than his curricular plans. Nevertheless, one report has suggested that Summers forced Kirby's resignation because of the "slow pace of curricular reform."[4]

Radical curricular change is hard to come by, but Harvard's multiyear effort may betoken a renewal that will move to other institutions. Yet the "national" curriculum has not been completely moribund over the past twenty years. A great deal of tinkering occurs continually. At departmental levels, for example, courses are constantly being redefined or added.[5] But mainly, as Gerald Graff has observed about curricular change in English departments,[6] institutions have tried to remedy the problems in the curriculum with add-ons such as women's studies, African American studies, Jewish studies, and gay and lesbian (or GLBT—gay, lesbian, bisexual, and transgender) studies that then must be integrated into the requirement system. Thus at Harvard the recommendation for an international experience needs to be folded into the more general set of requirements. Still, the proof of any new pudding lies in decisions at the departmental level, and whether courses developed there will bear the marks of any new plan.

Given the diversity of institutions and the complexity of their offerings, it is doubtful that unchanging and universal curricular decisions at the level of course content can ever be made for all of American higher education. What is not in doubt, however, is that the faculty needs to engage both with the campus community and with the general public in considering some very real problems. In talking about what they teach, and why, faculty need to use a language that is based on their experience in introductory classrooms, that is accessible to non-academics, that respects the normal student desire for guidance about the most significant or founding texts and ideas in their studies, and that is itself careful to mute the rhetoric of political and cultural warfare. Although faculty are frequently distracted by the strategies of conservative critics to get "liberals" out of education, their more important task is to convince students, and their parents, that introductory courses currently offered to students bring together profound philosophical themes and broad social relevance. In other words, they need to get the liberal back into education.

 ❧ ❧ ❧

 In laying out the history of today's curricular reform movement, I will forebear the conventional return to ancient Athens, the University of Bologna in the Middle Ages, or even nineteenth-century Harvard, Oxford, or Dublin. Instead I want to make my point of departure Berkeley, California, and the deliberations of the Carnegie Commission on Higher Education there, as reported in 1972 in *Reform on Campus: Changing Students, Changing Academic Programs.* At that time, and in that place, American higher education was recovering from the disruptions of the 1960s, and the Carnegie Commission report reveals that its leaders were attempting to respond to changes suggested by those disruptions. The commission was made up of the leading administrators of the day, and its report was written in large part by Clark Kerr, former president of the University of California.[7] In its "concluding note," the Carnegie Commission was optimistic about the possibilities for changing college curricula: "We see the decade of the 1970's as a period of innovation, as an era that provides unusual opportunities to improve the quality of academic life, and as a period when the energy for reform that has been released can be combined with the spectrum of available innovations to provide more vital intellectual communities." But, given the recent history of campus unrest, the commission was also defensive about any suggestion that curricular change was politically driven: "Whatever changes are needed should be undertaken for the sake of the students and for the sake of society, not for the sake of peace on campus."[8]

 But despite its protestations, the Carnegie Commission did conceive of curricular reform as deriving from social pressures—pressures that would eventually politicize the very reasonable changes it called for. Interestingly enough, the commission's program of curricular redesign was not in any obvious sense urgent at the time of its report. The massive survey of student and faculty opinion conducted as the foundation for the study revealed that at the beginning of the 1970s, both faculty and students were relatively content with what was happening in classrooms on their campuses. Finding that substantial majorities of students, graduate students, and faculty were positive about the state of higher education—only 12 percent negative among students, 23 percent among graduate students, and 8 percent among faculty (pp. 10–12)—the report strenuously spun the results as a mandate for change, concluding that in real numbers, the minority who expressed discontent should be taken seriously. It finally asserted that the current levels of dissatisfaction "are important aspects of campus life" (p. 11). In some ways the members of the educational establishment involved in the Carnegie Commission were promoting an agenda of their own.[9]

Accordingly, the commission set up a schema that would undermine by elimination or dilute by expansion the old system of defined course requirements for general education. It would emphasize the necessity to design courses that answered to the diversity of students, call for many more opportunities for student choice, and advise a new concentration on preparing graduates for civic and vocational life after college. Indeed, the report rejected not only the old "core" curriculum but also the notion of "breadth" in introductory courses, showing great disdain for the "survey" course as an instrument for giving freshman students effective overviews of particular fields of knowledge:

> We prefer, in fact, to drop the nomenclature of *general education* and *liberal education* because it carries with it connotations of past efforts at a general coverage of all essential knowledge. Such coverage has proved impossible, despite repeated experiments over the past 70 years. "Essential knowledge" no longer has the intellectual (classical) and/or theological core that once allowed a student to cover it all in one college career. We prefer the concept of a "broad learning experience." The major provides depth within a single discipline or related disciplines. Free electives provide a chance to follow specific interests over time. (pp. 42–43)

The emphasis on "experience" in the definition of the best motive for general education points to pedagogical as well as curricular issues within the commission's purview. And it is clear that those issues were linked to concerns for diversity—for serving new students from a variety of backgrounds and preparations. "The main development we see ahead is an effort at the creation of a more diverse series of optimal learning environments to meet more precisely the needs of each college-age person—diverse as these needs are and hard to accomplish as this goal will be—so that each young person will have an equality of opportunity through one form of education or another, to maximize the quality of his or her life" (p. 68). Thus American higher education's continuing concern for the inclusion of minorities in general education became embedded in the curriculum as well as in admissions policies.

Many colleges and universities reacted positively to the suggestions offered by the Carnegie Commission. Although they paid homage to its vision, however, the motives behind their loosening of general education requirements were mixed. As they acknowledged the ideal of responding to diversity among students, for example, they were also responding to growing disciplinary specialization among faculty and departments. With the increase in number of departments—whether spin-offs from the standard liberal arts departments or new combinations of them into interdisciplinary programs—came a need to generate student credit hours that would justify specialized course offerings. The power of being listed as one of the new "optimal learning environments" was motivation enough for departments to design syllabi that would be attractive to introductory students. The reward would be enrollment figures that could sustain the program and its faculty.

As the disciplines shifted, changed, and multiplied, so did the faculty who taught in them. Their graduate training had become more specialized and so did they. As a result, a new assistant professor in history who, for example, had spent five years completing an interdisciplinary history of medicine dissertation on the black death in twelfth-century Italy could hardly see herself teaching a course that required her to know the history of the world from the beginning to 1945. Further, the expansion of her knowledge in one direction—about medical diagnosis, epidemiology, statistical demographics, and the like—made even a chronological command of European history harder for her.

Although there is much justifiable criticism of faculty overspecialization, it is important to acknowledge the link between specialization and the expansion of knowledge. Research became more specialized in the last quarter of the past century because information and methodologies for interpreting it expanded in a number of disciplinary directions. And it is also important to remember how much excitement there was in new courses, much of it caught by students; they felt like pioneers who were complicit in uncovering new texts and new insights into how knowledge is established and achieved. Pre-med students who delved into the conditions underlying the black death were apt to become doctors who were *more* likely to continue to read history after college than those who spent time trying to figure out why they should know about the Treaty of Ghent.

Another motive for accepting the reforms of the 1970s was a rising doubt about the project of "introducing" students to universal knowledge all in one course or one year. Many professors began to find such curricular projects misguided in their assumptions about students as well as faculty. If it was questionable that a single faculty member could responsibly teach texts that reached from the Greeks to the moderns, it seemed even more questionable that students were prepared to absorb such texts. Although the choice of content in the literature courses that were the backbone of the liberal arts curriculum received the weight of attention through the wars about the canon, concerns were raised in other humanities departments as well. The sciences tended to avoid controversy, except in debates about the "new math" or whether general biology courses should require labs, but the humanities have been at the center of the curriculum controversies from the start.

At this point I would like to take the liberty of giving a bit of autobiography to illustrate the evolution of introductory world literature courses in the direction envisioned by the Carnegie Commission, indicating some of my own problems with it along the way. In doing so, I must note that as the course design changed, so did the class size, as discussed in the previous chapter. At the start, I taught the introduction to (world) literature in classes of 30 students; then, under the reform scheme, I had to teach the course in sections of 300. Eventually, a faculty revolt got the enrollment down to 150. There were always TAs, and working with them was one of the joys of the course.

When as a new assistant professor I taught the general literature course required for all for freshmen, we began by slogging through the *Odyssey,* caught speed through *Oedipus Rex,* limped through "The Death of Socrates," picked up a bit over selections from the Bible, and bogged down almost completely in Dante's *Inferno.* The second semester (which I rarely taught), launched off from *The Canterbury Tales* (selected), went well with *Hamlet* (using cuts from Olivier's version), managed to become somewhat morose through either Swift or Voltaire, became decisively gloom-ridden with *Crime and Punishment,* and then petered out over *As I Lay Dying.* I seem to remember that there was time for some modern poetry (selected). This "modern" course was more teachable, perhaps, but the closer its chronology came to the twentieth century, the less the faculty agreed on which texts ought to be included. Just about every member of the faculty, from assistant to full professor, taught one or another of these courses every year. Amid enrollment pressures in the 1960s, however, advanced graduate students had come to be assigned sections as well. Thus one of the reasons to turn the course into a lecture was the fear of its becoming a non-faculty course. My department maintained the notion that tenured or tenure-track faculty should teach first-year students. But frequently lamenting their lack of preparation for the course, some faculty became skeptical about the wisdom of its syllabus.

I longed to find from my senior colleagues the key to the successful teaching of Literature 101, for the quality of my students' understanding of the power of literature to examine and explain their experience seemed to me lost in the pile of strange names, obscure allusions, and difficult language. One helpful mentor suggested that I try showing some of Gustave Doré's etchings for Dante—"Doré for the *Inferno,* Blake for the *Paradiso,*" he intoned. I felt very uncomfortable with either, and so I was receptive to a second motive for resisting the requirement's content: the conviction that ordinary students could not learn from such a course more than an elementary smattering of literary lore and surface interpretation. They would get a passing familiarity with the authors and their times, perhaps, and a dim sense that they ought to be concerned with great themes (in this case, "the journey" was a handy rubric), but the more contemporary texts featured in my sophomore lecture course, "Introduction to the Novel," seemed to connect with them on a deeper level.

Nevertheless, I dutifully taught the Greeks-to-Dante version of the introductory humanities course often in the early '60s, rebelled against it in the late '60s, and became slightly nostalgic for it in the '70s. By the time the course was changed to feature each instructor's sense of what it was supposed to do and which texts to use, it was also competing with a variety of other literature courses offered by the comp lit department, by language departments, and even by some sections of religious studies. At that point, my self-designed lecture sections did not have the automatic authority given by their former status as requirements—even the School of Business had required them. Under the old dispensation, students *expected* difficulty and alien texts, whereas in the later one they were querulous about all the "foreign stuff." For one thing, the older version of the course required presentation of *lore*—essential information that students could get in usable form only from me (even though I may have feverishly swotted it up the night before). The later version of the course, however, concentrated on interpretation, and in that activity students have always suspected that one person's version is as good as any other's.

When I was chair of my English department in the 1980s, I decided one day to clean out the storage room to gain space for such things as computer supplies. There, hidden under a back table in the shadows, were two strange remnants from the Lit 101 course of the '60s. The first was a large poster, elaborately drawn by some student, of the circles of hell, featuring modern-day sinners in the various circles (Elizabeth Taylor and Richard Burton were placed by this student in the second circle, to accompany Paolo and Francesca). The second artifact was even more elaborate, a wooden model of the Globe Theatre. I could have dismissed these as quaint evidences of primitive, ineffective, literalist teaching, but then I remembered my own frantic grasping at some ploy to entice ordinary freshmen into some realization of the relevance and reality of Dante and Shakespeare and so reserved my judgment on former colleagues. With the passing of time, I had come to realize that even in our more sophisticated teaching of contemporary texts, familiarity with essential material facts might be worth a thousand interpretive angles.

I give as one example an episode from a group discussion I once conducted in a small section of "Introduction to Literary Studies," which was meant, under a new order of things, to introduce sophomore English majors to issues in the study of literature, with an emphasis on "theory." The day's job was to explore Faulkner's "A Rose for Emily," in the light of reader-response criticism. Thinking that it would be good to start by simply making sure that everyone appreciated what had happened in the story (or had actually *read* the assigned text), I asked for a simple summary of its events by members of my encircled class. My first respondent, bored by the whole thing, observed that in his opinion nothing much had happened in Faulkner's gothic tale. A second respondent was astonished by this judgment: "What about Homer Barron's skeleton that they found in Miss Emily's bed after she died?" she asked. "He was right there where she'd been sleeping with him all those years." The bored student came back, "Is *that* who that was? How did you know?" And the second replied, "Because they found the silver toilet seat, engraved with his name on it, that she had given him as a wedding present right before he tried to jilt her. It was right there on top of her chest of drawers when they broke in." The entire class snapped to attention: "*Toilet* seat?" they all said.

In a frantic rescue of the awakened students, the class, and William Faulkner from this serial misreading, I became aware that Faulkner's Yoknapatawpha County could be as strange as the world of the ancient Greeks. Of course, I pointed out that the betrothal gift had been a "toilet set," not a seat, and that the word "toilet" was Americanized from *toilette*, the French word for grooming. In the ensuing discussion of sanitary conditions and social conventions in the American South in the early twentieth century, I wondered if we wouldn't be better off discussing propless dramatizations of treachery and revenge in the House of Atreus. But my main curricular conclusion was that any text I could think of could be alien to one student or another. Each would require some background—information about either the times or the setting or the beliefs therein. And even so, students will always make mistakes that seem bizarre on first glance but turn out to be reasonable if we remind ourselves that one of the reasons to go to college is to find things out.

I will leave off the biography at this point. What I have tried to indicate through it is my sense that in the experience of ordinary faculty members, the changes advised by the 1972 Carnegie Commission seemed inevitable, but they became problematical as well. And if liberal ideology played some role in loosening up the curriculum, the main sentiments behind what happened were practical and pedagogical.

In any case, the curricular controversies of the 1970s actually seemed a recycling of age-old issues and therefore relatively predictable educational problems. But they subsequently became fixed at the center of a storm raised by critics in the political culture who believed that the core courses in a college education held the key to the beliefs and loyalties of the students taking them. Since the explosion of knowledge and research in all the disciplines was accompanied by an explosion of enrollments, the masses of American high school graduates who were going to college constituted an increasingly important sector of the new "knowledge society." Perhaps as a result of the Vietnam crisis and student demonstrations, however, critics of the curriculum expanded their worries about the transmission of what they viewed as the democratic traditions of American society; and so they worried that this mass of students was so impressionable that its members—future voters—would be indoctrinated by their courses in the humanities and social sciences. Meanwhile, many an experienced instructor—hearing of this alarm about impressionable students— only thought, inwardly, "I wish."

❧ ❧ ❧

Thus did the curricular reforms of the early 1970s prepare a setting for the kind of rearguard argument mounted by Allan Bloom in his 1987 critique, *The Closing of the American Mind*. It is important to note that in arguing against the state of the curriculum in the late '80s, Bloom relied on the philosophical premise that in the state of nature (read "entry into college"), all undergraduates are enough alike in their needs and their capacities to benefit from certain basic studies. Fleshing this out as an assertion of a radical equality that transcends ethnic or class background, Saul Bellow's foreword to Bloom's book invoked the power of college study less to define, elaborate, and confirm diversity than to liberate individuals from it.

Responding to Bloom's somewhat abstract account of the Platonic understanding of the liberation of discourse, Bellow offers some autobiography: "For a Midwesterner, the son of immigrant parents, I recognized at an early age that I was called upon to decide for myself to what extent my Jewish origins, my surroundings (the accidental circumstances of Chicago), my schooling, were to be allowed to determine the course of my life. I did not intend to be wholly dependent on history and culture."[10] Thus although some critics accused Bloom's book of elitism, it could be said to have made the claim for a form of liberation from the bonds of race and class that recognized aspirations by students to be free of determined identities as well as other oppressions. In this regard it met a need that can be overlooked in the proliferation of special courses for special people that had ensued with implementation of the Carnegie Commission report of fifteen years earlier. (I must note that I found my own introduction to higher learning in college a liberation from the limits of my identity as an Irish Catholic girl from West Virginia, and so I had sympathy for such a point of view when I first read Bloom's book. But rereading the book now, I continue to find it irritating for its stubborn and studied emphasis on education in terms of men and its relegation of women's progress to a debilitating cultural loss of "modesty." My reading of Bloom, then, enacts the polarities involved in the curricular debates.)

That Allan Bloom's critique of contemporary academe became a phenomenal best-seller puzzled many of its early readers, given the book's relatively dense and allusive excursions into the work of philosophical thinkers from Plato to Nietzsche to Heidegger. Indeed, some of his friends have suggested that no one was more surprised than Bloom himself.[11] But it is clear that the fame of *The Closing of the American Mind* derived from cultural and political strains that had been simmering in the years since the report of the Carnegie Commission. Bloom's book—with its unblushing rejection of "diversity" in favor of "merit" and its exalted talk about converting the souls of America's youth to the search for the good—was ripe to become a sacred scripture for the conservative movement. It was credible because it was grounded in the teaching experience of a real professor at a distinguished school, and the passion of its condemnation of the slackness of modern teaching fit well with a fear of the leveling effects of an educational system that insisted on making allowances for inferior preparation. But without the backing of political exhortation and action from well-placed public figures, Bloom's analysis would have been only one more distant echo from the halls of ivy.

The path by which debates about the "liberal" in education entered the popular mind may be traced through the history of the leadership of the National Endowment for the Humanities. Under an old-fashioned view that privileged the role of the liberal arts in expanding knowledge and enhancing democracy, the federal government created the National Endowment for the Humanities in 1965. The rationales listed in its legislative language pointed to a consensus in public understanding of the humanities in American democracy: "To fulfill its educational mission, achieve an orderly continuation of free society, and provide models of excellence to the American people, the Federal Government must transmit and [sic] achievement and values of civilization from the past via the present to the future, and make widely available the greatest achievements of art."[12] The first NEH chairs were chosen from inside the academy, and they spent their terms of office in relative obscurity. Their required reports were written without fanfare. In the course of the ascendancy of cultural conservatives in American politics, however, the state of the humanities curriculum began to loom as a significant feature of whatever permissiveness remained from the '60s. Ronald Reagan's appointment of William Bennett as chair of the National Endowment of the Humanities was a significant milestone, marking the insertion of the federal bureaucracy into the curricular debates of the academy. Nevertheless, Bennett's 1984 call for reform in *To Reclaim a Legacy* was a rather mild, and bipartisan, effort to undo some of the curricular tendencies promulgated by the Carnegie Commission. But despite being even in tone, Bennett's declaration showed some disdain for the faculty in a formulation that insisted on their lack of drive in planning and executing their mission. Bennett asserted that "A collective loss of nerve and faith on the part of both faculty and academic administrators during the late 1960's and early 1970's was undeniably destructive of the curriculum."[13]

Such pronouncements made way for the success of Allan Bloom's more thoroughgoing judgments, even though Bloom's book never mentions the National Endowment, or William Bennett, or indeed his successor at the NEH, Lynne V. Cheney. Nevertheless, Bloom's subtitle, *How Higher Education Has Failed Democracy and Impoverished the Souls of Today's Students*, foreshadowed the moralization of curricular reform that started under Bennett and became entrenched during Cheney's regime as the NEH chair. And Cheney took the animus against the professoriate even further. The linkage between threats to America's tradition of democracy and the dereliction of the academy may have seemed an incidental flourish in the subtitle of Bloom's book, and even in William Bennett's NEH report, but it became a major, and menacing, theme under Lynne Cheney's influence in the 1980s.[14] Not only did Cheney make conservative curriculum reform ideas a partisan project by continuing to imply that those who objected were nerveless, she also added the charge that the faculty were, in some way or another, unpatriotic.

The enabling legislation for the NEH required that the chair issue a report every two years, but Lynne V. Cheney took it upon herself during her term of office to issue full-fledged reports every year. These reports picked up on Bennett's lament for the loss of "a legacy," and they insisted on connecting that loss with a decline in teaching about American democracy. Thus Cheney's NEH reports tended to have titles and subtitles that echoed the premonition of cultural decline in Bloom's subtitle, pounding home her sense of the connection between the curriculum and Americanism with pointed epigraphs. Her first report was titled *American Memory: A Report on the Humanities in the Nation's Public Schools* (1987) and was prefaced with words from Lincoln's Second Inaugural Address: "The mystic chords of memory, stretching from every battlefield and patriot grave to every living heart and hearthside all over this broad land, will yet swell the chorus of the Union when again touched, as surely they will be, by the better angels of our nature." In 1988, her title was innocuous, though it made a sweeping claim of audience—*Humanities in America: A Report to the President, the Congress, and the American People*—and took its epigraph from de Tocqueville: "Imagine a democracy prepared by old tradition and present culture to enjoy the pleasures of the mind." The 1989 report, *50 Hours: A Core Curriculum for College Students*, was less tendentious, quoting only Mark van Doren.[15] And the 1991 version, *National Tests: What Other*

Countries Expect Their Students to Know, was relatively neutral as well, though it presaged the emphasis on testing that would become a hallmark of President George W. Bush's "No Child Left Behind" scheme. The 1990 report fit the combat mode, however, with the title *Tyrannical Machines: A Report on Educational Practices Gone Wrong and Our Best Hopes for Setting Them Right.* The fighting words in its epigraph were taken from William James's description of what happens to good ideas in bureaucracies: "The institutionizing [*sic*] on a large scale of any natural combination of need and motive always tends to run into technicality and to develop a tyrannical Machine with unforeseen powers of exclusion and corruption." Its text makes clear that the "tyrannical machine" in question is the liberal university system that has been impervious to William Bennett's "first stage of the education reform movement of the 1980's."[16] The second stage must reinstate the standard curriculum in literature and history.

In a litany reiterated time and again, Cheney's report gave "shocking" details about what students didn't know: "more than two-thirds of the nation's seventeen-year-olds [were] unable to date the Civil War within the correct half-century. More than two-thirds could not identify the Reformation or Magna Carta. The vast majority was unfamiliar with writers such as Dante, Chaucer, Whitman, Melville, and Cather. A 1989 survey . . . showed one out of four college seniors unable to distinguish Churchill's words from Stalin's or Karl Marx's thoughts from the ideas of the United States Constitution" (pp. 1–2). Lurking in this list is not only a condemnation of undergraduate ignorance but a warning that such ignorance could indicate naïveté about the errors of communism. This particular listing of student points of ignorance emits a slight scent of the old paranoia with its juxtaposition of Churchill against Marx, as if the cold war were still flourishing. Thus an implied third stage would be to sweep out the corruption of the tyrannical machine—essentially the hold by liberals on liberal education.

The appointments of Bennett and Cheney were somewhat unsettling for liberal members of the academy because both seemed programmatically conservative and looking for a fight. It is important to emphasize, however, that Lynne Cheney's early criticisms of what had happened to pedagogy and to the curriculum in higher education during the 1970s and '80s made a lot of sense. At the K–12 level, she called for well-written and interesting school textbooks, condemning the practice of draining all the aura of pungent language from elementary school readers. She also asked for less training in "methods" and more in content for high school teachers. At one time, she abhorred teaching to the SAT as misguided. She criticized higher education's fixation on publishing at the neglect of teaching, and she warned of the damage involved in exploiting teaching assistants and part-time faculty. She also deplored the decline of the humanities in the turn to vocational training. She often quoted Matthew Arnold's dictum that the function of criticism should be disinterested, and thus education should be "simply to know the best that has been known and thought in the world."[17] Although they would deem the word "simply" suspect in his formulation, some faculty members have recently found themselves meandering back to Arnold in thinking about how to make curricular choices. I actually heard his famous phrase uttered approvingly, and without hisses, before a large audience of practicing faculty members at a plenary session on the humanities at the Modern Language Association's annual conference in 2004.

Within Cheney's worthy observations, however, several themes surfaced that signaled her increasing alienation from the academy and her eventual wholesale rejection of it. One was the insistence that an acceptable curriculum must feature not only the noble works of Western culture but also a heroic version of American history. This insistence was backed by the considerable leverage of funding: Cheney's personal veto of some proposals after they had passed through the standard review process was a power move that could only raise suspicions that she was ready to apply the heavy hand of censorship.[18] Given the restoration of lost texts by women and minorities in the late '70s and '80s, moreover, her insistence on the old canon seemed a dismissal of many of the contributions by feminist and ethnic scholars—even though Cheney occasionally praised some of their work.

Another theme that was unsettling in Cheney's reports was her call to parents, students, and alumni to take curricular matters into their own hands. *Tyrannical Machines* was the first of her reports to emphasize the possibility of forcing a return to the old notions of a liberal education by doing comparison shopping for colleges and universities: "Prospective students and their parents need to exercise *in an informed way* [original emphasis] the choices available to them in higher education. . . . They should learn, for example, how to read a college catalog in order to determine if the curriculum is well conceived because that is an important indication of whether or not teaching is valued" (p. 51). Such advice might seem harmless, but its later metamorphosis into a positive appeal for outside intervention into the curriculum had serious implications for faculty governance and institutional autonomy.

More important than any other implication in her NEH pronouncements, however, was Lynne Cheney's insistent linking of her vision of the core curriculum to American democracy, for the political side to such insistence was the implication that "other" curricula formed by "other" educational experts were somehow undermining the nation's freedom.

Cheney's valedictory NEH report in 1992, *Telling the Truth: A Report on the State of the Humanities in Higher Education,* summarizes—in anecdotes about outlandish faculty attitudes and citations of ideological depredations on powerless students—the wars over political correctness in the late 1980s and early '90s. It is scandalized by French thinkers such as Foucault and Derrida, while exhibiting only a shallow engagement with their ideas. Once out of the National Endowment, Lynne Cheney continued her efforts to reform the curriculum with even more sweeping condemnations of the liberal status quo. She went so far as to approve a proposal by Newt Gingrich to abolish the NEH. And she wrote a 1995 book that appropriated the title of her final NEH report, *Telling the Truth,* but added a subtitle that combined wholesale indictment with a call to arms: *Why Our Culture and Our Country Have Stopped Making Sense—and What We Can Do about It.* With evident emotion, she recounted the negative reactions that one of her NEH reports provoked at an academic conference in North Carolina in 1988 and asked, "What had I done to deserve demonization by this distinguished group?"[19] The rest of her book answered that question with a parade of by now familiar narratives purporting to show that mendacity, literal and philosophical, permeates the entire American school system—K–16. Moreover, the "what we can do about it" phrase echoed her earlier advice to parents about comparative educational shopping, and so foreshadowed her founding of the American Council of Trustees and Alumni.

Although the National Association of Scholars had already been formed and functioned as an organization that backed the Bennett-Cheney critique of the post-1970s curriculum, Cheney's new organization was designed to follow a more activist program.[20] It sought to recruit college and university graduates, philanthropic groups, and board members to exert the power of the purse and of elective politics to implement its version of curricular reform. With a perfect talent for making a stir, for example, it staged a costumed event at Georgetown in 1996 that called on alumni and retired faculty to protest the English department's revision of requirements that did not mandate a Shakespeare course for all majors.[21] Several of its sympathizers were also appointed to the board of the State University of New York by the state's Republican governor,

George Pataki, and it was not long before they took a direct hand in trying to discipline controversial campus events and change the curriculum.[22] Meanwhile, an alliance in Congress backing Newt Gingrich's Contract with America cut the budget of the NEH by 36 percent. Clinton's appointee to the chair was Bill Ferris, a faculty member from the University of Mississippi whose southern origins, interest in local folklore, and ability to play country music on his guitar helped him protect the endowment. To do so he had to scramble, focusing on NEH roots in state and local humanities centers.

🙚 🙚 🙚

Lynne Cheney's question about the negative reception she received from members of the academy deserves more than a simple dismissal. Many of her ideas held common ground with those of centrist faculty on issues in pedagogical and curricular reform. Why, then, should their debate with her have become so hostile? Some of the blame lies in the lack of civility on the part of some prominent faculty members in their dealings with her. The exaggerations in their discourse and the animosity in their attitudes about the academic right were surely permitted under the principles of academic freedom, but they displayed a kind of rudeness fed by arrogance that can be one of the less attractive features of academic debates. More significant, within the academy the debates on the curriculum tended to be extremely abstruse, and very short on practical solutions. While Cheney's conservative versions of the best approaches and texts in good teaching were often naïve and expressed in the language of Parson Weems, liberal views were generally chaotic and formulated in barely translated French or German. The conservative prescription at least had the virtue of being plain and simple. Ordinary citizens could find many of its directives to be worthy of support through tuition and philanthropic dollars, even as opposing ideas seemed to flutter aimlessly along in endless course proliferations actually being taught by nontenured underlings.

For their part, conservatives could never forget or forgive an insult from the left, and so they seem to have became paranoid in suspicion of everything about the academy establishment—its theories, its intentions vis-à-vis diversity, and its pleas for understanding. Most important, in their trust in the sufficiency of familiar ideas and texts, conservatives tended to be self-indulgent and somewhat lazy. There were some exceptions, but generally the supporters of "tradition" read the new thinkers—especially those from the Continent—only to refute them, or didn't bother to read them at all. Unaware of the very real concerns about the power origins of canonized taste raised by subtle thinkers like Pierre Bourdieu, educational critics on the right could rarely engage the academics on the left with adequate understanding and nuance.[23] Finally, reformers like Cheney also seemed incapable of admitting the increased complexity of institutions of higher education—apparently modeling all education after a pattern available only in small liberal arts colleges. The masses of new entrants to higher education required some new approaches and, given the poverty of their K–12 training, no small amount of remediation. The conservative insistence on Plato for all sometimes looked silly in the light of such student needs. From another view, the insistence seemed one way of saying that those who couldn't absorb Plato should not have a chance at college at all.

Much of the ferocity between the two sides on curricular questions could be excused as a mark of the liveliness of debate if it had not become so linked with shadowy accusations of treason. These became especially troubling after the attacks of 9/11. Within weeks, ACTA had issued a report on selected antiwar campus meetings titled "Defending Civilization: How Our Universities Are Failing America and What Can Be Done about It." This document spoke of "moral equivocation" as equivalent to what it labeled as the faculty's impulse to "BLAME AMERICA FIRST."[24] It made the accusation that the tendency of many academics to hold back from condemning America's enemies actually betrayed a lack of solid conviction about evil, rather than the intellectual's natural tendency to seek nuance before certitude. Thus in a time of extreme national crisis, issues of the curriculum and its teachers moved from arguments like Allan Bloom's about the faculty's intellectual shortcomings into the far more threatening realm of the faculty's citizenship. As the curricular debates became the equivalent of doctrinal warfare, any reform suggested by either side would be charged with political implications.

Despite this sorry escalation of misunderstanding, I believe that the opposing curricular agendas of the Carnegie Commission report and of *The Closing of the American Mind* reflect genuine problems and indicate some directions for solutions. The sides should not, therefore, be taken simply to reflect party affiliations, religious leanings, or intolerance of diversity. There are too many middle-of-the-roaders among the faculty to permit the kind of invective and threatened retaliation that came to preoccupy curricular reform. Rather, the oppositions represent the inevitable dialectic arising from a number of contrasting impulses and aims for higher education in America. These include, as I have already suggested, learning versus teaching, but they also involve depth versus breadth, analytical skill versus content, theory versus lore, and individual revelation versus communal understanding. Since the precise fulcrum point for these polarities lies in the canon—the list of prescribed works, ideas, and systems of data to be learned by introductory students—I want in conclusion to move toward some observations about the nature and utility of canons.

❧   ❧   ❧

One lure of canons is their promise of a hierarchy of texts or principles that embody unchanging foundations for truth and action. That is the lure that most disturbs modern skeptics; they fear the extremism of such a view—its temptation to the security of permanence in times that call for change. Women's studies and ethnic studies have unearthed too much evidence that canons are determined by existing power structures and that they are likely to represent only partial values, no matter how carefully these are defined. It is clear that rigid canons not only are philosophically suspect but can be barriers to learning. Almost invariably they come to represent a nexus of value that must be known by all, ignorance of which will brand any individual as unworthy. Thus they can separate the haves from the have-nots, the upper from the lower, the learned from the ignorant.

A second promise of canons, on the other hand, is their identification of basic tenets or texts on which mastery of any field of study can be built. Canons can thus group together texts that have generated other texts, or ideas that generate other ideas. The almost defunct "survey course" was set up to present a descriptive inventory of the sources for basic knowledge in a given field. At their best such courses offered explanatory patterns for literature, history, and philosophy as well as the sciences. If canons are defined as such practical and provisional "lists," they can present a useful approach to helping minds develop, transmitting the lore of the surrounding culture, and establishing some community in mastery of information that has the authority of cultural familiarity and circulation. And although such lists can be stultifying if they are presented as definitive, even rigid canons can facilitate their own critiques. Modifying and rebelling against a set canon is often an essential creative act.

To take a case in point, the British critic F. R. Leavis was by temperament and social conviction a canon breaker and maker. He famously began *The Great Tradition* by proclaiming with utter conviction that "The great English novelists are Jane Austen, George Eliot, Henry James and Joseph Conrad—to stop for the moment at that comparatively safe point in history."[25] This proclamation triggered a flurry of publishing and research, not to mention curricular adjustment, in the 1950s and '60s. Studies of authors like George Eliot flourished while it was difficult to find more than a biography on such a writer as Thackeray. Until Leavis shifted his views in 1970 by adding Charles Dickens definitively to the list,[26] studies of the Victorian novel either followed his sense of the tradition or argued against what seemed a glaring omission. At worst, Leavis helped justify the neglect of a very great writer in college courses for a period of time. At best, Leavis's list clarified not only his own approach to fiction but also some important values in works that had not been carefully read before. And so even though a student like Margaret Drabble rejected the notion of the canon that he projected, she found his clarity of purpose and rigorous method to be a lasting influence on her own writing.[27] Discussions of a canon such as the one Leavis established can aid in the understanding of one or another text because it offers the clarity of comparisons. It also provides essential models to work against.

Because they have sought to recognize underrepresented cultures and have worried about reproducing class distinctions based on narrow criteria, some thoughtful faculties in the humanities have had valid reasons to eliminate established canons, and they have done so with varying degrees of vehemence. But elimination tends to end in defeat, for individual lists multiply, one list replaces another, and exclusionary preferences become embedded in the new canons as in the old ones. Even though scholars dedicated to the critique of culture are uncomfortable with assertions that one text or idea can be better than another, discussions of value seem unavoidable. Choices must be made: a course syllabus cannot be infinite. So we cannot avoid the question of what the criteria of selection will be. As a species, we are inveterate judges; conversations about relative value are not only natural in common discourse but essential in intellectual training. And so an informed making of discriminations is helpful for novices who might otherwise be lost in a welter of possibilities. Discriminations are vital for creative work, for example: artists tend to gauge their own efforts against other creations, and in doing so, they privilege intention and agency over unacknowledged cultural forces working on their creative psyches. The nation's writers, with a healthy dollop of caution, still value the "best poems" of the year, or the "best short stories,"[28] and so on through the National Book Award and the Pulitzer prizes. Indeed, to refuse to evaluate works or ideas can seem to dodge a creative responsibility.

Similarly, I believe that a refusal to acknowledge the inevitable formation of canons and an effort to avoid them can lead both to creative paralysis and to curricular instability. As Pierre Bourdieu has observed, "There is no way out of the game of culture."[29] John Guillory, the most subtle contemporary observer of this canonical debate in English (where it has attracted most controversy and been most divisive), has therefore called for a return to "the aesthetic" as an antidote to the problem of shifting determinants in academic thinking about canons. In doing so, however, he has cautioned that there must be extraordinary care to safeguard curricula from their origins in, and circulation of, exclusivity.[30] And so departmental faculty—charged with the design of the nation's liberal arts curricula—must make choices that are both pedagogically usable and self-critical. In the process, they must avoid several pitfalls.

One confounding dilemma is what to leave out. In his discussion of the curriculum when he was chair of the NEH, William Bennett tried not to be prescriptive, but he could not resist drawing up his own list of the works (or writers) that students should know if they were to be counted as liberally educated. Like many list makers, he got carried away:

> The works and authors I have in mind include, but are not limited to, the following: from classical antiquity—Homer, Sophocles, Thucydides, Plato, Aristotle, and Virgil; from medieval, Renaissance, and seventeenth-century Europe—Dante, Chaucer, Machiavelli, Montaigne, Shakespeare, Hobbes, Milton, and Locke; from eighteenth- through twentieth-century Europe—Swift, Rousseau, Austen, Wordsworth, Tocqueville, Dickens, Marx, George Eliot, Dostoyevsky, Tolstoy, Nietzsche, Mann, and T. S. Eliot; from American literature and historical documents—the Declaration of Independence, the Federalist Papers, the Constitution, the Lincoln-Douglas Debates, Lincoln's Gettysburg Address and Second Inaugural Address, Martin Luther King, Jr.'s "Letter from the Birmingham Jail" and "I have a dream . . . " speech, and such authors as Hawthorne, Melville, Twain, and Faulkner. Finally, I must mention the Bible.[31]

Such an expansive survey of texts could not be covered by any imaginable course, or set of courses, for ordinary undergraduates in today's colleges and universities—not if they are also to study the sciences, pursue a major, and follow their own bent in electing at least some "free" courses. Bennett's lack of realism points to a problem with any canonical list making; one item leads to other items, and there is no end to it. The only way to be safe is to include *everything*. But choices have to be made in context, and so the faculty curriculum committee must consider what its campus traditions are, how each of its departments can benefit an introductory program, and—an essential point—how the curriculum can be presented as something more coherent than an inventory of everything it would be nice to know about.

Another curricular thinker who has fallen into the trap of the endless list is E. D. Hirsch, Jr. In his book *Cultural Literacy: What Every American Needs to Know,* Hirsch shares the concerns of most of the conservative curricular reformers of the past two decades who believe that the teaching of shared texts is critical to maintaining American democracy. But his conclusions are, I think, less politically polarizing than theirs because his impulses are inclusive rather than exclusive. Hirsch more strongly emphasizes access to a community than specific political principles: "Any true democrat who understands this [the need for a shared 'national vocabulary'], whether liberal or conservative, will accept the necessary conservatism that exists at the core of the national vocabulary, which must serve all sorts and conditions of people from all generations."[32] Admitting that the pace of consolidating such a vocabulary—and he really works at the level of reading comprehension for elementary school children—would be "glacial," Hirsch has undertaken the task of providing shortcuts by providing extensive lists of all the bits of knowledge and common phrases as well as names and titles that should be committed to memory in order to make sense of learned and professional discourses. And so his book is a catalogue of *Jeopardy* proportions that seems a reductio ad absurdum of canonical possibilities.

From one point of view, Hirsch's sense of the need for "cultural literacy," the a priori information required for understanding, has some common ground with Pierre Bourdieu's finding that the success of dominant classes in education is based on their possession of "cultural capital." Both Hirsch and Bourdieu thus pose the axiom that knowledge is power and status. But while Bourdieu's solution is a critique of received culture, Hirsch's is a naïve effort at providing culturally approved knowledge pills for the ignorant. With its adoption by cultural conservatives, Hirsch's project has led only to further divisions in the canon wars.

David Lodge catches the quandary of the endless list through a game called "Humiliation" invented by the hero of his academic novel *Changing Places.* The aim of the game is to name a text that everyone but the contestant has read: the winning contestant will therefore be the one who has *not* read a universally known, canonical masterpiece. One of the untenured faculty members at "Euphoria State," the university in which the novel is set, becomes so overwhelmed by his "pathological urge to succeed and . . . pathological fear of being thought uncultured" that he finally volunteers the secret that he has never actually read *Hamlet!*[33] He wins the game, but his revelation is so shocking to his colleagues that he is denied tenure several weeks later. The Lodge episode reveals the doubleness of canons. They can be the currency for a "dominant" culture—one that can be vicious in its class exclusions and lacking in self-criticism. But ignorance of them is dangerous, even among those who are supposed to understand their limitations. Hirsch may have accepted this fact of life without sufficient questioning, but he doesn't kid himself about the lack of cultural capital being a genuine and often debilitating deprivation.

A further point in considering the curriculum is that the collective introduction to a common text or body of knowledge can be the basis for a community of learning. For that reason, one common effort is to remedy the lack of a core curriculum by assigning a single text for all new students to read and discuss in their first weeks of college. Significantly, however, the intense scrutiny aroused by the politics of the curriculum has put such texts under threat of censorship. In 2002, the University of North Carolina at Chapel Hill assigned an introductory selection from the Qur'an as the text for its summer reading program for freshmen. This program was designed to inspire faculty-led discussions with incoming students during orientation week. But some members of the state legislature took offense at the privileging of the sacred scriptures of a national enemy, and threatened to establish a law against state funding for *any* course that sought to teach about any single religion without giving equal time to other religions. After a brouhaha that reached the national media, things quieted down. But there was controversy the following year over the choice of Barbara Ehrenreich's *Nickel and Dimed*, a text that seemed leftist and even un-American to some critics. The following year, the university chose a book called *Absolutely American* about life at West Point. It was presumably a "safe" choice.[34] The North Carolina incidents, among others, indicated how much decisions on the curriculum are now part of a national politics that has become fractured and suspicious of its own diversity. Nevertheless, courses taken and texts read early on in a college career tend to reverberate positively thereafter. Their common content can give students markers for both building new understanding and entering into discussions with peers in the dorm or in other classes. The faculty also finds it useful to be able to allude to specific works that they are sure that their classes have read.

Thus, despite the inevitable dissensions about specific details of efforts to assign specific texts or subjects for introductory studies, I believe that the faculty is obliged to take the problem of curricular coherence seriously and defend its rationales in addressing it. In some cases, as at the University of North Carolina at Chapel Hill, the very controversy can become part of the assignment and so lead to the kind of "teachable moment" that Gerald Graff has proposed as the key to resolving curricular debates. We should, he argues, teach the controversies.[35] But I don't think Graff's solution, convincing though it is for practice, can address all of the issues about the canon. We must admit that there is a body of knowledge, constantly changing but always ripe for canonizing, that it would be helpful for students to know about. Faculty members, who frequently take their own knowledge for granted, should not only teach about the sources of the categories of this knowledge but also confront how its absence might affect the prospects of many of their students.

I mention an example from my own experience. In the days before canonicity became an issue in higher education, the English department at my school had put together and circulated a summer reading list for the state's high school students. Years later, when I was chair, the principal of a high school asked if the department could revise and reissue such a list. She said that her students needed to know what they might read during the summer. Hers seemed a reasonable request to me, and so I took it to our advisory committee. After an extensive debate, we finally refused her request because most members of the committee were uneasy with setting such reading lists. They bore the taint of the Book-of-the-Month Club and other old-fashioned efforts to bring culture to the masses. I obeyed the consensus of my colleagues, but with strong reservations. Indeed, in the heat of our discussion I pointed out that they themselves told their own kids what to read all the time; why not give the same advice to those whose homes didn't have any books at all? I had grown up in a community where professors were few and far between, and so we thought they knew more than we did—and if we ever got to college, they would tell us about all of it.

Exclusiveness can be a feature of canons, then, but it can also be a feature of the critique of canons. The deciding question is whether we conceive of book lists as restrictive or as invitations to join together in collective discoveries. The "cafeteria" curriculum that followed the Carnegie Commission's report of the early 1970s, and that represented the best compromises available in the context of faculty specialization, massive enrollments, and the expansion of the disciplines, avoided restriction but was less helpful in enabling collective discoveries.

Meanwhile, as the academy has avoided canonical guides for readers, other arbiters have taken over. We can let Oprah Winfrey stand for a current form of canon formation that avoids the fustiness of a panel of experts, instead presenting one person's choices and then inviting discussion about them. That such a process now takes place on television may tell us what a vital connection with the learning public we faculty in the humanities have given away in our disdain for popular opinion. Perhaps a caution regarding our own canons lies in the minor fracas that ensued when Jonathan Franzen, clearly an academic writer, had his novel *The Corrections* named as a choice for Oprah's book club. Emily Eakin summarized the terms of the Franzen-Oprah controversy in an article published in Britain's *Observer* in 2001: "he publicly questioned her judgment, suggesting to more than one interviewer that his novel's 'high-art' literary qualities made it a dubious choice for a programme normally associated with middlebrow fiction. His remarks started a national scandal. . . . Franzen is now busy trying to explain his way out of the gaffe, telling the *New York Times* last week: 'Mistake, mistake, mistake to use the word "high."' . . . Both Oprah and I want the same thing and believe the same thing, that the distinction between high and low is meaningless."[36]

The popularity of Oprah's book club is not isolated, for canon formation now takes place privately in the myriad reading groups that have grown up around the country in the past decade. The movement has been so successful that serious fiction is now published with materials at the back of the book to aid group discussion. Similarly, films issued in DVD formats frequently have all the trappings of a college course. Anyone who invests in the deluxe version of *The Lord of the Rings* will end up learning not only about how the movies were made but also about Tolkien's life and thought. There is an innate desire for discriminations, lore, and discussion, it seems. And what's good enough for the general public might be useful for the academy as well.

I could not gain consensus from my colleagues to support my own predisposition to value lists. As an associate dean in charge of the major curricular reform at my university in the 1970s I had done the kind of wheeling and dealing with departments that used the leverage of requirements to get them to offer courses that did important things, such as having students write across the curriculum. But I finally found the self-interested bargaining among disciplines in search of enrollments a worrisome principle on which to fashion introductory courses for our students. Despite my failures in administering greater coherence, I maintained a sense that we could do better. And so in a series of summer workshops on the liberal arts for faculty held under the aegis of the Lilly Foundation in the late 1980s and early '90s, I began to conduct polls among the faculty in my humanities seminar. I would tell my class—composed of professors from a variety of fields—that they were to consider themselves a curriculum committee. They were charged with designing a required freshman gen ed course in literature. We agreed that there was some value in having a common set of required texts from one class section to another, but the question was, Which ones? During our two weeks together we all read *Hamlet* and *Candide* and then a modern novel (after several experiments, the standard choice became *Beloved*). We also discussed the current debates about approaches to literature—through myth, reader response, gender and ethnic studies, and so forth. And we studied disputes about the canon. Then, on the last day, we held a runoff election to decide on five texts.

It was interesting to me that the group invariably reached agreement on three choices—the Greeks, Shakespeare, and Toni Morrison. We never had time to hammer out the specific plays for the first two, but *Beloved* was the canonical Morrison text. It was impossible, however, to get a consensus on the last two choices for our imagined common syllabus. The spectrum ran from *Don Quixote* to *Blade Runner,* and despite my pleas to at least consider making the Bible a fourth choice, I could not drive my "committee" further than the three common texts. I finally convinced myself that my colleagues were right to agree on a minimal core, while allowing variations on the fringe. I also thought that if my university's curriculum committee could reach such a moderate compromise—with faculty from outside English taking an interest and actually reading the assigned texts—it would be a good thing for our introductory students.

More important than the specific choices, after all, were the discussions that preceded the poll. All the members of my committee had to read at least one text they'd never studied before. Each had to think about, and explain, what he or she thought an introductory course should try to do for students. And finally, each watched as opinions were polled and gradually tabulated on a chalkboard during the final class meeting. Some gave in on one or another text as the results came in; others stood firm on at least one outlier that they couldn't do without. But the discussion was lively and collegial and interested in what would motivate as well as inform students.

I believe, from such experiments, that we can return to curricular reform with a renewed sense that making choices together is not only educationally sound but useful to our own learning about our teaching. I therefore believe that we should really engage in debates about what is "liberal" about education, without being distracted by the raging politicization of our choices by forces outside the academy. Our new efforts at providing a liberal education for our students must disavow an epistemology that links the reading of established texts with indoctrination—despite our own theories or external pressures. The fallacy behind the cultural conservatism of both Bennett and Cheney is the notion that bad curricula can pervert the loyalties of students while good ones can lead them to personal virtue. We know that the "liberal" in liberal education cannot make such claims. Even while hoping that knowledge and virtue might be related to one another, we have too much evidence to the contrary to make any such claims for our curricula.

We have seen that when he was chair of the NEH, William Bennett was preoccupied by the potential of lists of texts to inculcate good values. After he left the government as NEH chair and later secretary of education, he turned to lists again. In 1993, he wrote the best-selling *Book of Virtues,* and since then he has turned out a stream of morally uplifting catalogues of books and their spiritual uses. The titles are reflective of Bennett's thinking about the curriculum as a vehicle for moral improvement, leading from personal to public virtue: *The Children's Book of Virtues* (1995), *Moral Compass: Stories for a Life's Journey* (1995), *The Children's Treasury of Virtues* (illustrated, 2000), *Virtues of Family Life* (2001), *Our Sacred Honor: "The Stories, Letters, Songs, Poems, Speeches, and Hymns that Gave Birth to Our Nation"* (1997), and *Why We Fight: Moral Clarity and the War on Terrorism* (2003). The PBS animated children's program based on Bennett's *Book of Virtues* created a pantheon of talking animals to illustrate each one. The leader is a buffalo named Plato (Bennett was known as "Buffalo Bill"), followed by a bobcat named Soc (Socrates), a prairie dog named Ari (Aristotle), and—to include a female—a red-tailed hawk named Aurora. I have wondered why, since the list includes major Greek writers, a niche might not be found for Sappho, but I think I know. And I have also meditated on the fact that since virtue often needs a seasoning of vice to moderate its zeal, there should also be a rattlesnake—possibly called "Stoph," and modeled on Aristophanes. Such a balance would provide some reverence for skepticism, satire, and the antic uses of naughtiness.[37] The danger in efforts like Bennett's to set up national programs of personal earnestness was made evident when his attachment to gambling became public. Making claims for moral teaching can expose the teacher to unpleasant criticism for his or her own failings. "Teacher, teach thyself."

Nevertheless, our articulation of the value of liberal education must be pursued as we continue to assert its benefits. It is time to reflect anew on the formation of what we study and why. That reflection should not be in the form of easy generalizations but in curricula with specific aims and specific material designed to fulfill those aims. If this kind of reflection leads to some new canon, so be it. Critiques of the old canon have led to new approaches in the humanities—and an openness to the discovery of neglected areas of study, of forgotten works of genius. When any canon is imagined as a list of works that inform one another, it can be very useful. It can provide introductory students with reference points for future discovery, and it can enable professors to make cross-references from one course and one semester to another. Through it faculty members can compromise and cooperate in drawing some coherence out of the diversity of their fields. The trend in more and more schools to assign a single text to orient all entering students to college indicates that curriculum committees are making choices.[38] And the faculty deliberations during Harvard's review of the core curriculum demonstrate that faculty can also explain the choices they make. When any curriculum is liberal—exploratory, provisional to achieve clear purposes, illustrative of a range of creative options—the lists of required texts it establishes are good. When these lists harden into the tablets of the law, they become instruments of discord. The name-calling begins, and liberal education becomes intemperate, political, and illiberal.

CHAPTER FOUR

Distance Makes the Heart Grow Colder

Online Education

In 1995 the world of higher education was astonished by the appearance of a new concept of a university. It shone on the horizon as the "Western Governors University," and it promised to revolutionize college education as we know it. Rejecting the concept of site-based schools, it revised the notion on which land-grant institutions were originally formed—that each state would establish and support at least one public college for the useful education of its citizens by building up a site where they could encounter a community of scholar-teachers and a broad sampling of courses. WGU would offer access to all courses online. The notion of campuses without sites was thus a rejection of the Morrill Act's founding assumption that American education involved bringing students together in social space to prepare them for life in American democracy. Indeed, some of the backers of the burgeoning crop of distance education providers celebrated the "death of the campus," urging sentimentalists among the faculty to substitute the "clicks" of the PC for the "bricks" of the campus.[1]

In this chapter, I want to consolidate the themes already raised—the vitality of the campuses and classrooms of American colleges and universities, their vulnerability to misuse by commercial or political forces, and the need for their faculty to participate in making the kinds of choices that can preserve their effectiveness—by telling the story of the embrace of technology by the higher education establishment, too frequently as a replacement for rather than an enhancement of faculty work in the classroom. I want to show how the distance ed movement paved the way for a new array of proprietary schools that have staked their claim for acceptance on the promises of technology. Renouncing campuses, for-profit ventures have nevertheless adapted reformists' pedagogical and curricular criticisms to help lay their arguments for respectability and especially for traditional accreditation. They have promised that their courses, on or off the Net, would be learning-centered, standardized in curriculum, and testable. Now that the academic dot-com debacle is over, we are still in the midst of such related market-driven incursions. Glowing with the glamour of distance ed claims, these proprietary schools have managed to gain accreditation by relying on the eagerness of a weakened voluntary system intent on avoiding both the unpleasantness and the litigation that would follow a no.

And then, proclaiming that they would operate as tax-paying rather than tax-taking enterprises, for-profit schools have managed to convince the federal government that they should be able to tap federal grant and loan programs. These funds were originally designed to permit continuing students to complete consecutive college degrees in a reasonable span of time. Branding that motive as elitist and ageist (adult students cannot take time off for college), proprietary schools have had great success in lifting safeguards on course load and continuity standards for federal student aid. It is ironic that proprietary schools have gained access to student funding just as its general availability has been cut during the George W. Bush administration. As a result, the gap between those who can afford a four-year college experience and those who can take only one course at a time is growing.[2] Growing with it is the movement to privatize education, but in the peculiarly American way that entails public subsidies.

And so we are left to wonder what the higher education leaders who so eagerly signed on to the technology mania, clearing the way for the for-profit sector, think that American higher education ought to be. Do they believe that the content and conduct of market-driven courses should be validated by disinterested and trained expertise? Do they see any problem in the disarray among traditional accrediting agencies pressured to loosen their standards so that for-profits can sell their wares at home and abroad? Do they consider whether course creation should be protected by the norms of academic freedom? Are they concerned about the integrity of an academic establishment whose members are at-will employees? Do they imagine how the physical presence of a student in a classroom with a live teacher plays into a national commitment to education as a process rather than a commodity? Have they really thought about how courses designed for speed and ease would be conducted in cyberspace or in the office classrooms of corporate diploma mills? Have they taken the time to ask teaching faculty how technology could best be used in teaching, or what its limits might be? Finally, and most important, have they pondered the betrayal involved in turning American higher education over to the vagaries of the stock market?

It may seem ungenerous to beat a stable of horses as moribund as some of the long-gone distance ed schemes, but there is something to be learned from their day in the commercial and academic sun and its effects. For one thing, we should recognize how successful they have been in insinuating the vocabulary of the marketplace into arguments about the purposes of American higher education. Further, we need to judge the costs and benefits of their IT imperatives, for many schools now seem to accept major investments in hardware and software without question as budget expenditures. Moreover, dot-com education schemes have been carried along not only by universal confidence in the market but also by a presumption that all faculty skeptics must be either technocratic ignoramuses or retrograde protectionists. In so squelching all questions, the defenders of the new tech teaching have driven some of their faculty critics into extreme positions that have eventually undercut their motivation to explore creative pedagogical uses of technology.

We have come to a point in the history of American higher education at which a central question must surely be how technology should be brought to bear on one of our society's most critical challenges—its engagement with its adolescents. In the United States, an extensive system of low-cost and accessible not-for-profit campuses has come to represent our sanction of a substantial learning interlude for young adults and thus a compact between generations. In providing such sanctuaries and such interludes, we envision learning as a social and cultural as well as cognitive process. We thus understand that communication between and within generations is a critical feature of the identity formation of our young—a foundation for their active participation in the civic life of the nation. We need to ask about how the dissolution of this expectation, that students should be supported to live together and learn from one another during their time of apprenticeship, might undermine the cultural compact on which our campuses have been built.

This is the kind of question that the purveyors of technology in education have tended to ignore; and now that some of the dust has settled, faculty should ask it again. In doing so, the faculty must also consider afresh what advantages technology may actually have for those who want to reconstruct college teaching in ways large and small. But ultimately the question of machines for teaching and learning is a question of presence or absence. What substitutes for the human factor in the learning exchange are acceptable in an age in which the electronic hookup preoccupies our students in and outside of class? In raising such issues, I am haunted by the statement of a gifted student from an elite research university during a student panel on computers in education presented in 2000 to the Washington Higher Education Secretariat—a group of academic associations located in the nation's capital. She indicated that despite being wooed to her school's demanding pre-med program on the basis of her African American identity, she had found many barriers to her efforts to be both a good student and an activist for minorities on campus. No allowance was made, for example, when the exam schedule of a monster course conflicted with a campus-sponsored presentation on diversity that required her presence. Dismayed by her experience of anomie in a school that should have treated her better, she offered a formula for us to ponder: "If a faculty member can be replaced by a computer, he ought to be."

🐝 🐝 🐝

The group of governors of the western states who embraced the virtual learning craze in 1996 argued that the populations of their region are too widely dispersed to serve through local campuses. But a concern to provide access for students isolated in ranches, kitchens, or prisons was not their only motive. They also needed a solution to the budgetary problems looming in the form of Tidal Wave II. With budget-cutting governors of states such as Colorado, Utah, and Arizona in charge, the imperative to find a cheap way to deal with their students was as important as meeting the needs of a dispersed, rural population. And in considering the problems of new demographics in the new century, some states seemed more willing to build prisons than campuses. As a matter of fact, their protestations that the virtual university was intended to serve "nontraditional" students tended to mask some resistance to meeting the expectations of the many new college-age young people to be able to leave home for college as generations before them have done. Thus WGU's Web page claimed that "WGU was born out of a desire to make education more accessible to the citizens of the largely rural Western United States—an area where people may not live or work within easy driving distance of a college or university." But it then observed, "even if you do have a university nearby, you may not be able to take the time . . . to travel to and from campus for classes."[3]

After the establishment of Western Governors University was announced, rafts of other virtual universities were launched, from Jones International to the American extension of Britain's Open University to the ambitiously international Universitas 21. Their comings were heralded with fanfare; their goings were cloaked in silence. Some new online ventures were offshoots of other "knowledge" industries such as publishing and journalism. An interesting feature of these entries was their emphasis on acquiring the credibility of brand names—especially in the absence of accreditation. A venture that began as Universitas 21 presents an interesting, and tangled, example of the changing fortunes of the late nineties distance ed enterprises.

Universitas 21 was supposed to become the bijou brand in business education—allying itself in one now-vanished Web page with the "Columbia Business School, Stanford University, the University of Chicago Graduate School of Business, Carnegie Mellon University, and the London School of Economics and Political Science." At first, it worked avidly to get American university backing. Through a constantly shifting series of alliances, mergers and acquisitions, and redefinitions of mission, it at one time acquired the right to show links to the University of Michigan and the University of Virginia on its Web page. It also involved such universities as McGill in Canada and Melbourne in Australia. Its early Web page, no longer available, thus promised courses of study as guaranteed by the prestige of its sponsors: "The Company's core business is provision of a pre-eminent brand of educational services supported by a strong quality assurance framework." To emphasize the brand, the page invited potential ·customers to "see the university crest . . . and campus photograph" of each participating school. Interestingly enough, each photograph featured a stunning shot of some Gothic campus building, frequently populated by milling students. Thus the denigration of bricks and mortar in the new global competition morphed into cyber images designed to entice students to think that they could easily log on to a famous school's campus spirit as well as its intellectual resources.

It is a feature of the ephemeral nature of such Internet ventures that their Web pages can change without notice over time, and so the original Universitas 21 page eventually disappeared into the ether, marking the withdrawal of its main American university backers. By the fall of 2004, the Web page for Universitas 21 was skirting the issue of accreditation through branding; it now announced itself as "having developed a global quality assurance capability in higher education via U21 pedagogica, a wholly owned subsidiary."[4] Accrediting its own self, Universitas 21—renamed "U21Global" as of spring 2005—made the familiar claims about e-learning; it offered students a FAQ list, compiled at its office, now located in Singapore. Under the question "Will I learn as much in an online subject as I would in a traditional face-to-face subject," it replied: "Online subjects can actually offer a superior learning environment because they require the student to be more actively engaged in acquiring knowledge."[5] The faculty of this iteration of Universitas 21 seem mainly local to the Singapore area and few in number. Nevertheless, the U21Global Web page for its "Graduate School for Global Leaders" continues to feature flashing coats of arms from the schools it announces as affiliates.[6] Within the United States, Universitas 21 / U21Global now seems to have morphed into "Cerdean University."[7] The information market giant Thomson Learning, which invested in Harcourt University and then closed it, has become the corporate sponsor, and now lists the new entity under the URL "UNext.com." Thomson's corporate sponsorship has become, after all, its most important source of credibility. According to one of U21Global's press releases, its interim chair continued to claim academic viability through the business model: "the fundamental business architecture, brand value and market demand are right, and because Thomson is a superb partner, with the resources, skills, experience, infrastructure and focus in on-line learning necessary to leverage the brand value and accreditation capability of Universitas 21."[8]

Many new distance education schemes were proprietary, but some ventures were sponsored by traditional universities. Schools like the University of Maryland University College had mixed motives for seeking to virtualize their distance education programs. For one thing, they already had extension schools ready to go online. Indeed, the correspondence schools of traditional universities had been relatively neglected until the recent turn to technology. Now they found themselves less the orphans seeking refuge from the storm and more the baby drawn from the bulrushes—newly discovered, funded, and honored beyond their expectations. Their value may have derived from their ability to easily piggyback accreditation for electronic courses onto traditional ones. In past practice, they had been able to contract syllabi and course materials from departmental faculty, many of whom ignored their rights to their intellectual property and so would design a course for a small honorarium. Before online materials brought issues of copyright, franchise, and royalties into play, correspondence course development proceeded without much fanfare on campuses; now it could be hoped that online courses might be created through the same informal procedures—sidestepping troublesome demands for copyright and royalties from faculty. Finally, traditional extension schools were charged by their administrations to fight competition with competition.

In the late 1990s some administrators in the nonprofit arena feared that "distance education is going to eat our lunch." I heard this assertion, made with utter self-confidence as to its truth and only moderate anxiety as to its effect, from the chancellor of a major state university in 1998—even as I wondered why a perfectly respectable administrator could become so fixated on distance ed hype. I was unaware at the time that the most viable threat came from for-profit schools. But indeed, since nobody wanted to be stupidly left behind, such campus executives found themselves responding to deals they couldn't refuse. Several of them lost great sums money in trying to accept such offers. Duke, for example, hooked up with a Silicon Valley enterprise called Pensare, founded in 1996, to provide an online MBA. Pensare filed for bankruptcy in 2001.[9] Although there was some notion that Duke's Fuqua School of Business would buy the rights for a course platform for $1.05 million, by the fall of 2005, the Fuqua Web page was featuring online education for the MBA only in terms of global outreach. But even its Global Executive program has an essential residency requirement: "International residencies are an important ingredient in a global MBA program as they add to the value and richness of the classroom component by providing various lenses (social, economic, cultural, etc.) through which to view various economies and systems."[10]

With more than $5 billion invested in online education in the decade ending in 2002, there were many such offers.[11] The situation at UCLA in the mid-1990s was a case in point. David Noble has unraveled the clever network that sought to bring together old-fashioned university extensions like UCLA's with new businesses like OnlineLearning.net under prodding by alumni entrepreneurs and large show-business investors. Noble's adamancy against what he has called "digital diploma mills" has represented a singular effort from within the faculty to ask serious questions of the new age. For in the years during which electronic distance education was first launched, the unwillingness to analyze its impact on the deeper aims and motives of American higher education was palpable among some faculty, many administrators, and most vendors.

The hype in favor of the exciting new world was intense—backed by info-tainment entrepreneurs, validated by the high flourishes of NASDAQ, and well funded by lavishly heeled hardware, software, and Internet companies intent on dominating a new market. To get a sense of the range of interested parties, consider the membership of the Congressional Commission on Web-Based

Education chaired in that portentous year, 2000, by Senator Bob Kerrey (D-Neb.) and Representative Johnny Isakson (R-Ga.). The commission included representatives from Walden University (an online business college), the Private Equity Group of Chase H&Q, OnlineLearning.net, bigchalk.com, Sun Microsystems, and Fabrizio, McLaughlin and Associates (a lobbying and consulting group headed by the conservative pundit James McLaughlin). There were two university administrators: the president of the South Dakota School of Mines and Technology and the assistant to the vice president for research at the University of Montana. There was one CEO of St. Louis Science Center (a nonprofit science museum). Finally, there were two teachers—one a professor of technology and education from the University of Mississippi and one a high school teacher of poetry from New Jersey. Despite the nod to the school classroom and administration, however, the membership of this commission represented the array of commercial forces that enthusiastically supported distance education. Certainly the congressional leaders themselves were eager converts. I felt the heat of their enthusiasm firsthand when I testified before this group in the summer of 2000. I found my own skepticism to be more controversial and oppositional than I expected; indeed, in the hearing in which I testified, mine was the only dissonant voice raised in a chorus of praise. I was clearly singing in a choir from another church.[12]

The report of this congressional commission may mark the high point of the distance ed bubble. The failures of ventures that were prominent even in 2000 have by now left a landscape of dead Web links. Harcourt sank before it got launched. Universitas 21 continues to weave, ravel, and reweave new global identities and promises. A number of traditional school initiatives—among them those of NYU and Princeton, as well as Duke's—have been either withdrawn or scaled back. Most significantly, the Open University's effort to establish an American model—so likely a venture when it was announced in 1998—collapsed in 2001.[13]

🐌 🐌 🐌

Many of the distance education ventures of the late 1990s were financed and promulgated by the ascendance of another phenomenon in American higher education—the proprietary school. There have always been for-profit educational ventures on the American educational landscape—technical schools, the old-time "secretarial schools," and schools geared to training in specialized vocational spheres from auto mechanics to barbering. The new for-profits were different, however. They claimed an ability to give bachelor's or master's degrees equivalent to those from traditional colleges, but more efficiently. The promises made are distilled in the description offered by the Apollo Group—parent to the most successful of the for-profit schools, the University of Phoenix. Apollo's courses feature "centrally developed curriculum, trained practitioner faculty, and a continuous emphasis on customer service to produce a scalable and replicable model, localized to serve each country's particular needs. The outcomes of this model are supported by comprehensive evaluation and quality control systems that contribute directly to the enhancement and value of the program design and to the high level of service offered."[14] By promising flexibility of schedule, standardization of courses, "practitioner" faculty who have had hands-on experience, and assured outcomes certified by objective tests, the Phoenix program has played strongly to the prejudices and preferences of legislators and of some members of the higher education establishment. The appeal was vital in Washington as elsewhere—as seen in the embrace it received by Senator Kerrey's congressional committee and some foundation backers.[15] Their enthusiasm for new possibilities was admirable, but the for-profit movement made no bones about its own less progressive designs. Clearly it was intent on cutting away the frills from traditional, nonprofit education by eliminating full-time and tenured faculty and fancy campuses. Indeed, such schools implied that their being profit driven would itself assure the consumer of the satisfactions of efficiency as well as help the consumer economy by benefiting their shareholders. Further, these schools would save public moneys by operating without public support; they would be funded by stock offerings and fees; they would be self-supporting. Representing the world of business, these schools were embraced as having a thing or two to show the self-indulgent private sector.

In becoming the leading example of the new for-profit school, the University of Phoenix has embodied the successful attributes of a well-run corporation. It is listed on the New York Stock Exchange, it has established branches in prime space off the interstate highways of many major cities, its logo on the buildings it rents is impressive, and public roadways now accord it the official green-and-white directional signs once reserved for nonprofit colleges and universities. It invests heavily in commercial advertisement, it is familiar on television, and its pop-ups on its degree offerings are ubiquitous over the Internet. It is the latest thing out, and has been for a decade.

Phoenix's founder and his partner, both former faculty members at traditional schools, have publicized their discontent with conventional higher education and claimed that they represent a rejection of tired traditions. Jorge Klor de Alva impressed an interviewer in the late 1990s with his social vision, for example: "he characterized his move, in part, as a reaction against the self-referential, politically correct theorizing in the top liberal arts departments. He wanted to give working-class students a more substantial education to take back to their community, one that would help them in their jobs."[16] Such denigration of former institutions and colleagues has been pleasing to some of those academic reformers who locate the perceived failures of traditional higher education entirely in the ranks of the tenured faculty. For example, de Alva implied in a 1999 article on "technology and learning" that the demise of several e-learning schemes was the fault of professors: "The power of the entrenched faculty will make it difficult for traditional institutions to take advantage of new technology and adapt to the evolving needs of students."[17]

Advertising itself as an innovator in the heart of the system rather than another fly-by-night correspondence school, and emphasizing its intentions to revolutionize not only "learning" but the methods by which students would have access to learning, the University of Phoenix has managed to parlay its emphasis on distance and technologically assisted pedagogy into academic respectability. Indeed, de Alva's potshots at the faculty seem to be part of a conscious marketing scheme. Another striking example of this strategy can be seen in an article by Phoenix administrators Laura Palmer Noone and Craig Swenson published in 2001 in *Educause Review,* the journal for the "IT practitioner." It essentially accused faculty of teaching without knowledge of or care for pedagogy, of mistakenly insisting that student presence is necessary for learning, and of maintaining the myth that research and tenure are important features of higher education.[18] And so the University of Phoenix has allied itself with pedagogical reformers by insisting on student-centered learning and with curricular reformers by insisting that all of its courses give basic information with undeviating sameness. In the Phoenix curricula, there are no confusing variations of syllabi, it seems, and so no politically oriented views.[19]

Thus the University of Phoenix has been able to position itself as an educational leader not only by pioneering distance education but also by defying the claims of the traditional academy and accusing it of being careless about deserving students, inattentive to their differing learning styles, closed to adult learners, profligate with expenditures on full-time faculty, disdainful of tests that validate outcomes, and blindly insensitive to the market. In situating itself as an answer to these imperfections, the University of Phoenix has both shamed and seduced the higher education bureaucracy into welcoming it with open arms and few questions. Its leaders publish regularly in such journals as *Educause* and *Change*,[20] and they sit on the boards of such higher education groups as the American Counsel on Education (ACE). Most important, its representatives have gained considerable clout in the U.S. Department of Education.

Certainly aided by its market ideology, and possibly empowered by the kind of lobbying that makes a difference in politics, the University of Phoenix has installed itself not only in the higher education establishment but also at the very heart of the postsecondary education activities of the federal government. And from this position it has been able to influence laws dealing with the accreditation of higher education entities as well as with for-profit access to federal funding for students.[21] During the George W. Bush administration, its representatives have been given unusual national power. The assistant secretary for postsecondary education through the first and part of the second Bush term was Sally Stroup.[22] She came to the DOE from a position as director of industry and government affairs for the Apollo Group Inc. and the University of Phoenix. A pleasant and ebullient Washington professional—and an expert on student aid from her days as professional staff member for the U.S. House of Representatives Committee on Education and the Workforce—Stroup had a wary welcome to her position from the American Council on Education and other members of the Washington Higher Education Secretariat. Stroup's command of technical information and responsiveness to educational leaders were impressive, especially given their sparse communication with Secretary of Education Rod Paige, her boss during Bush's first term. But her position with Apollo threw into question her possible influence on DOE rule changes that have given proprietary educational enterprises access to federal student aid.

For example, in the fall of 2002, the department embarked on renegotiating the rules, as described by Ruth Flower, director of public policy for the AAUP: "One of the issues on the table was the 'twelve-hour rule,' a financial aid rule that essentially defines full-time students as those who are in class twelve hours each week. A student carrying a typical twelve-credit load usually meets this standard." Admitting the difficulty of measuring student effort in the context of working students who must take fewer courses over a longer period of time, the department began work on new definitions of full-time and part-time studies. Flower summarized the process and its conclusion: "The lengthy and tedious negotiated rule-making sessions, themselves marked by plenty of 'seat time,' failed to produce agreement. Nevertheless, the department is charging forward with a recommendation that the current twelve-hour rule be abandoned."[23] The twelve-hour rule was lifted by the Department of Education in 2002. Another rule that placed limits on federal student support was breached in the budget of 2006, when Congress eliminated the requirement that colleges must offer at least half of their courses and that students must take at least half their courses on a traditional campus to be eligible for student aid.[24] Some congressional backers of that action had received comparatively large campaign grants from political action committees of the industry. Furthermore, A. Bradford Card—brother of President George W. Bush's then chief of staff—was the chief lobbyist for the industry. Soon after the dearest wishes of the proprietary institutions were met, Sally Stroup resigned from the Department of Education; almost immediately after the 50 percent rule was changed, she announced her decision to return to work for the Committee on Education and the Workforce. The chair of that committee is Howard P. McKeon, who succeeds John A. Boehner, both of whom are ardent supporters of free enterprise in education and were instrumental in getting the 50 percent regulation changed. Attending to the "update" of the Higher Education Act in her new job, Stroup has claimed that her position will not demand the kind of neutrality required when she was assistant secretary for postsecondary education: "I would never recuse myself from those kinds of things that have a broad reach across the entire industry."[25]

Dropping the full-time requirement played to the interests of distance ed and proprietary schools, and so the interests of the for-profits seem to have overridden the ordinary course of deliberations. The suspension of the twelve-hour and 50 percent rules enables part-time students to apply for government grants and loans to pay the University of Phoenix or other such enterprises—despite the fact that such schools have renounced government handouts in past statements as against their free-market creed.

Now that the essential limits on government aid for students in the for-profit sector have been abandoned, of course, proprietary and distance ed enterprises can recruit students with the promise of government funding. Grants and loans for tuition offer sure profits. Most recently, there has been evidence that this benefit led to abuse. In fact, the Department of Education has fined the University of Phoenix $9.8 million for violations of rules against using federal financial aid to recruit students—especially unqualified students. Stroup recused herself from the investigation that led to this finding.[26]

The for-profits point of view in the DOE also continues to be represented in the person of Laura Palmer Noone, the current president of Phoenix. Noone has been chair of the Department of Education's National Advisory Committee on Institutional Quality and Integrity (NACIQI); her first three-year term ended in 2004, but she was reappointed as a member for a term ending in 2007. According to the department's Web site, this committee's mission is to advise "the Secretary of Education on matters related to accreditation and to the eligibility and certification process for institutions of higher education."[27] The committee has obviously had a major role to play in legislative issues that most concern the University of Phoenix: access to accreditation, transferability of course credit, and access to student loans and Pell grants; it also has helped foster a general acceptance that any supposition that education should involve any long-term, residential, or on-site experience is a retrograde idea.[28]

Thus in the name of innovation guided by the market, that most reliable of modern sources of value, the federal government's credibility as a disinterested sponsor of not-for-profit higher education has begun to unravel. Self-governance by the regional accrediting agencies has also been infiltrated by market arguments for accrediting for-profits. Divided already by warring regional factions, and by presidents who had grown restive under their mandates, these voluntary agencies began to lose their moorings in 1994 with the breakup of their organizing institution and its replacement by a new agency, CHEA (the Council of Higher Education Accreditors), designed to maintain some kind of coherence in the American system of accreditation by accrediting the accreditors. Since then, the main regional accrediting agencies have gradually assented to the arguments of the proprietary schools for changing the focus of their assessments from "inputs" to "outcomes." The input/outcome dichotomy is another of the high-sounding polarities that "reformers" have used to further their attempts to accommodate the profit motives of proprietary schools. The shift argues that what matters is not depth of understanding but whether a student can pass an exam.

There are, of course, real problems in defining higher education—especially its dimensions of temporality and locality in an age of new possibilities. Ruth Flower addressed these wisely in her 2002 column on the twelve-hour rule: "The dilemma is both simple and inescapable: to choose the right tool, there must be agreement on what is being measured. So far, such agreement has eluded not only Congress and the Department of Education, but also higher education administrators and faculty." But then, in a note of appeal to the faculty to reconstruct, and redefend, a view of education as something more than vocational credentialing, she added: "The Department of Education is now prepared to suspend some of the minimal measures of education, perhaps clouding accepted definitions of terms such as 'college degree.' This step makes it all the more important for faculty to strengthen their role and their voice in academic decision making, in order to preserve the integrity of higher education."[29]

Getting faculty involved in accreditation becomes increasingly difficult as agencies pick and choose among which faculty to engage in accreditation visits, and as faculty themselves are busy with disciplinary pursuits. Meanwhile, accrediting agencies seem less and less interested in faculty opinion and more and more cowed by the threat of litigation. In 1995, the American Bar Association bent to a landmark consent degree with the Department of Justice after its accreditation authority was challenged by new and proprietary law schools.[30] The most recent flash points have been in the southern region, where Auburn University sued the Southern Association of Colleges and Schools for threatening its accreditation by finding flaws in the board's governance of the institution and where Benedict College, too, has sued over its loss of accreditation. Though these actions are rare, traditional accreditation agencies have responded to pressure by shifting their emphasis to "outputs" rather than "inputs"—in other words, they have shown themselves willing to seal, with approval, a raft of distance ed schemes that feature technology as a substitute for the human element in education. For example, in 1998 the New Jersey Commission of Higher Education turned down a University of Phoenix petition for licensure in the state because library support, beyond a minimal online set of texts, was absent; it granted a limited license in 2003 after Phoenix set up a collaborative deal with a small college library in the interim.[31] Thus accreditation of such schools has moved forward, and any deficits in their capacity to meet national standards are seen as remediable by buyouts of resources from struggling campuses, employment of part-time teachers, and application of instructional technology to teaching. The New Jersey deal for Phoenix featured a reduction in the state's usual requirement for "face time" with faculty.

☙ ☙ ☙

My credentials are clearly and determinedly humanist. I am an English professor, but I am not by that token a complete Luddite. I have processed the words on this page on a computer. I have used the resources of the Web to gather information found herein. I have also taught with computers. It is my contention that many promises can be delivered by technology, and that a failure to embrace them will damage the futures of our students.

Nevertheless, I have come to qualify my enthusiasm for the uses of technology with some observations about how students learn—especially those late adolescent students for whom computers have come to be seen as an adequate tool for absorbing a total college curriculum. It is true that more mature students are a major part of the target clientele for online companies, but no online company will forswear the traditional student market in the long run. Indeed, the University of Phoenix, which once required its students to be at least twenty-three years old, has now dropped that criterion. Particularly in light of the global potential market, it is clear that what is left of distance education after the dot-com fall in the United States will turn to aspiring young people around the world with promises of a full education online. Such an education will be defined, it seems, as the sum of a multiplicity of course credits without undue attention to their relationships to one another. And, as we have seen, in entering the undergraduate market proprietary schools have relied on mechanistic ideas of education.

One of the most significant drawbacks to online courses is a human one: students who enroll have a hard time finishing them. At one time, registration forms for the University of Phoenix raised some tough questions in a self-survey that it offered potential customers. That self-survey, like the findings of a number of research-based studies, suggested that information technology cannot motivate most students to stick with the course in the absence of a teacher. The self-survey is no longer featured on the Web site, but there is a cautionary stricture: "While convenience and flexibility are unsurpassed, online learning does require a high level of discipline and does not allow students to 'coast.'"[32] To be sure, retention is a problem for conventional colleges these days as well; students are likely to shift, drop out for a time, and drift from one place to another. The estimates of college dropout rates hover around 25 percent. Yet the estimate for online course losses is far higher—upward of 50 percent.[33] Completion rates are higher for short courses that update the skills required for professional jobs—recertification for a CPA, refresher training in computer technology, and the like. But these are specialized courses, and often of limited scope. They serve immediate and tangible job interests. Even so, some vocational educational experts have come to see that "there really isn't a substitute for the human touch."[34] Such conclusions point to the need to consider how individuals actually respond to forms of instruction offered without the mediation of a live teacher. As we turn to that consideration, I will venture a bit of biography as illustration.

My first experience with distance education came when I enrolled in a traditional, snail-mail correspondence course with my older sister many, many years ago. We had been forced to drop out of college for a year in order to conserve the family finances. Given our isolation in a small West Virginia coal town and our anxiety about ever finding a way to get back to college, my sister and I were perfect candidates for distance education. We signed up for a course offered by Loyola College of Chicago (one of the early leaders in distance education). I cannot find much trace of that course in my memory now as I try to recall it, and neither can my sister; we even disagree about whether it was a history or an art appreciation course. We do agree on the lingering tinge of regret that we never finished, though. We sent a couple of lessons in, and there was a sympathetic response from an unknown grader. Nevertheless, the demands of our current lives took over.

For most people, completing a course of study is a struggle between desire, distraction, and inertia. It takes a teacher to help jump-start most of us, and to keep us going. If I, a highly motivated student, had such a feeble relationship with the achievements of study in a structureless environment like a correspondence course, what must be the situation for "regular" students? Motivation is one of the prime engines of education, and in that line I have learned that good intentions are no substitute for definite deadlines and the knowledge that an expectant individual is waiting—in person.

I managed to get back to college the following year, and I finished all the courses I took there. Even though I had a full-time job teaching fourth grade during my first semester back, I enrolled in a weekend class to begin making up for my missing year of college. I trudged to a college classroom at a local university every Saturday morning to hear a lecture about Europe in the sixteenth century. I was overwhelmed with the fatigue from teaching energetic nine-year-olds from eight to four, five days a week, but I completed the Saturday course. The professor was not very good; indeed her lectures were dull, and the Saturday mornings were always rainy and gray. I managed to complete the work was because I knew the professor was waiting for me.

Having taught a correspondence course in children's literature myself when I was just starting out as an assistant professor, I became even more convinced that whereas I could enforce the boundaries of time and expectations of performance in person, I could not do so from afar. Most of my correspondence enrollees lapsed as students, and eventually so did I as teacher. The sporadic pace and lack of continuity were deeply unsettling to my sense of pedagogy, and the pocket money I was paid simply wasn't worth the anxiety. Since that unsatisfying episode as a distance educator, all my teaching has been in person, and my written assignments have served as fulcra in the always-active dialectic between the abstraction of free-form mental exploration and the cognitive need for a mastery that has to come to some final end point. My conclusion from biography and experience, then, is that distance education is a possibility for highly motivated students, but that even for some of them, completing a course will be very difficult. The latest news from current practice is that motivation is a highly volatile issue not only in distance education but in other forms of on-site technology-assisted educational innovations. Even there, the presence of a teacher is a significant factor for keeping students on task.[35]

The idea of providing the total education of adolescent undergraduates through distance learning or a major reliance on on-site technology is another matter altogether. In their case, the need for an immediate, human presence is not only a matter of providing motivation. It is also a matter of paying attention to the social as well as the cognitive dimensions of education. Indeed, one research team has recently asked whether the reliance on computers for teaching might not recapitulate the famous monkey experiments of the early 1960s, in which the replacement of simian parents with wire mock-ups led to mental breakdowns in the young chimps.[36] Failure to finish is one of the hidden practical debilities of distance education. But it is important to consider the psychic effect of such failure—not to mention the financial cost to enrollees.

"Just click on and begin learning," the University of Phoenix once promised on its Web page. For many learners such an invitation to intellectual ease has been equivalent to the results of the old NordicTrack invitation to bodybuilding: payment of a hefty fee by mail, vigorous exercise on the new machine for a week or two, lapse, and then a gathering of dust on the contraption in some basement or attic. The actual practice of distance education has other complications as well. Some recent criticism has noted students' frustration when the technology doesn't work, for example. And another study of an online graduate course took the students' reactions as well as their test scores into account. This survey of student response, going beyond collecting the bare facts about completing and gaining a certain grade in the course, discovered problems because the researcher included personal satisfaction as a variable. Students' criticisms matched those of their teachers as recorded in other studies: both miss the visual cues from a personal presence, the nuance in the instructor's and students' communication, the reactions of others in a group. Even when such students and teachers persevere in online classes, they all warn of the need for extraordinary self-discipline to finish the course.[37]

Persistence is one of the features of learning that most distance education programs tiptoe by, but other troubling psychological difficulties with the use of technology are only now becoming manifest. One such difficulty is the addiction to Internet surfing and game playing. One review of the literature published in 2004 suggests that "58% of students suffered from poor study habits, poor grades, or failed school due to excessive Internet use. Increasingly, college administrators are recognizing that they have put all this money in an educational tool that can easily be abused."[38] Educators are also concerned that a student's ability to hide away in the computer lab may keep him from learning social skills in his education.

🐝   🐝   🐝

Along with and because of the psychosocial problems attending an education marked by the absence of real instructors, we must discuss problems of cognition, verification and integration of information, and application of skill as we consider the possibilities of technology not only in the ether but also in physical spaces on campuses.

The Net is wonderful for finding and providing information, but not for aiding its sustained incorporation. In point of fact, reading is still an essential skill for gaining knowledge from the Internet. Many of the Web pages in the humanities are highly text dependent, even though they also provide visual and sound enhancements to the texts they offer. Indeed, it looks as if online magazines and journals will replace the hard copy of today. My online research for this book has yielded essential articles, legislation, and archival material, enabling me to avoid the time and distraction of trotting to the library and taking notes by hand. Nevertheless, longer texts—monographs and novels, for example—seem less amenable to electronic substitutions. With a book, you can sit at a table, lounge in a chair, read in bed. You can mark it, dog-ear it, skip, and return. It is a *vade mecum*, an object to take along the way—as we see on airplanes or commuter trains where almost everyone has a book to read. Most important, the continuing, connected discourse of the printed page is of incalculable value as we ask students to enter the world of rational and consecutive discourse.

Another realm in which technology has proved its power, at least in my experience, is in the various hypertext pages on the Web. George Landow of Brown University has been a pioneer in setting up such pages, and in thinking about how their interactivity and the ability to move from one link to another may make for new kinds of discourse, if not new mental configurations. Landow's contribution to Web knowledge through the Victorian Web Page (www .victorianweb.org) shows the possibilities of the Web for gathering and organizing masses of information. But his meditations on the ways in which hypertext might reconfigure traditional creativity and learning leave some questions for a pedagogy concerned with extrapolation from data, synthesis of information bits, and informed interpretations.[39] In fact, despite the far-reaching potential of technology-driven education, the high-tech feature of computers most often utilized in today's college classrooms is PowerPoint. Anyone who has sat through a lecture beamed onto a screen soon discovers that in the hands of most users, PowerPoint tends to be a throwback to the familiar outline, just as many Web pages are highly textual. More significantly, the use of such IT techniques may create new problems. Edward R. Tufte, an expert in information design and the visual display of information, sees the PowerPoint convention as instilling a rigid cognitive style in students: "Rather than learning to write a report using sentences, children are being taught how to formulate client pitches and infomercials."[40] PowerPoint is not the only computer invention that can be adapted to pedagogy, but its drawbacks point to our failure yet to assess how technology can benefit learning, and we should beware the intoxication with the new that can blind us to its limitations.

Given the difficulty of absorbing lengthy texts and the ease of clicking from one bit of information to another, technological pedagogy needs to consider, beyond plagiarism, the disciplinary dangers of Internet information. Readers of *Ulysses* will recognize that a truly great artist like James Joyce never rejects out of hand any of the bits and pieces of information picked up during an ordinary day. The question for students, however, is how to critique such casually accumulated information, and how to organize it into larger and more accurate and coherent bodies of knowledge. John Seely Brown, one of the most interesting recent thinkers about learning through technology, has asserted that the random surfing and cognitive multitasking of young students is entirely natural and actually expands their range; and if it also reinforces short attention spans, so much the better in "a world of fast context-switching."[41] However, Brown recognizes the limits of technology when it comes in canned forms, like instructional CDs. Rejecting these, he concentrates on the social contexts of testing and combining and applying the bits of knowledge made available by technology. He coins the phrase "learning ecology" to indicate a new world of virtual and real, cross-linked communities that technology can enable by easing trade in information, stories about how to make things work, and ideas. These create a rich mix of intellectual and creative possibility—but only if they are managed well. "Of course not all these conversations, even if focused and well intended, lead to productive learning. . . . [J]udgment, navigation, discernment, and synthesis become more critical than ever."[42]

As a pioneer in the field, Brown is extremely enthusiastic about the potential of Ethernet learning communities, and he does not undertake to explain in any detail how "judgment, navigation, discernment, and synthesis" can be ensured in them (he does mention peer review as a possible instrument for providing "warranted beliefs" before they are entered into a database).[43] Given the plethora of blogs and the penetration of advertising into media "info" these days, I believe that all teachers must become as adept in helping students to criticize the new media as to navigate them. Without such criticism, a cultural Gresham's law will let the bad drive out the good in the reconstruction of history, the interpretation of literature, and the understanding of science through technology. *Sesame Street,* the most successful technological attempt at teaching in our time, gives a forewarning of the way commercial interests can intensify this tendency. At one time, that program was almost the only children's instructional programming around. Its proliferation of letters and numbers differentiated it from other television, even though some experts complained that it sold the ABC's like toothpaste. But now its Saturday morning competition from massively commercial children's programming is only confusing; what is knowledge and what is commercial manipulation?

Relying on the Internet or media for basic knowledge leads to another difficulty beyond nuance, accuracy, and manipulation. It presents the problem of sustainability and balance. Acquiring advanced knowledge, especially technical or scientific knowledge, is a struggle. One simply can't read once and pass on. Understanding is more complicated than absorbing the images projected on a screen, because knowledge is the product of a process of assimilation and negotiation over time.[44]

I have already suggested that insofar as technology can aid this process by engaging the student in testing and hypothesizing, it will be a great benefit. It is already a benefit for writers because it eases their task in revising and correcting, which is a way of thinking online.[45] On the other hand, those who cannot stop revising can find themselves overwhelmed with the possibilities. For the computer, by not paying attention to the limitations of common life, fosters almost infinite revision. The ever-growing World Wide Web presents another kind of infinity, and one of its harms can be recognized in the computer nerd who dismisses any reality that is not on the Internet. Students and faculty members on our college campuses know of such lost souls, who use the computer to escape the demands of social life on campus, who have been kidnapped by the Net—lost in endless possibility without consequence. A recent study has confirmed that students involved in the Net to the exclusion of other social interaction have become more introverted and less expressive.[46]

My greatest worry when I think of technology within the social contexts of traditional higher education is that many of the proponents of a totally computerized campus believe that a large number of students don't need any other kind of campus at all. They would argue that online discussions are adequate to create learning communities, as defined by John Seely Brown. But they neglect the other benefits of physical presence that campuses provide, with their wide spectrum of learning contexts. The technology boosters have convinced themselves that returning women students, for example, don't want the bother of coming to a campus when they can fit courses in among their household chores at home. They also view working students as concentrating so intensely on their jobs that the niceties of campus life might be merely distracting. But the students I know, and not just the late adolescents among them, express the need for a specific time and place in which to learn, and for particular company. Desperate housewives need the change of venue that an orderly campus provides. Students who must work part-time should reap the rewards of networking with other students and alumni no less than those who can pay for four consecutive years on campus. No matter how we dream of greater egalitarianism through technology, we must admit that the campus is a site for creating social as well as cultural capital. Many of the biographies of those who have risen to political power in this country attest to the reach of the social and intellectual connections they have made in college. The growth of state and regional campuses has provided some social cohesion for those who could not attend the Ivies or the state flagship campuses. Are these advantages to be denied the next wave of students, who have very little access to powerful social networks to begin with?

🐝 🐝 🐝

The best teaching I have ever done, or observed, has happened when a class comes together—in agreement or argument or wonderment—to understand not only the subject but one another as well. They can test the level of their understanding by what other members of the class seem to get or not to get. They can test the power of their own intellect by trying to explain something to a lost classmate. They can sort through interpretive possibilities to find the one that seems most powerful in unlocking the problem at hand. This kind of learning, up close and personal, is not only an antidote to substituting the arid amassment of fact for a conceptual grasp of implications, it is a cognitive necessity for integrating knowledge fully and flexibly. And though I may seem to be talking only of English classes, where interpretation requires free exploration, I remember the objections against computer learning from electrical engineering professors at a conference on technology and teaching several years ago; these faculty members were adamant that they could not teach their engineering students unless those students had the broad background of understanding that transcended facility with geometry or algebra. Without such a foundation, there may be some attainment of rote skills, to be sure, but there will not be the problem-solving self-assurance that can lead learners from one difficulty to the next possibility.

This is not to say that the power of technology to enhance teaching is not exciting and pedagogically rewarding. Indeed, I would be suspicious of any critique that ignores its ability to increase communication among students and teachers. Technology is essential, but not in isolation. I cite another example from my own experience. The last time I taught a women's studies course at my home campus was in 1992. The campus Internet system was relatively new then, and ordinary students were not yet online. I decided that one of the best ways for me to help empower the women in my class was to get them computerized, so I worked with the computer center to enroll my female students who had not spent their early adolescence playing Pac-Man. I had an introductory session with them in the computer lab, showing them how to enter an electronic classroom that would continue and expand class discussions.

At first the electronic discussion traffic was slow, but it picked up as a result of one class crisis. A student who had missed one lecture on women's history by one of my teaching assistants had objected vociferously in class to the assistant's subsequent lecture—without realizing that what she objected to had indeed been covered in the class she missed. Her classmates put her straight on that electronically, and there ensued a vigorous online give-and-take that covered what would have required at least two class meetings to say. It also saved me from being in the difficult position of having to defend my assistant alone, without the support of the students themselves. The major benefit of the electronic venue was a surprisingly open, combative, and emotional set of exchanges among students. I do believe that this freedom was inspired by the atmosphere of the class itself, where lectures were shared and small group discussion sessions encouraged participation. But the electronic extension of the classroom gave many students an additional forum; there were seventy of them, and they couldn't possibly have raised all their questions, or made all their statements, during the fifty-minute class periods. The full effect of this electronic community became evident during a tragic episode on our campus at the end of the semester: a double murder and suicide during finals week, as a student and her boyfriend were killed by her stalker. The campus was roiled with anguish, and my students were especially concerned because we had studied women and violence during the course and because some of them had direct experience of stalking. Burdened by such awareness, how could they cope with this event after the class sessions were over? Since the electronic classroom was still open, the students logged on, and we talked there about practical measures to take, about counseling possibilities, and about our common sorrow. Further, students from this particular course have remained online with me long after the course was over. Several years ago a "Hi, Professor Burgan" popped up on my screen. It was the greeting of a student from the course who had found my name by browsing on the Net. She told me that she still remembered one class and was using its insights in her career.

Let me note in this episode a mixture of pedagogical themes that point to the fullness of technology in teaching when it combines the intimacy of human interaction with the ease of the Internet. First, the student attained the skill to use the Net in her college class (though nowadays she would come to class already wired). Second, the instructors were interested enough in her experience as a learner to engage her variously—in lectures, in small group settings, and online. Third, the process of learning continued after the class was over and that continuation affected both the student and the teacher. In our last communication, we shared understanding and acknowledgment across time and across our generations. My student's learning inspired her to celebrate its worth. And that celebration in turn validated me by communicating her sense that my own calling to be an educator has made a difference. In appreciating one another, we modeled the interchange of pedagogical trust that made the class we participated in more than three credits toward a diploma. It was a compact that enabled one timid young woman to gain the kind of security of insight that she could then put to use in her own life.

Motivation, complexity, credibility of information, and the social contexts of learning—these are the pedagogical problems often ignored by current advocates of technology as the solution to higher education's problems of access and cost. When faculty balk at technology, they do so because their experience cautions them to maintain skepticism about such simplistic promises. Virtual universities undermine their professional status not only as purveyors but also as creators of courses, their control over the information they organize and assess for transmission, and their notion of education as involving an ongoing relationship between themselves and their students. And that effect on their professional ethos is a final barrier that distances the faculty themselves from technology in teaching. Although one hope for technology was that it could "enskill" faculty by making them more sophisticated in its uses, the actual result of the for-profit use of technology has been to cut costs by de-skilling the faculty. It is no wonder that faculty members are leery of a system designed to replace their expertise and initiative with per-course tutelage and piecework pay. As Gary Rhoades has indicated in his book on the "managed" faculty, any use of technology will tend to exert managerial control over workers—especially if technology aids in the replacement of continuing, full-time faculty with part-time instructors.[47]

Not only do the prophets of information technology ignore education's communal foundations, but they even celebrate the unbundling of the faculty into robotic entities who can be contracted as "content providers," "assessment experts," "mentors," and "performers." As I think back over all my experiences as a learner and teacher, however, I am convinced that although enhancements are possible, there is no replacement for the human classroom. The effort to tell us that we can do the job of educating more cheaply through mechanization rests on a grand illusion that would lead to the ultimate dehumanization of the most intimate of our cultural activities. For when we talk about education, we are talking about basic acts of cognitive refinement, intellectual discipline, socialization, and identity formation. These must take place in the presence of one human being with another—and if they do not, the hearts of students and teachers will grow colder indeed.

CHAPTER FIVE

A More Perfect Union

College and University Governance

In the past ten years, governance has become a topic of concern among the critics of higher education.[1] As we will see, tenure has been on the minds of these advocates of radical change as well, but governance seems an issue more likely to generate productive dialogue because there is agreement among professors, as well as board members and university presidents, that college and university governance rarely lives up to its own ideals of balanced collegiality. There is a consensus that higher education is an extremely complex operation with multiple aims, interest groups, and traditions, and everyone agrees that the trick is to get the parts to work together without becoming buried in muddle. There is also some basic agreement—though it is not unanimous in every quarter—that faculty participation in governance would be a good thing if it worked.

At the same time, our mutuality of concern harbors some conflicts. Lately, the lines of governing authority have been defined with a fiercer sense of opposition on all sides. In the debates of the past decade, a list of complaints from the administrative side has become routine—charges that the tradition of faculty consultation is outmoded, that its anachronism is marked by inefficiency, that modern choices have to be made quickly and will probably go against some interest that has become entrenched under the old order, and that the faculty tend to be less interested in the good of the whole than in the fortunes of their own specializations and careers. From the faculty side arise rebuttals that carry an equally broad animus. Faculty tend to believe that boards are packed with business entrepreneurs whose notions of the aims of higher education are limited by the lore of their MBAs, that most college and university presidents have no idea about the nature of teaching and research, that presidents and other administrators cover their own lack of vision with erratic lunges after management or curricular fads, and that the true character of their ambitions is now to be seen in their fixation on national rankings, the increasingly astronomical pay packages they command, and their tendency to move from one presidency to the next.

These are, of course, self-defeating attitudes on both sides, and the self-defeat does not derive merely from the fact that by relying on stereotypes, each side simultaneously insults and misapprehends the other's realities. More important, such attitudinizing overlooks the vital need in today's higher education for a full mutuality in deciding on aims and in driving our institutions toward achieving them. Those who call for simpler times when everyone worked together are just as deluded as those who call for simple lines of authority that can enforce neat, quick, and binding choices. Thus we exchange charges and countercharges in a most witless way, when what is really needed is a more thoroughly grounded view about how the very nature of employment has shifted, establishing new variations for the responsibilities of leaders and followers, managers and employees, boards and presidents, presidents and deans, provosts and professors. Not to mention those of professors and other academics—counselors, librarians, information technologists, lecturers, lab assistants, teaching assistants, and the burgeoning ranks of contingent faculty.

In this chapter, I want to look at three modes of administering colleges and universities—management as defined by the business culture (recognizing that management models change as often as auto models do), traditional shared governance, and academic unionization. All of these have been tried and found wanting in one way or another, even though it may be that sensible versions of each could work together successfully. But it is also clear that for any one of these modes to work, faculty must become invested in it.

If the arrangements for governance in higher education require a better grounding in the faculty, that need arises not because the notion of cooperation between the main constituents—boards, administrations, faculty—in higher education is outmoded but because its potential in these troubled times has not been realized. Indeed, the tradition of shared governance in higher education may provide a surer guide for managerial problems in complex institutions than its critics realize. There are two main reasons for this hypothesis. First, the nature of the American workforce has changed from a preponderance of manual laborers to a preponderance of knowledge or professional workers. Professional workers cannot be expected to automatically toe the lines set by managers; they are used to independence and the autonomy promised by their training. Second, all of our institutions have become more complicated, layered by competing interests and beset by change. They defy the ability of any one manager to comprehend their challenges all alone. Those enterprises that have tried a more centralized, top-down model tend to regret it afterward as, for example, Hewlett-Packard regretted the much-publicized ascendancy of Carly Fiorino in 2000—and then her departure in 2005. In the light of such spectacular flameouts in the world of business, the model of governance in which areas of responsibility are well-defined, but also shared, may be seen less as an ideal and more as a shrewd strategy for a more workable kind of management for what the management guru Peter Drucker has called the "knowledge society."

🐙 🐙 🐙

The traditional formula for governance in academia derives from the outline of board, administrative, and faculty duties that forms the basis of the American Association of University Professors' 1966 statement "College and University Government." This outline blurs the divide between "owners," "managers," and "employees" in higher education because it establishes governance roles for all three, even though, as we will see, that blurring has provided legal cover for prohibiting faculty unions on most private college campuses. In the 1966 statement, developed in consultation with the American Council on Education and the Association of Governing Boards, AAUP sought to delineate intermeshing activities among the main administrative and faculty entities and (whenever possible) the student body. The guiding notion was that members of the college and university community—called "stakeholders" in business-speak—should be mutually interactive and respectful of one another's interests, as founded on and serving a common pursuit that is crucial to human progress: the acquisition and transmission of knowledge.

Recognizing the fiduciary obligations of the board in overseeing the welfare of the entire institution, the AAUP statement of governance nevertheless argues for dialogue with the faculty on vital issues. And so also, acknowledging the administration's duties in making sure that programs are run efficiently and within fiscal parameters, the statement advocates consultation with faculty in areas where such matters as budgetary planning bear on the educational programs and mission of the school. To the faculty, the 1966 statement assigns the care of educational standards—including the admission of students, hiring and review of faculty, review and implementation of the curriculum, and participation in the immediate self-governance of departments and schools.

Such definitions are clearly elastic, and they have been refined and elaborated over time. In their moderation of tone and modesty of claims, AAUP's statements on governance seem collaborative in intention, and even innocuous in implication. But the 1966 statement's inventory of the foundations for governmental authority in our colleges and universities met with reservations from administrative groups from the very start. The American Council on Education and the Association of Governing Boards "commended" the statement in 1966, but declined to endorse it. And although it has become the source document for any discussion of academic governance since that time, there have been some defections from its principles and its details.

For example, the national Association of Governing Boards recently attempted to devise its own formulation of a new order with an emphasis on the limits of faculty consultation and debate. The AGB's resistance to the notion of shared governance was initially expressed in an essay by a blue-ribbon task force that spent a year studying and taking testimony and ended up writing a report on "the academic presidency."[2] In that document, the AGB concentrated on college and university chief executives and found that they were beset by pressures from all sides and therefore unduly challenged in their mandate to make decisions for the good of their institutions. The answer to such pressure was a new emphasis on "leadership." According to the report, the very notion of shared governance was an irritant to the managerial sense of unimpeded leadership, which had come to be devalued as an essential requirement for running complex institutions. I am confident about the irritation because I found it to be intense when I testified before the task force in the fall of 1994. Then I found myself under fire from a number of the panelists for representing a retrograde faculty that didn't do what they were told and wrote too many articles on Shakespeare. (It may be helpful to note that in the ensuing argument, I gave in a bit on this second indictment.)

When the report appeared, subtitled "Stronger Leadership for Tougher Times," I realized that it was guided by a notion of the academic president as the agonistic hero of the academy's struggles with change. Its criticism of governance in higher education seemed to be inflected by assumptions derived from the management attitudes embodied in the tales of captains of industry widely publicized in the 1990s best-seller lists—lists that were often populated by the memoirs of such famous managers as Lee Iacocca. In that mythic mode, the story of American economic success centered on brave leaders who were willing to make tough choices—usually having to do with cutting out some portion of a corporate enterprise. One of the most famous memoirists was "Chainsaw" Al Dunlap, whose 1996 book *Mean Business: How I Save Bad Companies and Make Good Companies Great* was soon replaced by Jack Welch's *Jack: Straight from the Gut*.[3] In truth, as a run-of-the-mill faculty member, I was not familiar with the CEO species. In meeting with faculty and board members, I did notice that the businesspeople and lawyers had impressive shoes that they actually shined; notwithstanding our differences in dress, however, our encounters were usually cordial. The emergence of angry CEOs at the AGB session alerted me for the first time to an almost reflexive enmity between some business entrepreneurs and the faculty.

Despite the fallen idols of the past several years of corporate mismanagement, books about authoritarian CEOs continue to sell an image of leadership as highly individualized, and very muscular, self-advancement. In this modern form of hagiography, corporate leaders have become the great hope not only because of the gains in profitability that some have engineered but also because of their insistence on efficiency, accountability, and immediate success in the institutions they have so famously led. The fact that so many have left weakened businesses in their wake seems not to have registered deeply in the public consciousness. In the minds of boards and administrators there lingers a similar ideal of the heroic college president who will cut through the red tape of traditional governance by articulating clear goals, forcing their attainment, and making the classes run cheaply. Certainly that is the ideal advocated by the AGB study of the presidency.

It is notable that with the flamboyant failures of so many of the leaders of the 1980s and '90s, the level of their compensation has become a major issue both for stockholders and the general public—though seemingly less so for corporation boards. Over time, the ratio of CEO compensation to the salary of the average employees under them has risen sharply.[4] And despite failures to meet stated goals, boards seem to find it unthinkable to dock executive pay. While some failed CEOs have been fired in full public view, their severance compensation has become even more of a scandal than the level of their pay. Higher education boards, never to be left behind, have adopted similar compensation and severance practices—with resulting unhappiness among the faculty. Inves-

tigations of exorbitant compensation for failing work led to the downfall of the
president at Adelphi University, and there have been notable controversies about
generous severance arrangements for presidents at the University of California
and Indiana University, among other schools. Recently, in order to keep up with
the private universities able to put together enormous salary packages to bring
in the next great leadership hope, boards at universities like Michigan have gone
to the private sector for supplemental funds to increase the presidential salary.
The same kind of side deal has been fashioned to take care of the other top-
of-the-line salaries in higher education—those of the football and basketball
coaches. Faculty have been troubled by the uncoupling of athletic salaries from
their more modest pay scales, but they are even more exasperated by astronomical presidential pay. Presidents are supposed to be less grasping than coaches.
Roger Bowen, the current general secretary of AAUP, has hazarded the novel
idea that executive pay be established "at a ratio that does not exceed something
like four or five times the average faculty salary," arguing that such caps on presidential salaries would accentuate the fact that leadership in the academy is
about idealism and service rather than competition and market bidding.[5]

The search for and hiring of presidents is, indeed, one vital academic activity that illustrates the gap between governance and managerial ideas. Faculty
understand that it is the board's prerogative to hire and review the president,
but they always push for a substantial faculty presence on the relevant search
and review committees. Although faculty representatives can be as eager as
board members to pull a hiring coup that will bring a distinguished academic
leader to campus, they tend to distrust professional headhunters as costly and
insensitive to academic qualifications. They also dislike the secrecy of such
searches because secrecy prevents them from seeking references from colleagues elsewhere. Finally, they worry that a search process run on a CEO
model too often prefers outsiders to inside candidates. Whatever the case, the
current spectacle of rotating presidents, those who perch at one school while
waiting for an offer from a better one, is unseemly and expensive. Faculty
believe that a more reasonable process—a shared process—would be cheaper
and would yield better results.

I tried to convey these beliefs to the AGB presidential study group in 1994,
but I emerged from our conversation with the realization that I had a lot to
learn about the managerial mentality. And once aware of its penetration into
the leadership of the academy, I began to understand the origins of some of
the initiatives on my own campus and throughout the nation. Indeed, I was

so struck by managerial discourse that when I was invited back to my campus to talk to an English graduate class about academia several months later, I urged the students to widen their reading to include the management best-seller lists. I observed that while George Eliot's *Middlemarch* or Dickens's *Hard Times* or *Bleak House* might tell them much that they needed to know about the formation of the bureaucracies in which they would find themselves as professors, they had better get to know contemporary sources as well. I further observed that management best-sellers had become the substitute for novels in the reading of travelers; they were always on sale at airport bookstalls, for example. Actually, they offered some of the attractions of Victorian fiction under a new guise. For one thing, in setting up a hierarchy of management heroes, they indulged in narratives of poetic justice for winners. Moreover, they tended to outdo Victorian fiction in their didacticism. And they have also become extremely pious in numbering the virtues and vices of organizational practice. First there was Steven Covey's "7 Habits of Highly Effective People" (now extended to the "8th Habit, from Effectiveness to Greatness"), then "6 Steps to Financial Independence," "5 Easy Steps for Creating Wealth," the "5 Dysfunctions of a Team," and the mystical "Six Sigma Way"—to give only a few examples.[6] Finally, these texts could be Darwinian in their insistence on business "red in tooth and claw": one of the most successful managerial handbooks of the nineties was *Reengineering the Corporation: A Manifesto for Business Revolution,* which advocated downsizing with a kind of glee that seemed overdetermined in its animus against employees. Given the array of dismal failures of this program, the authors have subsequently offered their mea culpas in various venues.[7]

The traditional governance ideals of continuity in leadership, deliberation in decision making, the invitation of a wide range of opinions, and suspicion of short-term thinking may seem inefficient in a corporate setting obsessed with the challenges of market volatility. But the chaos that ensues when these practices are disparaged may be illustrated by the failures of governance that have beset non-academic sectors in the past several years. The collapse of Enron is only one example of the problems with the new management ethos in a complex enterprise. So is the failure of intelligence agencies within the federal government. In each case, it seems that the managerial system was geared to resist interference from lower ranks, even though the employees of these institutions possessed superior education and training. The upper reaches of the Enron Corporation could command the best and brightest among financiers, accountants, and managerial staff. And the high standards for admission to such government agencies as the FBI, CIA, and State Department are legendary. Instead of seeking full and independent participation of such gifted employees, however, these corporate entities seem to have fostered intense personal competition and extreme company or departmental loyalty, ignoring established regimens of checks and balances. Enron devised no fora for open debate—only pep sessions. Further, it gave little protection to skilled employees who might ask questions, raise objections, or plead some higher good than the bottom line; such workers faced a threat of being fired, or not being promoted.[8] Within government agencies like the FBI, retaliation is limited by civil service regulations; nevertheless it seems that naysayers even in the heart of our national security agencies risk their careers when they speak.[9]

In these instances, the failures of business and government to preserve their own internal checks and balances have presented challenges to market theorists. Alan Greenspan is one of those who have mused on where the system failed, and it is remarkable that although he has used such words as "credibility" and "character" in his remarks, he tends to imagine these as unenforceable values except through the monetary valence they acquire when they are violated: noting that "investment firms are well aware that security analysis without credibility has no market value," he has suggested that credibility will eventually become a commodity attractive to those investors who have been burned badly enough to demand it.[10] This proposal seems to me naïve in its trust that market demands are self-policing.

The problems with corporate credibility have also risen out of failures to appreciate the new nature of workers and of work. In some tech workplaces, management has "flattened out" in order to benefit from the collective ingenuity of programmers and inventors. Sophisticated, independent-minded, and highly trained workers require modes of participation within organizations if the benefits of their initiative and imagination are to be realized. Further, the complexity of the organizations requires more rather than less discussion and debate from within. Without such debate and discussion, the actions of parts may never become clear to the whole; departments may spin off out of control and out of sight. Thus decisions that seem right in the short run may never be assessed in the light of long-range developments.[11]

In drawing these generalizations, I take as my text a passage from Peter Drucker, who has emphasized the shift in our postindustrial society from manual workers to "knowledge workers." In a key passage in one of his most influential books, he extrapolates the future of governance under a double guidance—from the managers, on the one hand, and from the experts who work for, with, under, over, and beside them, on the other:

> The transformation of institutions into "double-headed monsters" in which there is both a business management and professional groups (whether accountants, market researchers, salesmen, engineers, or quality control people) will force us into new, and fairly radical, organizational concepts. Business organization as we know it has developed fundamentally in the shape of a pyramid, with a "command" function mitigated by the emergence of "staffs" who were "advisory" rather than "command." Increasingly, the hospital or the university will be a better model than the traditional military, perhaps even for the military itself. Increasingly, we will see organizations as concentric, overlapping, coordinated rings, rather than pyramids. There is need for "top management" and there is need for an ultimate "command"—just as there is need for a skeleton in the animal body. There is need for a clear locus of decisions, for a clear voice and for unity of command in the event of common danger and emergencies. But there is also need for accepting that within given fields the professionals should set the standards and determine what their contribution should be.[12]

But despite Drucker's stature in management circles, the administrators in higher education seem drawn back again and again to an outmoded military or business model, and just at a time when that model will no longer suffice. The needs of the skeleton displace the needs of the flesh, and so the body works against its own health. When higher education leaders adopt the pyramidal business model for academic governance, they may therefore be participating in a misreading of contemporary work and the contemporary workforce. They underestimate the value of professional training and expertise among the academics who work in colleges and universities. And rather than seeking the expression of this training and expertise in coming to creative decisions, they find the input messy and irritating. My contention is, as a matter of fact, that despite all of the failings noted by its critics, academia has been better attuned than the corporate world to the changes in modern work and workers because of its system of shared governance founded on the expertise and responsibilities of each sector.

Later in this chapter, I will return to the AAUP's description of traditional shared governance, and how faculty governance works—and doesn't work— in practice on campuses. Indeed, I will make a plea for faculty to understand how critical a role they play in taking part in enlightened management. For now I want to concentrate on the governance critiques that have issued from boards of trustees like the ones I ran into on the AGB commission, as well as from other advocates of corporate governance models.[13] These managerial types seem ready to accord faculty some say in curriculum and in the personnel decisions that are part of the tenure system, but they are skeptical of faculty governance in other areas. James Duderstadt, former president of the University of Michigan, has summarized the common view in the chapter "Governance and Leadership" in the book about the future of higher education that he wrote after leaving the presidency. The issue, he says, is "whether the current shared governance characterizing universities can achieve the capacity, the flexibility, to respond and adapt to a rapidly changing world."[14] This view is shared by the general public in its harboring of the stereotype of the absent-minded and therefore impractical professor—except when the professor is Peter Drucker.

The giveaway about the source of business critiques of academic governance is that they are usually couched in the language of management fads. The belief in management has become almost a secular religion in some academic quarters; management axioms are lifted whole from the *Harvard Business Review* or the business best-seller list of the *New York Times* and deposited in the strategic plans of one institution or another.[15] The faculty responds with almost automatic opposition when jargon from these sources articulates administrative planning. There is no surer way of arousing faculty satire than using such terms as "stakeholder," "value added," "total quality management," or "accountability measures" in describing the actors, methods, and aims of university governance. These are especially obnoxious to faculty in their acronym forms—notably TQM, as well as RCM (responsibility-centered management), BRP (business reengineering process), MBO (management by objective), and the infamous PIs (performance indicators—called "pissies" by faculty in the Cal State system). For many of the faculty I've worked with, the shorthand of such acronyms simply masks the irrationality of trying to solve problems with slogans.

As the decade of the 1990s proceeded, the issues of governance continued to play a major role in campus disruptions—especially as the corporate mandate to assert clear plans and overwhelm resistance with force, if necessary, was acted out in several famous cases. The firing of a number of long-term faculty at Bennington College in the name of defining a new mission for the institution was perhaps the most infamous example.[16] Despite continuing controversy, the determination of a segment of the higher education establishment to "let Bennington be Bennington"—and thus to substitute for faculty tenure the depressed and variable academic employment market in the arts—has helped the college survive.

Equally significant was an effort by the board of overseers at the University of Minnesota to undermine faculty tenure as a feature of a major reengineering of the entire campus. There, a management overhaul was initiated in response to a group of problems in the medical school. The effort to address these problems was conducted along the lines set up by the philosophy proposed as a cure-all in *Reengineering the Corporation* and implemented by the consulting firm of its authors: Michael Hammer and James Champy.[17] The provost for the medical school operations at Minnesota had become a convert, and he persuaded the state legislature and the board of overseers to join him in going around traditional governance in favor of the dictates of reengineering—one of its mandates being decisive downsizing everywhere. The initiative led to a general faculty revolt. By the time the Minnesota "tenure wars" came to a head, the provost had left to head another major university and the chair of the board had resigned. In true managerial fashion, the board responded to the faculty unrest by hiring another outside consultancy. It went to a Washington, D.C., law firm, which rewrote the tenure code to include an entry requiring the faculty to behave with "a proper attitude of industry and cooperation with others within and without the university community."[18] This awkward formulation was taken as a direct challenge from the corporate world to faculty professionalism, and so it was immediately printed on the badges used in a drive for faculty unionization. The drive to unionize barely failed—by 26 votes in a ballot of 692 to 666—but the threat was sufficient to bring the university into a compromise in which it reaffirmed its commitment to faculty tenure and to shared governance.

Since the mid-1990s, advocates of faculty governance have tended to look at the Bennington case as a defeat and the Minnesota case as a victory. Whatever view one takes, however, the fact is that poor faculty governance in each institution was in part responsible for the crisis. At Bennington, there had been a long history of faculty opposition—widely chronicled in outrageous accounts of Bennington's traditional free spirit—that gave the president and the board ample pretext for a general and continuing purge.[19] At Minnesota, the faculty had become compliant about handing over the issues to the administration for solution, even when there were scandals in oversight of prominent faculty entrepreneurs. The tenure system for clinical faculty in the medical school had also become a burden that spilled over onto the rest of the campus. Given the instincts of an impatiently business-minded board leader, a clash was inevitable.

ஃ   ஃ   ஃ

In Minnesota, the challenge to academic tenure and governance inspired the reemergence of faculty leadership. In describing the way that shared governance should work on a college campus, it is useful to note that the instrument of governance that had lapsed before the crisis at Minnesota was the one that was supposed to bring together the faculty from across all the segments of the campus—the faculty senate. Countering this instrument of unity, the effort to reengineer the campus sought to confine faculty to their roles within their school units, broadly conceived, while at the same time erasing the unit boundaries that had given individual faculty a base of power. According to one faculty member who was then in the Academic Health Center, these plans were presented to faculty on overhead slides at meetings with reengineering staff, but requests to be given copies were denied.[20] It seems that faculty culture was to be subsumed under the complexity of newly defined units whose appointed leaders were answerable to one centralized administration, advised by a circle of program directors or deans. This was one variation of a managerial strategy that has weakened centers of faculty power by creating new units for decision making that are dominated by chief executives and middle managers. In Minnesota, however, such managerial aspirations awakened faculty governance. The "faculty consultative committee" of the senate rose to the occasion, and eventually helped all sides reach a series of compromises. The other aid to resolution was the faculty's decision to mount a collective bargaining campaign. While the vote for an AAUP union fell short, the campaign itself so alarmed the board that its president resigned, and Mark Yudof, the new president of the university, sponsored an AAUP conference on governance in the first year of his administration.

The Minnesota case was not a total victory for the faculty, but its sound and fury energized alarms about governance in academic discussions on the Internet and in disciplinary societies across the nation. Its final resolutions indicate that despite faculty inertia, all politics is local. Shared governance can draw forth a great deal of time and energy the closer it gets to the level of faculty practice, not only in the realm of tenure but also in the realm of departmental identity and prerogatives. There, too, it can be as territorial and as self-interested as are departmental competitions within corporations. This competitive interplay is one of the sources of the intensity of faculty self-governance, but departmental self-interest is also a reason for administrations to foster faculty senates. They can provide help in bringing faculty from various departments to consider the welfare of the entire campus.

The most self-interested level of academic governance is the department. Departments are by nature opportunistic, territorial, and sometimes provincial. They are frequently situated as rivals with one another for the resources that can help them thrive—faculty lines, clerical assistance, technology upgrades, and the like. Competing departments and programs can drive the dynamics of colleges and universities, though in the development of what Sheila Slaughter and Larry Leslie call "academic capitalism,"[21] departmental efforts to garner resources from research markets can undermine collegiality. One of the most divisive areas for interdepartmental conflict is in tenure decisions. Cross-disciplinary tenure committees at the school and higher levels are critical to maintaining some common level of judgment on the identity and quality of the entire faculty—but when members of those committees make judgments according to their own disciplinary understandings, antagonisms arise. Humanities faculty tend to be extremely suspicious of members of science departments who may make tenure or other resource judgments without understanding the priorities elsewhere. Thus I have heard colleagues in English complain that the science side of the campus thrives while the humanities side runs downhill; this was one of the issues raised at the fora of the 2004 Modern Language Association meetings on the future of the humanities.

Deans and presidents expect a good department to be loyal to its discipline and thereby to bring scholarly intensity and professional credibility to the institution. Those who fault the academy for lacking an active sense of entrepreneurship have never sat in on budget sessions at the school level. I have done so both as an associate dean and a department chair, and I can testify to the salesmanship of many department heads—and the dismay among colleagues at the laxness of those leaders who do not fight for their colleagues. But I have found that wise department leaders also keep an eye on the welfare of cognate departments, because they may find themselves looking for alliances some day. In the current intellectual ferment of the disciplines, they may be looking toward future interdisciplinary possibilities as well.

The second most active level in faculty governance occurs in school or college committees. In larger institutions schools work in the same competitive way departments do, but they tend to be even more competitively positioned within the entire institution. When they command grant money or major student enrollments, their deans can become feudal barons. One of the critical tests for chief academic administrators is at once to let talented and aggressive deans build fine programs and to provide protection for more vulnerable and possibly less well administered units. The dean has middle management—the department chairs—at her beck and call, and the chairs can bring the power of their faculties with them. The dean may also have a staff of important academic administrators—associate and assistant deans, registrars, counselors, budget trackers, and that most powerful person in the unit—her personal administrative assistant. With these forces, a powerful dean can thwart a president's best-laid plans.

Faculty members view work on departmental committees as part of their profession. And they are also willing to serve on school curriculum, tenure, promotion, and policy committees to preserve the welfare of their departments. But the entire structure of department and school is designed to make collaboration more oppositional than cooperative. It is here, indeed, that one of the academic management fads of the late 1980s and early '90s threatened the balance in academic governance on a number of campuses.

In the '80s, the complexity of university campuses, and especially the need to find support for each unit as state and private support waned, led to the concept of RCM, or responsibility-centered management. Animated by a notion of "every tub on its own bottom," it aspired to get each school to begin raising its own money through accelerated grantsmanship, entrepreneurial efforts to increase course enrollments, intensified philanthropic outreach, and cost cutting. As David Kirp tells the story in his book on corporatization in the academy,[22] the trend began at the University of Pennsylvania and then moved to the University of Southern California. Both of these were private schools that confronted severe budgetary shortfalls, especially in some of their professional schools. Before long the idea that each school would raise the bulk of its own funding had spread broadly through the public sector. It came to Indiana and then it went to the University of Michigan. In each case, according to Kirp, it had its problems; and in Michigan, after the departure of an enthusiastic president, it has faded away. At Harvard, where it has long held sway without the acronym, it has been the bane of new presidents, and Lawrence Summers was only the latest of those worthies to try to get it under control.

In my own work as chair of an English department at Indiana, I began to hear the phrase "seed money" whenever I sought funding for a troupe of visiting Shakespearean actors to spend a week in our classes. At every campus funding source I approached, the notion seemed to be that if I was given several thousand dollars one time, I must grow the money to do the same thing a second or third time. I found that arguing with some dean each year was the best I could do, and I began to wonder what kind of "seeds" an English department had that I could cultivate. To start that kind of gardening, I would have to hire a grant writer to help me. Doing so would require our dreaming up claims that our efforts would do more than enlighten our current students; we would have to hype our mission and, perhaps, distort our program. In English, there are few program grants available. Most of the research money in the humanities goes to individual scholars in the form of fellowships, as it should do.

There were many doubters about RCM when it came before Indiana's Faculty Council. The fear was that such a system would encourage one department to compete against the other. Moreover, it seemed clear that the science departments and professional schools, already privileged because of their grant overhead funds, would collect even more resources through their enrollments of job-hungry majors. English would survive, I believed, but I and my colleagues worried about smaller departments—language departments being in the most danger. Later, at a governance conference at the University of Michigan during a time when it was considering the institution of RCM, I heard the director of an area studies program lament the move. Slaughter and Leslie have shown that in the past twenty years, the impulse to "devolve" the budgetary function to departments dependent on academic capitalism has become stronger in the entrepreneurial university—at the expense of community and centralized control. Thus there is a contradiction between the mandate for cultivating a faculty community and the tropism of university ambitions toward research and technology centers that command the most resources. In the end, Slaughter and Leslie sponsor a notion of devolution through market incentives stipulated in public funding for undergraduate teaching; they see such an intervention as the only escape from the iron hand of the market that has directed research universities to activities that mainly serve research, technology transfer, and designated public service.[23]

Perhaps because of the decline of faculty governance on most campuses, critics of the imbalances in higher education tend to neglect the possibility that one force for community might be the faculty senate. The concept of a faculty senate, designed to bring faculty from all schools on the campus together to deliberate on common matters, has been integral to the traditional notion of shared governance in American higher education. When senates work, they are sources of unity rather than dissonance. In most cases, this faculty body can have representation from sectors other than the faculty; indeed, in some cases the president of the institution actually presides. On many campuses, the faculty body is also supported by the provision of office space, a telephone line, and secretarial help. Its elected leader usually obtains some release from other duties to serve. A faculty senate can hardly survive without some administrative support, but the faculty component is intended to be clear and predominant. Ideally, the faculty senate as a centralized forum for faculty debate entails a transcendence of unit and disciplinary lines, because it deals with larger issues of professional concern.

One such concern is the hiring and review of the president and other major administrators. Another is the setting of the academic schedule and calendar. The faculty senate also has a say in the awarding of degrees—including honorary degrees—as well as other all-campus academic affairs. Faculty senates usually press for authority over athletic programs, and however ineffective they have been, faculty senate committees on athletics are not uncommon. Most important, faculty senates seek to play some part in budgetary matters, and in well-functioning schools they help the faculty understand the school's financial situation. When the faculty senate is fully engaged in these matters, problems like the ones at Minnesota rarely arise.

The drawback to effective shared governance through all-campus elective advisory bodies is that faculty senates have been having increasing difficulty functioning under the stress of internal competition between the governing instruments of departments and schools. We have already seen that the faculty tends to be more interested in governance at the school and department levels than at the total campus level. An Association of Departments of English study of faculty governance summed up the problem in a report it made in 2001: according to one department chair, junior faculty members "are eager to be elected or appointed to the executive committee because they understand that that committee in fact governs the policies and life of the department. Beyond the department, I work in a corporate university, and that's where I think faculty governance has almost disappeared. It's very difficult to encourage junior or senior faculty members to be involved in the university's supposedly representative bodies."24 The consequent insularity of life in departments makes it easier to solidify the top-down model of governance.

And so a lapse of interest in senates characterizes governance on many large campuses. This decline in centralized faculty governance has been influenced by a number of internal academic myths and prejudices. For one thing, the faculty senate tends to be dominated by "old-timers" who remember the days when things were different and continually look backward. Despite their long service to the institution, these permanent fixtures of governance may have neglected the one thing needful—the cultivation of their own replacements. When replacements do appear, their eagerness to make a difference may label them as "professional faculty politicians" who serve with the most suspect motive—the desire to become an administrator. Thus their efforts to work with administrations may be seen as betrayal—cooption—rather than a sharing of governance.

Because roles in faculty governance are unsteady, a genial senate can become suspect by faculty while an oppositional one can be shrugged off by the administration. Given that the faculty share in governance is a matter of tradition as well as mutual idealism, it can be devalued with relative ease by its own constituents as well as the administration. When that happens the senate ceases to become an effective policy body and turns into a debating club for academic theorizing or a rest home where campus historians tell stories about better days.

In most cases the senate is some combination of these elements, but it still tends to be loyal to the ideal of campus democracy. The committees of the faculty senate are usually effective when they help formulate policy on campus standards, defend campus services such as libraries, open an important avenue of communication with the administration, and stick to the particular charge set before them—even when they do not take the initiative. Because the faculty are not managers, however, there are functional problems with governance at the level of the faculty senate. They cluster in three main areas: agendas, expertise, and time.

1. *Agendas.* Most senate agendas need to be set by an administration that cares about what the faculty thinks. It's the administration that knows what's happening. It's the administration that begins to frame plans for the future. And the administration is also informed by differing

initiatives (or problems) from departments, schools, and the campus. One administrative strategy can be to solve issues unilaterally. Another is to let them alone, hoping they will go away. The best way to work with issues, however, is to recognize, frame, and present them to the faculty senate. Indeed the most important role of the administration in faculty governance is to enable its work by helping it set its agenda.

2. *Expertise.* It is important to remember that nobody teaches governance in graduate school PhD programs. Most faculty members have only the vaguest notion, left over from high school, of *Robert's Rules of Order.* Further, some faculty have a knee-jerk disdain for "management" because they see the corporate model as heartless and soulless. That faculty senates survive despite such ignorance about reasonable procedures is itself noteworthy. The health of faculty governance may depend on its leaders devising practical courses for faculty on good practice not only in managing but in deliberating together efficiently.

3. *Time.* The faculty runs on an academic year that compresses its time for deliberation into nine or ten months. Usually, the summer is devoted to research or heavy summer school teaching, and the senate and its committees do not meet. Administrations run the risk of faculty revolt if they issue new policies after graduation—when the faculty is off campus. Timing is everything in the academy. Changes must be debated, which means that they should be introduced early in the fall. Decisions are rarely so exigent as they are made out to be, and in a crisis faculty leaders can be called together electronically. Nevertheless, one of the administrative offenses against shared governance is beginning major organizational changes without warning, in the summer, under "emergency" conditions.

※   ※   ※

It is in those schools where faculty governance has had to work with a very low measure of administrative generosity that faculty have turned to unionization as the ultimate solution to their issues with their institutions. Indeed, the rise of academic unionizing may be seen as a faculty attempt to gain and employ managerial know-how in response to administrative encroachments on their expectations of having some measure of self-management. That they do not resort to collective action in governance more often may be explained by academic employees' lack of education in the technical details of management—in matters such as finance, account management, employment law, and retirement and health care benefits. Most faculty do not have the time or incentive to become well enough informed to deal with such matters through campus governance when they trust their administrative leaders. Thus, if the administration lacks the skill to manage well or invite mutuality in governance, the faculty's recourse may be to adapt modes of participation that enact specific and definitive arrangements with the administration. The case at the University of Minnesota shows that the faculty may react to managerial faddism, authoritarian style, and arbitrary downsizing by threatening to establish a faculty union. And currently, in light of the growth of academic employees outside the personnel system governed by tenure, and thus outside the protections that tenure offers, a number of national unions—industrial as well as professional—see higher education as a fair field for organizing.

"Unionism" tends to be a dirty word in administrative discussions of governance in higher education. Most boards and many administrations find the idea of faculty collective bargaining scandalous—a violation of the notions of academic standards, collegiality, and independence. And many faculty also respond negatively to collective bargaining, for the same reasons. They may also find the bread-and-butter issues in most union bargaining to be counter to their notions of professional altruism. Both the 1998 AGB "Statement on Institutional Governance" and the Association of Departments of English's 2001 report on governance reveal suspicion of faculty unionism by trustees and faculty as well.[25] Nevertheless, the impetus to unionization has remained strong, despite the difficulties posed by current law. Unionization of full-time faculty in private colleges and universities across the country has been all but halted by the Supreme Court's Yeshiva decision of 1980.

That decision found that Yeshiva faculty could not organize for collective bargaining because they themselves were "managerial." Since that time, full-time faculty at private schools have been denied all the protection of the NLRA. In simple terms, the justices ruled that through the tradition of shared governance, faculty were supposed to have a majority say in the curriculum, in hiring and retaining colleagues, and in setting the standards for grading and graduation. Given that so many of the managerial activities of higher education were theirs alone to exercise decisively, how could they bargain against themselves? This impasse derived from the 1935 National Labor Relations Act's bipolar segregation of the interests along lines of opposition, setting management against labor. But the simple oppositional model of labor relations has been unable to protect the growing professional sector in American labor. And indeed, under such bargaining strategies as "win-win" or "mutual gains" bargaining, the notion of "labor versus management" has come to seem outdated and unproductive. Such conflict became an issue early in the Clinton administration when Secretary of Labor Robert Reich set up the Commission on the Future of Worker-Management Relations, chaired by former secretary of commerce John Dunlop, to investigate innovative ways to bring better concord to labor relations.

When the American Association of University Professors testified before that commission in 1994, it proposed that the shared governance ideal of the academy could present a model for the new modes of professional work and management brought about by the knowledge society. It asserted that the National Labor Relations Act of 1935 built a wall between workers and management, leaving little margin for the natural interchanges between them. Professional work in the academy required the individual's allegiance to ethical ideals and standards that could often override commitments to wages and conditions of work. Scholars could, and often did, risk their livelihoods by hewing to the truth of their discoveries. The law, then, should be revised to present a third category in the labor-management relationship for professionals, who should not confront the barriers to unionization set up by the Yeshiva decision. AAUP's position could thus be seen as a version of Peter Drucker's projection, quoted above, of the new kind of organization demanded in a knowledge society—one that "accept[s] that within given fields the professionals should set the standards and determine what their contribution should be."

After Yeshiva, a number of faculty unions in private higher education were decertified; but in states that have enabling collective bargaining legislation for public colleges and universities, many faculty in public institutions have turned to unionization. They have looked to securing the traditional protections of academic freedom through the tenure system, and they have looked for better control over their stake in the institution—seeking hands-on engagement in setting institutional priorities.

One often-ignored reason for the faculty's choice of collective bargaining in university governance is that the culture and expertise of unions can improve faculty effectiveness and efficiency. The definiteness in the procedures and rules set up in union contracts offers more clarity than less formal modes of institutional agreements can do. Collective bargaining draws on an expertise that, at its best, can match the expertise of managerial know-how. Union dues also fund staff assistance to faculty leadership, thus ensuring effective continuity and communication with chapter members. Finally, nationally affiliated higher education unions may also have a powerful voice in state legislatures and on the national scene. The current dismal state of public funding for education also lends added allure to "industrial strength" unions, like the United Auto Workers—which has entered the field of unionization for teaching assistants and adjuncts, notably at the University of California and NYU. No matter what the internal politics of these contemporary unions and no matter how their membership and influence have been eroded, many faculty imagine that these unions can bring extra clout to their interests.

Despite the appeal of the collective bargaining approach to academic governance, few have researched its particular benefits and its problems in higher education (among the exceptions are Patricia Gumport, Ernst Benjamin, and—especially—Gary Rhoades).[26] Since the mere mention of unionism tends to be greeted in managerial circles with suspicion if not outright hostility, ignorance among those who have not worked on union campuses makes it difficult to open a genuine discussion on the subject with the administrative side.[27] On the faculty side as well, the thought of unions can conjure up unrealistic images of solidarity, picket lines, and *Norma Rae* triumphs. This romance is ignorant of the relevant legislation as well as the bargaining practices of most unions—where a strike is usually considered a sign of failure. The fact is that knowledgeable faculty leaders on "mature" unionized campuses can sometimes be far more cooperative with managerial initiatives than those on union-free campuses.[28] They know the realities of budgets, they have studied various modes of negotiation, and their participation in self-management has made some of them less tolerant of faculty obstructionism than are colleagues in less well-defined, more traditional systems of governance.

In the AAUP model of unionism, the faculty senate is not replaced by a collective bargaining unit but rather supported and informed by it. Interestingly enough, however, some leaders on the union side of the issue are uncomfortable with faculty senates and the idea of their sharing of governance. Unions have long been suspicious of "company unions," and in their testimony before the Dunlop Commission, they tried to draw a very clear line between working with management and being coopted by it. In addition, some union leaders may believe that the union bargaining in drawing up and implementing the contract is sufficient to ensure faculty rights; faculty senates are only ancillary and should not involve themselves in matters like the conditions of academic work—teaching and research. In that regard, the AAUP's stance differs from that of organized labor. The national Association of Governing Boards, representing administrative views, has also argued against the faculty senates' cooperating with faculty unions. The AGB believes that participation by some individuals in both the senate and the union give faculty interests too much power; they see the combination as an invitation for faculty to "double dip" in governance. Thus, in its 1998 "Statement on Institutional Governance," the AGB made clear that union leaders should not be involved in the traditional structures of internal governance: "If a collective-bargaining contract governs the terms and conditions of faculty and staff employment, the board should consider a formal policy regarding the role of union officials in institutional governance. Specifically, the board should articulate any limitations the existence of a bargaining agreement may place on participation in governance by union officials."[29] And so we can imagine a paradoxical alliance between the AGB and National Education Association in which both agree that unions should stay out of governance—on the one hand because union leaders are viewed as having agendas and loyalties at variance with those of the administration, and on the other hand because forms of cooperation with administrations are seen as constituting a style of faculty organization that privileges the notion of compliance and trust over legally enforceable agreements.

I believe that any simplistic claim that unionization, old style, will absolve the faculty from the need to participate in their faculty governance structures is mistaken. Rudimentary dialectics, whether they come from the managerial or the union side, cannot help in governing modern service institutions cooperatively. And cooperative governance is absolutely necessary to preserve an independent academy in the United States. Without such an academy, the search for truth will be managed, governed, and bargained for, or bargained away, by the most powerful interest. Thus I believe that the faculty share in deciding on the aims and procedures of our colleges and universities must be reclaimed under any of the three modes I have mentioned here—traditional governance, managerial governance, or unionization. Some campuses are devising new structures of cooperation in which management and faculty do meet together to decide on program directions and needs. Some of these have been drawn up to avoid the oppositionality that can become a habit in faculty senates and faculty unions. In many cases, a president—especially when starting out on a campus—can try to bypass the elected faculty representatives either in the senate or the union by creating specially appointed blue-ribbon task forces. Again, the motive may be a desire for smooth discussion and simple agreement. But such moves inevitably invite faculty suspicions. Whatever structures of governance evolve, they cannot function well if the faculty has not had the right to choose their own representatives within it and if that representation can be vetoed by administrative power.

That being said, the current state of higher education calls upon faculty to become more active in whatever form of governance they choose. The demise of faculty involvement in oversight of their schools suggests that academics have participated in the horror suggested by Drucker's "double-headed monster" image. They seem distracted by self-interest and disciplinary ambition from understanding the new academic workforce and the new organizational configurations in their institutions. Most critically, many of those who have the power of tenured appointments seem oblivious to the de-professionalization of the American professoriate caused by the accelerated "temping" of their ranks. Whether academic managers and faculty realize it or not, their automatic turn to the employment of contingent faculty to meet short-term enrollment demands is the single most destructive force in faculty governance today. As Gary Rhoades has pointed out, "There are more subtle ways of reorganizing the academic work force, of reallocating and reducing faculty resources, than by retrenching faculty. There are more efficient and less politically problematic ways that have more dramatic results. Hire more part-time faculty. They are cheaper. They make it easier to shift faculty resources from one unit to another, for they are easier to hire and to release. In hiring larger proportions of part-time faculty, managers are renegotiating the position of faculty as a full-time professional work force."[30]

If professional interests and standards are to take precedence over profit, the faculty must unite and organize under one model or another. Administrators should sponsor a new mandate for faculty governance, knowing that their institutions can only benefit from receiving informed advice and consent. And faculty must understand that they should participate in governance wisely— with good will, civility, and efficiency. If such a mutual approach were undertaken, the stakeholders in higher education could participate in creating a "clear voice and . . . unity" that Peter Drucker calls for in the management of our complex campuses in these turbulent times.

CHAPTER SIX

Superstars and Rookies of the Year

Academic Competition

Twenty years ago, when I first started thinking about the competitive games we play in recruiting faculty in higher education,[1] I was struck by a television halftime spot in the University of Alabama's football game in which the president of the university appeared balancing a football in one hand and a book in the other. Peering into the camera at the supporters of the Crimson Tide, he solemnly assured them that soon the book would rise as high as the football in Alabama's national rankings. I have not followed the University of Alabama's academic standing closely in the years since, but my general impression is that the book is still fighting with the football for parity in Tuscaloosa. What was significant to me then, and continues to be today, is that the analogy between sports and academic success has absorbed the imaginations of presidents, provosts, deans, and chairs in their efforts to hire and support their faculty—and, on occasion, to conduct raids on other institutions in order to maintain a winning team in research and scholarship. More significantly, the language of sports competition has infiltrated the minds of faculty as well—many of whom may ask themselves after they've signed on, "Will I make the cut?" "Did I make the A team?" "Should I declare myself a free agent?"

In my earlier observations on the phenomenon, I had some fun with the language of sports, especially the seasons of competition for faculty in the academy and athletes in the outside world. There is usually a concentration on college athletics during March Madness; all kinds of schools can compete in basketball, whereas the competition for participation in postseason football contests has been limited both by the resource demands of a football program and by the big-school orientation of the Bowl Championship Series. Perhaps the excitement on campus when our team wins causes us academics to turn to the contests in our own domain with minds steeped in sporting metaphors.

While spring is the time for March Madness, it is also the time for recruiting faculty. The rookies tend to be recruited during midwinter; their wooing is keyed to the schedules of disciplinary meetings where job seekers congregate for interviews. But the competition for them extends further, with acceptance deadlines set by most schools for mid-March. Given the degradation of the academic job market in most basic disciplines, it may seem a wonder that there is so much fuss and bother about hiring a few assistant professors, but the intensity is high because the chances to hire are so rare. Graduate departments are always on edge as well, wondering whether their reputations will be upheld by star students landing positions. And departmental standing in schools without graduate programs can be burnished by bringing in a bright new candidate who would not have considered joining such a lesser league in earlier times. Spring is also time for recruiting full professor superstars—a far more circumspect and complicated process. Although there may have been nods and becks and wreathed smiles throughout the year, the deadline for a professor's telling a home institution about resignation is May 15, and spring may thus be full of news about offers and counteroffers. Both the winning and the losing departments wait with excitement.

Around the time of March Madness, it is also time in the academy for handing out trophies for achievements of the intellect. The earlier announcements of the Nobel prizes were like the Winter Olympics—we gradually lost interest as it became apparent that Team USA had not taken away most of the gold. Administrators in every school of the nation await the annual lists in the *Chronicle of Higher Education* to see what the home team players have won in the national research competitions staged by the National Science Foundation, National Endowment for the Humanities, Guggenheim Foundation, American Council of Learned Societies, and MacArthur Foundation. Some schools even covet the Teacher of the Year Award sponsored by the Council for the Advancement and Support of Education.

If the results in such prestigious leagues are not satisfactory, there are consolation prizes. There are, for example, the various department or program rankings (most of them either highly impressionistic or dated), the numbers of Rhodes scholars or Marshall scholarship winners among undergraduates, the rise of entering students' SAT or ACT scores, and the "best" lists that used to be the sole province of *US News & World Report* but have now spread in various guises to other publications. Canada's *MacLean's* has always ranked Canadian universities, and *Business Week* has ranked MBA programs, but such media outlets as *USA Today*, the *Princeton Review, Kiplinger's*, and the *Journal of Blacks in Higher Education* have entered the game as well. Campuses have to wait for midsummer or fall for these standings to come out, but they can be savored throughout the year. And then there are other, smaller awards to rejoice in. In 2005 and 2006 the Web page of the University of Alabama celebrated students who claimed, respectively, five and six of the eighty-plus spots on the annual *USA Today* All-USA College Academic Team—"the most of any school in the nation."[2]

The use of the language of sporting competition in our talk about success in the academy could be seen as a harmless verbal game if it did not so deeply imbue real institutional impulses, in ways often either unexamined or shrugged off as inevitable in today's market for talent. But just as the phenomenon of championship, record-breaking competition has gone bad in sports, so it threatens the academy as well.

In this chapter, I want to define this threat in terms of uneasiness about the academy's adherence to what has been called "the winner-take-all society," for the economic and social damages of that paradigm of competition can be reflected in faculty careers as well as those of sports stars, business aces, and operatic divas. I also want to look at how such a system works against the recruitment of new faculty who will be able and willing to work for the total good of their schools. Further, it is important to assess how the system harms continuing faculty as well. When schools depend on achieving a national identity by luring superstars to their staffs, the results can be demoralization among long-term professors, erosion of loyalty, failure to collect on institutional experience, and, sometimes, really bad bargains. Most important, there is intrinsic damage done to institutions when the superstar syndrome becomes a mind-set that overrides other values. Most critics decry the neglect of teaching and service in schools that stake their bets on "winning" through pursuit of research alone. My analysis suggests that when the academy believes that there are only a few stars, a few discoveries, a zero-sum game in wisdom and mastery of knowledge, the greatest damage is done to research itself.

❧   ❧   ❧

Ten years ago two professorial economists, Robert H. Frank and Philip J. Cook, wrote an important book that described a growing trend in labor and wealth distribution that they labeled the "winner-take-all market." That market is best defined by a phenomenon that they called "reward by relative performance," a system unlike the classic one studied by most economists because it does not reward "absolute" performance itself but performance in the context of comparisons with that of other workers.[3] Their book, *The Winner-Take-All Society: Why the Few at the Top Get So Much More Than the Rest of Us*, is slightly out of date now, but it has remained in print since 1995 because it has seemed ever more prophetic and relevant in the days of Tyco, Enron, unimaginable CEO pay, and baseball-on-steroids. Although seeking in traditional economist fashion to find some benefits in the new market they describe, Frank and Cook inevitably concentrate on the negatives:

> Winner-take-all markets have increased the disparity between rich and poor. They have lured some of our most talented citizens into socially unproductive, sometimes even destructive, tasks. In an economy that already invests too little for the future, they have fostered wasteful patterns of investment and consumption. They have led indirectly to greater concentration of our most talented college students in a small set of elite institutions. They have made it more difficult for "late bloomers" to find a productive niche in life. And winner-take-all markets have molded our culture and discourse in ways many of us find deeply troubling. (pp. 4–5)

The market phenomenon that Frank and Cook describe inheres within the academy in a number of ways.

For one thing, the book's chapter called "The Battle for Educational Prestige" details the effects of such a market mentality on students—their competition for narrowing opportunities to join the social and academic networks of elite schools that can promise excellent jobs and professional school access. Frank and Cook describe the familiar patterns that have led ambitious students around the country not only to pay Stanley Kaplan a lot of money but also to immerse themselves in sports and extracurricular service activities that might look good to college admissions officers.

More significantly, as the focus on "winning" schools grows, the distribution of academic talent becomes skewed to the detriment of the founding notion of American higher education as an instrument for spreading opportunity in many places. Frank and Cook comment, "Education's growing role as gatekeeper has given rise to increasingly intense competition for admission into the nation's leading colleges and universities. Whereas it was once common for the brightest high school students to attend state universities close to home, increasingly they matriculate at a small handful of the most selective private institutions of higher learning" (p. 148).

Frank and Cook are economists, and accordingly they look for the money, viewing student competition for elite schools as leading to higher tuitions everywhere. They argue that to keep in the race, universities must hire the research faculty who maintain the institutional prestige that filters down into the rankings that students watch so closely. Probably they overstate the impact on tuition of the competition for name faculty. Students have only vague notions about where a school's reputation comes from, and high tuition rates are not necessarily fueled by faculty salaries, as research by the National Commission on the Cost of Higher Education has shown.[4] Faculty salaries have, in fact, remained relatively low in the aggregate, compared with salaries in other professions.[5] Rather, rises in tuition rates are caused by a number of other factors: loss of state and federal support, cost of tuition subsidies, technological upgrades, and sharp increases in managerial expenditures to meet increased bureaucratic demands. As the National Commission reported in 1998, faculty productivity may have increased rather than decreased in the current market. After all, a steep salary for a superstar can be accommodated under an all-too-prevalent formula for replacing permanent with temporary professors; universities can pay for a super salary by cashing in two or three lower-rank positions for one big hire. Such a budgetary move might even free up moneys for part-timers to do the teaching. Once students have landed in a prestigious school, they actually might not know the difference.

Nevertheless, the competitive market in higher education may have some effect on tuition. The National Commission report only suggests that possibility among all the others: "The simple truth is that no single factor can be identified to explain how and why college costs rise. The Commission suspects that part of the underlying dynamic is the search for academic prestige and the academic reward systems governing higher education. This institutional emphasis on academic status is reinforced by a system of regional and specialized accreditation that often encourages increased expenditures by practically every institution."[6] It is important to note that the commission on college costs emphasized that "practically every institution" is involved in the prestige game; thus students pay in smaller schools as well as in research universities. And so when we think about the faculty winner-take-all market, we should extrapolate from the situation at elite research universities to the smaller schools that have entered that market, having given in to the irresistible temptation to imitate.[7]

Putting the National Commission's tentative conclusion in context, we may note that although super salaries can be derived from research grant overheads and philanthropic moneys, the competition for such outside funding can generate high costs as well as high payoffs for institutions. Thus although research funding may not draw from tuition dollars, it still has an impact on undergraduate students. For one thing, the search for outside funding has generated a large administrative substructure that has become ever more costly. For another, the intense competition for research dollars preoccupies not only administrators but faculty themselves. One of the criteria for a university's entrance into the sacred ranks of the AAU (American Association of Universities) is, after all, the amount of research funding it generates. Thus everything must stop to meet an NSF deadline. And at the student level, letters of recommendation must give way to grant writing; managing a research team is more important than conducting a seminar; major researchers hired in the research market may never teach the classes that undergraduates take. Consequently no matter where funding for research comes from, students also pay a price.

In an additional feature of the race to excel, some state schools compete with out-of-state private institutions by mounting honors colleges and programs to tempt superior students to stay at home. But even within that student-centered motive there lurks an element of faculty competition; just as schools promise honors students access to star professors, so they also promise superstars the prospect of teaching only the most gifted students on the campus. When one of these elaborate super student efforts—complete with special dorms, special courses with special teachers, special lecture series, textbook grants, and a junior year abroad—was suggested for my own state university some years ago, members of the board were appalled that faculty members resisted. One of them said to me, "Don't you see, Mary? We just want to recruit good students with the same deal we provide for the football and basketball team." I told him that I thought the student athletes should be treated like the other students, and so should the honors students—some special programs, yes, but not whole enclaves for them, isolated from the rest of the campus. He seemed dumbfounded.

In recruiting students, institutions should be aware that young people's participation in the admissions competition may lead less to inner satisfaction than to a spring season of tense waiting for bids. And the dismal result is that even though most good students will get into good schools, many of them will feel like failures when the college they really wanted turns them down. In the end, however, one of the most significant features of faculty bidding wars is the impression they leave. That impression is that the academy's fascination with superstars drives up tuition by bringing in overpaid faculty who never teach. No matter how exaggerated in detail, the scenario is widely accepted (in state and federal legislatures, for example) and continues to undermine the reputation of higher education in general.

Leaving behind the question of the toll on students, it is important to analyze the workings of the winner-take-all market for faculty. I believe that it is driven by the same kinds of forces that Frank and Cook discuss when describing competition in "the cultural arena." This arena—the area of national life that is most affected by media exposure—has given rise to many intensely competitive and wasteful markets. While the focus on singular talent in the cultural markets—music, film, publication, TV, and now higher education— has always been present, the possession of such talent has been accentuated in our time by instruments of mass reproduction. The wide distribution of the performance of a great talent tends to drive out the merely good; Frank and Cook note that the gap between first and second in this kind of market may be extremely slight, but it means fame for the winner and obscurity for the loser: "One characteristic of such competitive markets is that they translate small differences in performance into large differences in economic reward" (p. 121). In turn, the rewards for extraordinary performance become more alluring when they are magnified by the acclaim of media outlets that are ever more insistent on finding success stories. In earlier days, for example, a good musician could make a career performing in good orchestras for the enjoyment of live audiences within a limited geographical reach; but now the recordings of spectacular players can be heard everywhere in the world. As a result, there is not enough work to let good but not famous players support themselves in musical careers. In higher education, there has been a similar effect from a crowded job market. But because students need individual assistance in basic courses and teachers are not totally replaceable by reproductions in various media, the ranks of non-tenure-track faculty have swelled.[8]

The limiting effects of mass reproduction on "good" work and the riches it brings to "outstanding" work are further intensified because each individual tends to compete, no matter how narrow the market has become. Everyone wants to be a winner, and research shows that most people think of themselves as either above the ordinary or capable of beating the odds. That is why the competitions of so many "reality" TV shows so nearly approximate the excitement and pathos of the academic labor market—and in so many ways. After a period of arduous testing, the final decision will be arbitrary. I remember one graduate student confidently telling me that he had taken a non-tenure-track appointment with the expectation that "I'll write my way out of it" and into a permanent position. But rather than expanding opportunity, the multiplication of contestants in a winner-take-all market may instead intensify the "take-all" effect.

One important question for higher education is how contestants for academic jobs should have found themselves in such a market at all. One answer may very well be that *all* markets these days are winner-take-all markets. Another is that both the reach of higher education and the number of its past, present, and potentially future members are far greater than they have ever been.

Be that as it may, the academic job market has become susceptible to the effects of the excited public exposure that marks cultural worlds like show business. There have been famous academics in the past, but since the 1960s, they have tended to be idolized in venues with more public scope than scholarly journals and high-brow publications. The *New York Review of Books,* founded in 1963, became a new kind of media vehicle for academic criticism, for example. The *Chronicle of Higher Education* began as a relatively staid journal for administrators in 1966, but as its success grew exponentially, it also came to circulate news of the styles and fads in various disciplines and institutions. In the mid-1980s, *Lingua Franca*—a somewhat more gossipy publication—became a kind of fanzine for star ideas and star performers in higher education. It ceased publication in 2001, and it may be that when the excitement drained out of the humanities job market, so did the glamour of new intellectual movements and figures.

More important, however, have been changes within the general national media, where attention to faculty projects and fortunes has received greater play and possibly affected the market. I have already talked about the heroes and villains in the public conflicts between conservatives like Lynne Cheney and her antagonists in the academy. In light of such continuing controversy, the popular press is more likely to give one or another faculty member the full treatment. The *New York Times* has a special tradition of trolling the annual meeting of the Modern Language Association to discover what's hot and what's bizarre. In these days of decline in the humanities, its MLA story is likely to be condescending, but it has in the past lionized the humanities stars—even reporting on their clothing choices. It still takes news of the academy and its leading lights very seriously. Most recently, it featured a full article in its magazine on a young black economist at Harvard, designated a "baby star" by one of his colleagues.[9]

Yet the multiplications and magnifications of success in a winner-take-all market can become so confusing that rational or philosophical choices about value are either overwhelmed or formed by the market's own self-generated hype. Such formations lead to some qualms, even among market economists, about their traditional embrace of a free market as panacea. At this level of their analysis, Frank and Cook sound a little like French sociologists: "although Adam Smith's invisible hand assures that markets do a speedy and efficient job of delivering the goods and services people desire it tells us nothing about where people's desires come from in the first place. If tastes were fixed at birth, this would pose no problem. But if culture shapes tastes, and if market forces shape culture, then the invisible hand is untethered. Free marketers have little to cheer about if all they can claim is that the market is efficient at filling desires that the market itself creates" (p. 201). The relevance of such thinking to the market for faculty seems to me inescapable, since so much of the theorizing in the humanities and social sciences in the past twenty years has been about the social construction of value systems. Nevertheless, as David Lodge has illustrated so trenchantly in the satirical competition for an international chair in literary theory that drives the plot of his novel *Small World,* a few stars maneuver for the prize—openly or subtly—while hordes of fascinated secondary contenders watch. It is typical of Lodge's comic plotting that the UNESCO chair finally goes to a professor who has looked like an also-ran, so that in fiction at least, modesty gets rewarded.

We should pause to consider the nature of "winning" in the realm of ideas. It is clear that in the pursuit of knowledge and understanding, especially in the sciences, a few talented individuals manage to sweep the competition by contributing some new discovery or interpretive theory. According to Thomas

Kuhn, such new "paradigms" are rare, and should be honored.[10] But in physics or biology, breakthrough discoveries frequently build upon the foundations of "normal science." And so it follows that if competition to be a paradigm shifter clears out the ordinary work of scientists, then daily, necessary maintenance work will be neglected in favor of strenuous efforts to reproduce and test and refine, and even refute, some bit of the winning discovery.

An ongoing and key difficulty for science is finding support for lines of research that do not seem to promise immediate rewards. The "disease du jour" effect in national science policy is one manifestation of this problem. Another is the spectacle of scientists engaging in unseemly races to decipher a puzzle that has become ripe for solution because of the work of many different researchers. Although it is a very old story, the cracking of the structure of DNA is instructive here. Rosalind Franklin did the painstaking, "normal" work of science in her X-ray crystallography, a scientific endeavor that does not win trophies but "merely" enables the successful competition for them. James Watson's account of his and Francis Crick's appropriation of some of her work in their race to win the Nobel Prize in *The Double Helix* is a fascinating chronicle of how great ambition and a little duplicity can combine to sweep the boards in winner-take-all markets.[11] More recently, competition in the publishing industry has ensured the monopoly on publications by global conglomerates, feeding on the need for ambitious researchers to cut up their findings into as many articles as possible and to create new journals in small specialties. Universities have been all too willing to support such tactics in order to gain whatever scholarly recognition they bring. In my own field, like many others in the humanities and social sciences, interpretive theoretical breakthroughs have focused much scholarly energy on attempts to reproduce one or another paradigm in ever new elaborations and applications. Indeed the publications of such efforts in every disciplinary field have become so voluminous that a point of diminishing returns has been reached, and the MLA has called for some kind of moratorium.[12] More significantly, since tenure and promotion committees have come to depend on the editorial decisions of such journals to confirm the quality of faculty candidates for advancement, they now search for alternate "outside" certification. And so in scholarly publication as well as in the popular media, the values of the status market prevail.[13]

Another form of currency in the academic market is status achieved through systems of ranking or institutional classification. The competition for a place in one or another of these spotlights is perhaps the most effective driver of the academic market for faculty. The *US News & World Report*'s annual rankings of colleges are criticized, but the criticisms have not stopped the bragging by any college or university that gets in the top ten—of the country, the region, the state, or the category. There have been efforts to maneuver higher education out of the ratings game, as happened when the Carnegie Foundation for the Advancement of Teaching revised its classification system in 2000. But the rankings creep back in, one way or another, and institutions seem always ready to position themselves on the best possible perch within them. Thus the University of Richmond, a school that announced its ambitions publicly in 1998 when it inaugurated a new president, William E. Cooper, successfully changed its Carnegie placement in 2004 from university to liberal arts college so that it could fare better in the *US News & World Report*, which adapts the Carnegie classifications to categorize the schools it ranks.[14]

The fact is that most rankings of colleges and universities tend to be subjective—a sample of group opinion about institutional reputations. Further, new names rarely appear at the very top. There have been some additions in the middle, especially as research universities in the South and Southwest have come into their own, but major institutions tend to remain safely in the top ten or twenty. Indeed, both to establish that point and at the same time give more substance to the internal assessments of research universities, John Lombardi, now provost at the University of Massachusetts, launched a new research center, "The Center," at the University of Florida in 2000. Lombardi's institute was designed to define and provide both hard data and nuance to make possible institutional classifications that would be helpful in defining institutional missions rather than in painting schools as abstract successes or failures.[15] Lombardi's own effort to measure universities in order to improve them—especially the University of Florida, which he headed as president from 1990 to 2000—evolved into his center's eventual creation of a new list of the "Top 25."

In a refreshing departure from the usual rhetoric about "excellence" and "greatness," Lombardi and his research team chose measurable variables that had a simple clarity. He argued that no matter what the other admirable features of a particular school might be, determinative benchmarks in all areas of their excellence would be program size and money. Other measures, such as the quality of students or the distinguished nature of the faculty, ultimately derived from these variables. Once the money and size parameters are settled, according to Lombardi, more nuanced judgments can be made about improvements—but only after other simple-enough criteria for reward are established. His is a hard-nosed view, but Lombardi's toughness does set some limits to the over-heated efforts always to be in the finals—the "big dance," the "sweet sixteen," the "elite eight," and the "final four."

Yet even when the clarity of a sharp-eyed administrator[16] is brought to bear on the rankings, their intrinsic flaws as markers of educational value remain. My concern is that a competition that marks only a few as winners—ten? twenty-five? fifty? a hundred?—can actually distort the nature of winning itself. The system and rhetoric of cultivating winners go beyond diminishing the morale of fine institutions; more important, they hijack the values we expect from higher education. As Frank and Cook remark, "winner-take-all markets have molded our culture and discourse in ways many of us find deeply troubling."

🙚   🙚   🙚

What are the structural effects of this extreme competition in building the faculty for colleges and universities? The first place to find them is, of course, in the system for bringing in the new faculty—those "rookies" upon whom the burden of the future work and reputation of the institution and the profession will rest. The agonies of finding and keeping academic jobs, the "real" jobs marked by the promise of tenure, have become very well known over the years. There have always been tales of those caught in the "publish or perish" trap, but now the emphasis is on the suffering involved in getting a probationary job in the first place—given the armies of unemployed PhDs. The academic labor market has been decimated by outsourcing. Efforts to retrench in the 1980s and '90s by offering golden parachutes to those who would take early retirements have backfired, since junior replacements were rarely recruited to replace re-tirees. Instead, faculty retirement schemes tend to be opportunities for down-sizing—and the freed salary money is captured to use elsewhere. There was once a worry, after the cap on retirements at age sixty-five was lifted, that faculty with tenure simply would never retire. Although a few who insisted on hanging on forever may have caused some problems, more often than not, when faculty could afford to retire they did. Academic job scarcity has resulted not from holdovers but from the decisions of institutions to hire only sure win-ners—putting temporary stand-in faculty in place until the phenom comes along.

At the very first stage of the recruitment process, then, the faculty job mar-ket is narrowed by the tendency of administrations to meet budgetary stresses by putting a freeze on hiring new candidates for the professoriate. One growing alternative is to take new PhDs on spec, possibly as post-docs, to see how they might turn out before converting their appointments to tenure-track—which means lengthening the probationary period before granting tenure. The expansion of post-doc positions from the sciences into the humanities in recent years reflects this current tendency to make all new personnel decisions provisional.[17] When departments finally get permission to hire a junior colleague, the stakes are therefore very high. And the process can become toxic.

The psychological health of search committees can disintegrate as the hiring season intensifies. After years of starvation, a feeding frenzy may ensue. Intergenerational pathologies reveal themselves unexpectedly. Faculty members who joined the department in days before the emphasis on research can become defensive and extremely fierce about whether new colleagues will meet stringent new standards for teaching, for the same deans who ask for ever more research productivity also look at the market and ask, "Why can't we have it all—research *and* teaching?" Publication by a respectable though slightly stodgy press can suddenly become a sign of mediocrity among those who track the latest venues for the latest ideas. And then intermediate faculty members who have already leaped very high hurdles to get tenure may demand radical originality from new colleagues. Retracing a familiar argument can seem a mortal flaw, even though most dissertations end up doing just that. Failure to make sweeping claims can be a sign of academic timidity. Skirmishes can break out among theoretical factions, leading number crunchers to become adamant against hiring ethnologists. And vice versa. Academic pedigree can come to seem more important than the record itself: status satisfaction tempts a department to hire a "promising" novice from one of the coastal elites rather than fastening on the greater experience of applicants who've become all-around candidates through their postgraduate work in a variety of institutions. Despite recognizing the difficulty that candidates have in finding academic positions immediately out of graduate school, search committees can be turned off by their employment elsewhere; "experienced" may carry the connotation of "used."

Unless the institution works on a tradition of fostering and cultivating new professors, then, departments hiring at the entry level tend to focus on short- rather than long-term considerations. The conundrum, however, is that short-term achievements do not always predict lifelong productivity. Comets soar in a blaze and then vanish in darkness. So too a one-note researcher may make a genuine mark in the first six years, but fizzle in the second or third decade if she is unable or unwilling to move to other tasks when her project has played out or emphasis has drifted to other fields or methods. Since the long-term capacities of new professors must be somewhat unclear, it is good to search for academic talent that demonstrates a variety and malleability of focus. Wise recruiters know that the ongoing work of the faculty is likely to demand a range of abilities, and hiring on very narrow grounds may fail to keep all the needs of the institution in view.

Yet despite the recommendations of common sense, the recruitment of new faculty in today's academic market frequently tempts departments or schools into foolish tenure practices. We have already examined how the criteria for professional success have been narrowed; the process has been accompanied by the ratcheting up of standards for granting tenure. Some departments hire only candidates for whom tenure seems likely, and they work hard to make that likelihood a reality. Other departments hire with the intention of testing new faculty ruthlessly, turning the tenure probationary period into a survival test. In such cases some unspoken consensus may conspire to isolate those hires who look to be in peril after a year or two. Unsure of what of reasonable standards should be, departments impose tenure requirements that many of the current faculty could not have met. Such a system leads to a penetrating odor of bad faith in a department, and the faculty members who survive the system are likely to seek revenge.

Of course, some departments and some very elite schools make no pretense of any intention to lead new faculty to tenure. They assure themselves that their past practices make that intention clear, and that the privilege of taking a junior appointment within their precincts is such a stamp of excellence that their hires will have no trouble in moving on to good schools when the time is up. Such departments forget the likelihood that their untenured faculty may hope against hope—and against history. During the first five years of the appointment, roots go down, the work goes well, the school's address opens doors, and colleagues are pleasant. Who wouldn't dream of being the exception that stays on—and who wouldn't wake up embittered when nothing one has done really counts at the end? And because peer departments are usually not in the market for hiring associate professors, the "transient" then has to start all over again.

The malaise among probationary faculty in highly demanding departments may be intensified by another problem in the recruitment process—the offering of promises that are not honored in the long run. Obviously, no institution can recruit good faculty without painting a rosy view of his or her future in its arms. But the glow can fade when research leaves are cut, money for conferences becomes unavailable, and the promised lab lacks vital equipment. More significantly, optimistic talk about standards for tenure may change in the middle of the probationary period. A new dean or chair may be brought in to "shake things up," and her new interpretation of old standards leaves the candidate no time to try to measure up in his fourth or fifth year. Assistant professors often get stuck in the fault lines of those administrative transitions that are designed to accelerate the school's competition for higher rankings.

But perhaps the most pernicious institutional failure vis-à-vis junior faculty is the tendency to neglect the previous season's baby star while recruiting the current "rookie of the year." The salary offers for new faculty tend to rise faster than the rate for others, and so intermediate colleagues find their juniors nipping at their heels financially. Given resource scarcity, "late bloomers" may find themselves bereft of support and even recognition. This is especially true if their careers come to a pause after they've achieved tenure—what is known in the trade as the "associate professor slump."

Some seasoned observers of the academy have commented on the "missing middle" in its departments and schools. They point to the near total absence of associate professors or to the demoralization of those who hold that rank for more than a few years. Frequently such faculty have come to some impasse in their research and need time to change direction. The long struggle to achieve tenure may have left them gasping for new air and a break from anxiety about striving for the nearest prize. Some will wish to take advantage of the breathing room to look around the institution and find what other opportunities it might offer. And, not coincidentally, many associate professors can only think of having, or caring for, families after winning tenure. At this stage in their life cycle, too, they may desire to spend more time on public advocacy or service. The achievement of tenure and promotion should mean not the reinstitution of one more hurdle to jump but a respite for regaining breath, strength, and purpose. Meanwhile, there are important programs to run, teaching skills to consolidate, and advances in their fields to master beyond that last research project. In point of fact, every department needs a phalanx of faculty members who have the security of tenure and some space to turn their attention to matters other than research.

In past times, the rank of associate professor has provided individuals who could fulfill such functions. But in the winner-take-all market, their contributions are never enough. There are many reasons for a department to be lacking in associate professors, but when the main one is unrelenting competition for rookie stars, the institution is probably in for trouble. After offering buyouts to get full professors to retire, it may find itself with no one left to do the work—advise students, staff committees, participate in faculty governance, teach undergraduates, and even teach graduate students. One of the most misguided moves in many departments seeking to attract desirable rookies is to promise graduate courses to the new hires, relegating lower-level courses to regular faculty. The rationale is that the new stars are up on the latest discoveries and theories. What does such a rationale say about the continuing faculty? And how wise is it to foster a system that forces maturity on novices while turning a blind eye to veterans who don't keep up? Finally, such a system deprives new ideas, and new faculty, of the mature critique they may need to become something more than the relics of the latest fad.

🐛 🐛 🐛

Although the acquisition of new faculty can become a questionable contest, the winner-take-all competition in the academy becomes trickiest in the hiring and cultivation of senior faculty. I have called institutional fixations on this process "the superstar syndrome" because I believe that the drive to hire and retain only a few high achievers is often counterproductive, especially for wannabe schools that shop for stars indiscriminately—ignoring missions, budget constraints, and the continuing faculty who have managed to give the institution whatever distinction it already has.

The superstar syndrome is usually marked by two group obsessions. The first, evident in competition at the entry level as well, is an avid desire to climb onto a higher rung in the rankings. The second, less recognized because it is internalized and usually less conscious, is the fear of descent into the academic abyss—stepping down a rung or even falling off the ladder altogether. In the presence of such a fear, each new achievement carries with it the seeds of possible decline. Success is never at ease with itself; it always hears the competition coming up behind. And even at the highest level—as at Harvard—its anxieties can lead to a vulgar dependence on the opinions of others rather than the security of relying on its own judgment. Harvard has a practice of circulating to outside scholars the names of those it may want to hire, asking for rankings "both in absolute terms and relative to one another." The result can be exasperation and disdain from the reviewers as well as grave doubts about the independence of the institution. When asked to make such rankings, Leon Fink, professor of history at the University of Chicago, has rightly observed, "Rather than rely on reputation, as defined by outsider rankings, better to trust to close readings of the candidate's work, as well as the direct encounter afforded by the job interview. Be satisfied when you have found an outstanding scholar-teacher and don't worry whether she is at the very top of anyone else's list."[18]

The fear of falling in the academy ignores the natural cycles of achievement and rest before renewal; it is attuned instead to the sounds of other institutions following their own bent. It is true that an institution's process of comparing its standings with that of peers is a powerful lever for extracting resources from deans, members of boards, philanthropists, and legislatures. A healthy concern about quality is incumbent upon good administrators, and poetic license in proclaiming impending doom unless adequate resources are made available is a respectable ploy among the truly talented leaders of first-rate departments. The problem arises when such rhetoric becomes internalized. Then the fear of falling behind in the future denigrates the achievements of the present, and a department, a school, or a whole institution can become very sick at heart.

In its most important effect, such anxiety provokes resentment among the continuing faculty—those upon whom the reputation of the institution has been built. The hiring of a superstar off the prevailing salary scale can deliver a tangible message that what they've spent careers achieving doesn't quite measure up. Further, such hiring may awaken an impulse among continuing faculty to test the waters elsewhere themselves. And thus a bidding war can erupt between the inside and the outside stars that leads to higher demands on every side. Such inflationary contests are involved in the academic process known as "meeting outside offers." Trying to control this process, an institution may set aside funds to meet offers, even if doing so means ignoring salary scales to keep a superstar from leaving. It can be devastating for a school to lose one of its native "greats," even in times of budgetary stringency. To be sure, some argue that counteroffers are helpful to continuing faculty in the long run because a rising tide lifts all boats. But such maneuvers can backfire. In some schools the legend is that the only way to get a good raise is to get an offer from some other school. I have known deans and chairs who have actually encouraged their faculty to seek outside offers so as to provide leverage for bringing new money into the salary pool. Administrators may guard against this ploy by stipulating that outside offers must be from peer schools, or better, if they are to be met. At least one school, MIT, has a flat policy against meeting outside offers. But the fact of the matter is that when distinguished faculty shop around, they may find an offer that they really can't refuse.

The recruitment of outside superstars also poses dangers. The most frequent downside is that institutions fail to assure themselves of receiving full value for their investment. Many senior faculty members move to new positions with the best of intentions, and fulfill all the promises they seem to offer, but some are genuine prima donnas who require exceptional care. If the reason for hiring at the senior level is to expand a program or start an extraordinary initiative, the faculty member brought in to lead must be at once forceful and generous to his or her colleagues. One way of showing collegiality is to shoulder a fair share of work; another is to be publicly active on campus. Permitting a star to hide away from the rest of the campus, and especially from students, is always counterproductive. When an especially expensive hire is made on any campus, the spotlight automatically turns onto the beneficiary. Any irregularities in the hire or the performance of the new faculty member can have devastating consequences. Many years ago, the faculty rebelled when the University of South Carolina sought to raise its profile by hiring non-academic celebrities, and a great deal of scandal ensued. And the "tenure wars" at the University of Minnesota in the mid-1990s began with the fiscal misconduct of one superstar in the medical school as well as the discovery of double-dipping by another superstar in the philosophy department (forsooth): he was discovered to be commuting from an appointment at another institution. Interestingly enough, the response of the board in the Minnesota case was to try to renegotiate tenure rather than to seek out the root problems through better oversight of special allowances for special faculty. It was a form of poetic justice that the general public sided with the continuing faculty in the resulting controversy; the local press editorialized about the danger of losing their collective contributions to the general health of "the U" under the new scheme.

The effects when star hiring becomes the single approach for advancing in quality and reputation can reverberate widely throughout the institution. There can be a fostering of intramural competition, for example. One department can try to outwit and outplay other departments. All will, of course, exaggerate their needs and falsify their possibilities, in order to get a super line. Indeed, some departments paint grandiose visions on the basis of a single hire, only to discover that one super hire is usually not enough. And so superstar programs can become constant drains. Or they can be left high and dry—the creations of the ambitions of single individuals, never integrated into the cognate areas of study that might help them survive.

Another problem is mission creep, the tendency of ambitious schools to leave their real work behind as they try to imitate the activities of those in higher echelons of the academy. Once a faculty member guiding me on a tour of a school I was visiting commented, "We used to be a teaching college, but now we're not. We're a university." "Isn't that a shame?" I thought. I knew that when it was a normal school, this institution turned out generations of effective elementary and high school teachers for the region; it had good faculty whose expertise was carried into classrooms around the state. As a "university," however, it lost its local ties, becoming only one aspiring school among many. Further, since research was the coin of its institutional self-regard, it now found itself burdened with many faculty members who were not inclined to do the kind of teaching and service that its earlier mission required. Meanwhile, an extremely wise chair in one of its departments had accepted his unit's role as a farm team and used it unapologetically to build his faculty. He hired excellent people who could not get a nibble from the fast-track job market, but whose potential he was discerning enough to recognize. He brought them to the school for the several years or more it would take for them to prepare to move on. Some left, some stayed, and so he gained not only a talented and energetic staff but the gratitude of many young faculty elsewhere whom he helped to move along in their careers. His institution became known by them and respected.

და   და   და

Hiring new faculty—at either the junior or senior level—is one of the most important activities of any educational institution. It is also an activity that can bring departments and administrations together in planning for the future and in agreeing on mutual aims. It promises an influx of new life, new approaches, new ideas. And good hiring practices enhance an institution's reputation among faculty at home and elsewhere, in the graduate programs or departments from which new hires come. There are rankings that never reach the pages of *US News & World Report*: those are assigned by the consensus among most faculty of which schools are good places to be in.

Although it is obvious that I am extremely skeptical about the benefits of unbridled competition, I do not scorn ambition, and I realize that models of genuine achievement can fuel the desire to excel in positive ways. Further, I know that in some fields, in the sciences especially, truly impressive advances in research require more than one distinguished figure—that there is such a thing as a critical mass, not only of equipment and technology but also of gifted people. Finally, it is clear that departments and universities cannot, and should not, prefer a complacent stability over dynamic change. One way to avoid complacency is to bring in not just good new people at the rookie level but the occasional senior person who has the authority to challenge the work as well as to change the aura of a program. Departments and programs may not always be able to fill important slots by promotion from within, and while ongoing faculty make important contributions, they need a jolt from time to time. In addition, some migration of scholars from one school to another is natural and necessary for many good reasons—the development of new institutional initiatives that suit their special talents and aims, the presence of research supports that smaller schools cannot offer, the opportunities for the kind of collaboration that cannot be carried on at a distance. Individuals may grow stale in one venue and need either to change places or to be challenged by new colleagues. And shifts in family situations may make moves necessary.

The question is how to manage such healthy growth and development reasonably and within the parameters of a specific school's mission and resources. The question is also how to avoid the excesses that overstress the talents of new faculty, embitter the work of those in the middle, and fail to ensure the institution's realization of full value—generosity, collegiality, and loyalty from newly installed stars.

Remedies for violations of common sense in recruiting and hiring are hard to come by, given the realities of the inevitable competition. Frank and Cook quote James Tobin's useful admission of the problem: "The most difficult issues of political economy are those where goals of efficiency, freedom of choice, and equality conflict. It is hard enough to propose an intellectually defensible compromise among them, even harder to find a politically viable compromise" (pp. 211–12). In the midst of such conflicts in academe, however, the faculty must make choices.

It is the faculty that has been charged by the logic of its expertise to make wise judgments in hiring and granting tenure to colleagues. In the past, the assurances of equity in these processes have been embedded in the culture of the professoriate; now, in the "winner-take-all" context, it is up to the faculty to preserve their institutions from the unbounded competition that may override their own best judgments. How can they do this? First, they must defend the independence of their programs by refusing hires that do not fit the best interests of their departments. A dean or provost might tempt them to go for a star in one area when they really need a couple of new faculty elsewhere; they should stick to their own priorities by offering good reasons, presenting alternatives, and just saying no. They must also refuse shortcuts in judging candidates for positions; this means that although they read a candidate's letters of reference with respect, they must make sure that the final offer will arise from their own study of the dossier, interviewing, and group discussions. Like Professor Fink from Chicago, they will refuse requests for ranking even as they take the time to write letters of recommendation that are both accurate and generous in assessing candidates for academic positions. Knowing that a tenure-track position is precious, they will invest it wisely, having in mind that the wisdom of their choice is the basis for the institution's trust in them. This kind of trust is at risk in the current winner-take-all market, and so it is a great irony that tenure, with its aim of opening the professoriate to faculty of promise, now threatens to become simply another superstar perk.

Finally, of course, in their collective meditations on their status as teachers, scholars, and servants to the profession, faculty members must realize that excellence is always admirable, and that admiration is not always envy.

CHAPTER SEVEN

The Case of the Firecracker Boys

Academic Science and Academic Freedom

Who owns the findings of research? Does the current system for funding research distort the nature of hypotheses and the soundness of results? Has the emphasis on commercially exploitable discovery separated academic science from the university's root concern with the general welfare of humanity and of the planet? Given its dependence on funding outside the ordinary university budget, has academic science lost its concern for teaching science to American students? Even more fundamentally, has the assertion of scientific opinion become irremediably politicized in the current "public epistemology"—one that holds no conclusion to be free of ideological bias? Indeed, is the public beginning to assume that university experts should *not* be concerned with the welfare of humanity and of the planet—that they should present data to policy makers without conclusions, since conclusions constitute interference in politics?

In light of the infiltration of the market and politics into such hard sciences as physics, biology, chemistry, and medicine, I will argue not only that the university is responsible for offering conclusions but also that individual researchers must be free to sponsor their judgments fearlessly. It has been suggested that science is self-correcting—kept honest through the mechanisms of its system of peer review. But in the past fifteen years, the extensive networks of consulting and the funded research of reviewers have called peer review itself into question.[1] After all, peer review is reliable only when it engages the judgments of professionals who have no interest other than vetting the authenticity of completed research and claims made for it. When that autonomous assessment is undercut by other interests, credibility necessarily suffers. That is why universities must be the ultimate preserve of scientific credibility.[2] And they therefore must find ways to conserve some budgetary margin to support the continuing work of scientists whose funding is threatened.

Further, just as many university scientists organized themselves in earlier times to educate the public about dangers generated by advancing technology, I believe that they must now redouble their efforts. The old dangers remain, but they have been joined by others that are even more insidious, as not just the conclusions of science but the very belief that science can have *valid* conclusions is under attack. I have already discussed (in chapter 3) the process through which conservative criticism of humanities and social science professors has shifted from analysis of what they taught to accusations of their political bias and then to condemnation of them for outright disloyalty to the country. In that debate, some more moderate elements have suggested that science deserves less scrutiny because it has fewer ideological leanings, relying as it does on material evidence and trust in logic.[3] Nevertheless, some critics of science, on the right and on the left, have suggested that science itself is politically biased. Academic scientists, the most privileged faculty in higher education, will need help from their universities to counter such efforts to undermine their findings and suppress their conclusions. They must also find support from their colleagues in the arts, humanities, and social sciences, for the health of science, and indeed the intellectual vigor of all the disciplines, depends on the deliberate and informed mutual reengagement between scientists and their colleagues throughout the academy.

☙ ☙ ☙

As background for the questions and propositions about academic research in this discussion, I begin with the response of the faculty and administration at the University of Alaska in 1958 to a research offer it couldn't refuse. The offer came from the atomic physicist Edward Teller. Teller, then director of the Lawrence Radiation Laboratory in California and in alliance with the Atomic Energy Commission, was an advocate of Project Plowshare, a scheme set up in the late 1950s to investigate and test uses of atomic energy for peacetime purposes.[4] The story of Project Chariot—his efforts to use atom bombs to carve out a harbor in Alaska—has been told by Dan O'Neill in *The Firecracker Boys,* a gripping narrative of the events that took place between 1958 and the end of the project in 1962. O'Neill's book details the political, commercial, and academic contexts of the venture, including Teller's ardent salesmanship and the efforts of the AEC to find scientific backing for his plan.

In Project Chariot, Teller's idea was to use atomic bombs to make a harbor at Cape Thompson in the northern reaches of the newly established state of Alaska. Assuming that the territory above Cape Thompson as well as all surrounding land was essentially uninhabited, sterile, and vast enough to sustain atomic experimentation, Teller and his colleagues began by setting up an unpublicized experimental station at Ogotoruk Creek in 1958. Running into some resistance from citizens in Alaska at the start, Teller launched a publicity campaign to cultivate the local business leaders with promises of commercial development in the areas of oil and mineral exploitation and transport. Teller's enthusiasm for nuclear projects, especially in connection with high-tech weapons and defense systems, has long been acknowledged as the source both of his infectious energy and of his continuing efforts to persuade the federal government to expand the uses of nuclear technology. He brought this fervor to Juneau, Anchorage, and Fairbanks to such groups as local service clubs and chambers of commerce, and before long he incited a great deal of excitement about putting Alaska on the map—a useful move, since it had only recently gained statehood. His enthusiasm and that of his colleagues was so high, and their promises so lavish, that they were likened to boys playing with firecrackers.[5] In response to whatever anxieties were expressed in the community, Teller and other leaders of the project promised thorough studies of environmental and social impacts before they launched the bombs.

To calm fears about the possible effects of radioactive fallout, which then were little known, the AEC established a bioenvironmental committee composed of national scientists to bolster the project with scientific backing.[6] To the president of the university at Fairbanks, the officials at AEC also promised funding for local researchers; preliminary studies on the feasibility of the project were to begin in the summer of 1959, with more support to come once they got under way. The chair of the biology department at the time was urged to protect the contract for the good of the university. Indeed, the AEC spoke of future largesse, including the establishment of an environmental studies program—a proposal advocated by the University of Alaska faculty—and an AEC official arrived to offer contracts even though proposals for grants had not yet been written.

The University of Alaska was a small school, but it did have a committed group of biological scientists. Brina Kessel, the biology department chair, was an ornithologist and later wrote important studies of the birds of Alaska. Other members of her department were active in the conservation movement in the state. Albert Johnson was one of the pillars of the department and served as a leader of Project Chariot—later leaving for administrative posts. L. Gerard Swartz was a senior professor who was also actively involved in studies for the project. In addition to these scholars, the AEC provided funding to bring into the project two more faculty members in biology and botany, plus an independent field researcher in human geography.

The scientists who began studying the flora and fauna of Alaska near Cape Thompson seem to have had the typical ethos of Alaskan experts at the time. They were field researchers who savored outdoor life. Their deepest satisfaction came not from analyzing specimens in a laboratory setting but in braving the elements of the far north on-site, and frequently in forbidding weather. The new researchers jumped at the prospect of funding to carry on their studies. As William Pruitt observed, "There are a number of people who, over a period of quite a number of years, had been trying to do Arctic research—field biology—living from hand to mouth, trying to pick up grants here and there. So that when this rather magnificent grant, or contract, came through, of course they jumped at it. Sure. You know, a good field biologist will do damn near anything to get back in the field again."[7]

Pruitt had not joined the University of Alaska faculty until the 1959 contract with AEC was in prospect, but the national head of the operation was intent on having this extraordinary scientist on the team. Thus, as a new associate professor, Pruitt was made head of the mammalian investigation at Cape Thompson with the expectation that he would teach biology classes as well. The other two scientists who signed on were Leslie Viereck and Don Foote—both advanced graduate students who had unusual experience in Arctic regions and enthusiasm for fieldwork. Viereck suspended work on his PhD in plant biology at Colorado to take advantage of the research possibilities in Alaska. His appointment with the university also carried the expectation of teaching and service to university programs—especially the herbarium. Foote, who was pausing in his work on his PhD in human geography at McGill, was not employed by the university.

Remarkably, the wives of all these men were also scientists who not only endured the harsh conditions of their husbands' work but participated in that work. Don Foote actually commenced his married life with his work on Project Chariot, having wed his Norwegian colleague on the way to Alaska and then set up a very rugged winter home for her within the Eskimo community at Point Hope—thirty-some miles north of Cape Thompson. These researchers tended to work on their own in the field, and each had independent observations to report. The other scientists from the University of Alaska had other assignments—Al Johnson was to head the botanical research, and Gerard Swartz was to study cliff birds under the federal contract—and they strongly backed the work of the three new hires. Scientists in the state Department of Fish and Game also became involved in the scientific questions they began to raise about the atomic bomb proposal.

When the University of Alaska scientists hired to perform an environmental impact study for Project Chariot began their work in the late summer of 1959, they had no idea that the AEC was planning to "shoot" the atomic bombs within the following year. That ignorance points to one of the first sources of conflict: AEC publicity constantly ran ahead of the research. Teller and his colleagues had launched the project with wild claims about its usefulness as well as its safety; and although these had to be modified as some glimmers of reality set in, the backers of the project were intent on achieving a quick explosion before either the skeptics gained more ground or the funding lapsed. Because the field scientists were engaged to begin work in the fall of 1959, they could not gather very much data before the projected shoot. Thus their suspicions grew when they realized that their project was intended more as cover to justify an already-reached conclusion rather than as a genuine search for the kind of understanding of nature in the Arctic that would warrant—or forbid—such an invasive operation as nuclear explosions. Each time the University of Alaska scientists resisted the rush to approve the project, they were given private reassurances subsequently contradicted by public announcements that were both premature and inaccurate. Finally, they reached an impasse with the officials of the AEC, and in June 1960 they wrote a formal letter to register their disagreements with the official line of the AEC's Bioenvironmental Committee.[8]

Eventually the new president of the University of Alaska, William R. Wood, fired Leslie Viereck and William Pruitt, there being no tenure at the University of Alaska in 1960. His philosophy was relatively simple; as he told Brina Kessel, the acting chair of biology, when she tried to represent her colleagues' concerns to him, "the AEC has bought the material and it is theirs to use."[9] Kessel, a relatively inexperienced faculty member at the time, seems to have tried to thread her way between a president who was vitally interested in obtaining government support for institutional research and cranky colleagues who had become alienated from the AEC officials. In addition, Al Johnson, one of her advisers, was away on sabbatical. She was taken aback by the president's willingness to get rid of recalcitrant faculty.[10]

Viereck obliged the president by resigning under pressure; Pruitt's exit from Project Chariot was more public. It stemmed from his publishing Viereck's findings, along with negative findings of other researchers on Project Chariot, in a bulletin of the Alaska Conservation Society. From that point on, feeling herself and the authority of her administrative structure betrayed by a public declaration, Kessel claimed for herself the right to "edit" Pruitt's official AEC report. She did so in ways that weakened his objections to the commission's predictions about minimal damage to the food chain by the projected shoot at Cape Thompson. Again, the controversy turned on the issue of who owned the research done under the AEC contract—the university, its federal funders, or the scientists. Pruitt wrote to his departmental chair with obvious passion: "The ultimate responsibility for any scientific writing, whether intra-agency report, contractual report or open publication lies with the author. Your statement that the document under consideration is a final contractual report and not publication in the scientific literature imputes different degrees of accuracy or logical rigor."[11]

The archives of the American Association of University Professors do not reveal much about its response to the case of Viereck and Pruitt; in 1963, Pruitt lodged a complaint that he was being blacklisted, but the Association at the time seems to have focused on issues of process rather than substance. The lack of records indicates that the national office did not carry out a formal investigation; nevertheless, Pruitt has reported that the view of the Association accommodated the stance of the president of the University of Alaska, to wit, that "the general supervisor of this project was accountable for the accuracy of the facts and findings and for the opinions and conclusions derived from these findings."[12]

Although the national AAUP was not responsive to the issue of the individual scientist's rights in the early 1960s, the president of the local AAUP chapter at Washington University in St. Louis was. That chapter leader—Barry Commoner—was a botanist who had become extremely interested in environmental hazards caused by nuclear experimentation. He and his colleagues, especially Michael Friedlander of the physics department, published responses to Project Chariot in conjunction with their own research for the Committee for

Nuclear Information. The publicity they generated helped begin an outcry that eventually led to the suspension of Project Chariot in 1962. Commoner was especially concerned about radioactive fallout and the food chain, which the CNI was in the process of investigating through a study of baby teeth in the St. Louis region. Of special interest was the presence of strontium 90—a radioactive isotope—in the milk supply and whether it had an effect on calcium absorbed by infants. The conundrum was that although alarming levels of the element were found in cows in the lower forty-eight states owing to testing in Nevada, the amounts in reindeer in Scandinavia and caribou in Alaska—areas removed from testing—were much higher. Eventually Commoner realized that the key to this phenomenon was diet: the northern mammals foraged on lichen and sedges, plant life that has no roots and therefore derives its nourishment from the atmosphere and its contents. This revelation led Commoner to the realization that each ecosystem has its own characteristics and that science and engineering must become environmental, taking into account much larger geographical and ethnological sweeps than they had done before. The efforts of his group in St. Louis, as well as grassroots efforts among Alaskan Eskimos and environmentalists, helped stop the project. The suspension of Project Chariot illustrated the successful enactment of one of Commoner's essential principles: scientists should give ordinary citizens the scientific information necessary to help them make critical policy decisions. His Committee on Nuclear Information was thus an outgrowth of his teaching role as an academic scientist.

❧   ❧   ❧

It is important to understand what happened in Alaska fifty years ago because it reveals a persistent pattern in the exploitation of academic science. The reactions of individual scientists to the dangers and their efforts to find ways to resist have in many cases been exemplary as well. But although scientists like Barry Commoner have been successful in giving the public the kind of information required to stave off egregious mistakes in scientific overreaching, such efforts have become more and more difficult as the dependence of science on government and industrial funding for research has increased.

One reason for the difficulty is the mystification of science—*rocket science* has become a term for expertise that is beyond common understanding or skill—which has twin underlying causes. One is the formulaic hieroglyphics involving massive calculations that block understanding by those who cannot "do the math," and the other is secrecy. As Donna Demac has noted in her study of the "rise of censorship in America," enforced silence about the Manhattan Project was extended after World War II, "long after nuclear energy had entered the commercial marketplace and could no longer be considered a state secret. ... [The] main effect was to inhibit informed public debate on the use and hazards of nuclear materials, and to set a broad precedent for the propriety of strict government control of information."[13] The slippage between government and corporate secrecy, state secrets and trade secrets, is one of the continuing features of American science.

Under either government or corporate control, the results of scientific research can be both guarded and masked by their complexity and mystery. One of the key questions for science faculty in our time, then, is how to inform the public about the implications of their advances. For the fact is that accurate science continues to be marred by the same kinds of conflicts that beset the Alaskan researchers in the late 1950s. The tragic explosion of the space shuttle *Challenger* in 1986 is a prime example of what happens when the rigor of science is sacrificed to external expediencies, and disinterested science is reduced to holding an inquest after the disaster.

Explaining what went wrong in the remarkable "Minority Report to the Space Shuttle Challenger Inquiry" in 1986, Richard Feynman singled out as the root cause the dominance of management over science. His televised illustration of the fatal problems with the O-rings on the shuttle's rocket booster—he plunged one into a glass of ice water to show that it lost elasticity when cold—became famous. But his analysis was more significant than his showmanship. He pointed out that the leaders of the National Aeronautics and Space Administration pushed engineers not to be too definite in their calculations so that their enterprise could justify itself to members of Congress. First Feynman noted the weakening of scientific care under the pressure to keep to a launch schedule "in order to ensure the supply of funds." Doubts were eased by a continuous stream of exquisite calculations that were not as precise as they were claimed to be. Feynman also observed that the managerial imperatives demonstrated "an almost incredible lack of communication between [official supervisors] and their working engineers." To avoid such serious lapses in the future, Feynman advised that NASA should hew strictly to scientific accuracy and modesty of claims, as a matter not just of what was owed to the public but also of self-protection. In concluding, he made a very important generalization about science: "For a successful technology, reality must take precedence over public relations, for nature cannot be fooled."[14]

As in other episodes in which academic scientists have been involved in reporting on problems in the public uses of science, the independence of the skeptical voice was crucial. Feynman's minority report could be audacious not only because its author was a brilliant analyst but also because his position as a professor of physics at Cal State was secure. And his personal fortunes were untouchable, for he was the only member of the investigating committee who had no contractual relationship with NASA. Barry Commoner and Michael Friedlander were similarly situated when they raised questions about safety in Project Chariot. They had the security of tenure at a research institution that had a long tradition of protecting the academic freedom of its faculty.[15] Many other academic scientists who have sought to inform and warn the public ever since the end of World War II also seem to have relied on the protection of tenure. Some of them were too famous to suffer retaliation, of course, but the self-policing of American science by tenured scientists has been a remarkable, though sometimes sorely tested, phenomenon. Working from the secure base of their university laboratories and within the tradition of professorial autonomy, researchers have been able to mount counterpressures against censorship.

Thus the greatest threat to their academic freedom does not arise from the possibility of being fired, as the researchers for Project Chariot were. Too often, the threat lies in researchers' self-entrapment in the funding networks that are necessary to help them pursue their disciplines. Maintenance of funding, which Feynman saw as a top priority for NASA and its space program, soon became the primary concern of academic research as well.[16] Before the 1980s, as we have seen, there had been interactions between the military-industrial complex and the university. To be sure, the Manhattan Project ended up in a government campus in Los Alamos, but it began at the University of Chicago. Although Los Alamos foreshadowed major federal funding for and control of big science, the federal involvement was spread to a number of universities after World War II. The federal provision of big money for university research that started slowly in the 1950s and then gathered force for the next thirty years also represented the growing cooperation between government and private enterprise. There were famous commercial spin-offs from the space program, like CorningWare, and the cornucopia of unexpected benefits from that program supplied part of the impetus for corporations to seek development collaborations with universities. The enormous variety of scientific interests on the nation's campuses was an enticing field for commercial exploration.

Businesses had always been interested in having universities prepare employees for their enterprises, and they had always provided some student support as well as philanthropic underpinning for research and teaching that might train new workers in their fields. Before long, however, business and national interests became so intertwined that funding by corporations became another element of outside backing for academic research. A member of Canada's National Sciences and Engineering Research Council summarized the change in focus in a comment in the committee's report in 1985: "Industry can no longer afford to do all of the long-term research it needs to survive; thus it is no longer looking at universities simply as an inexpensive source of trained people, but also as a vast reservoir of expertise, which can perform that urgently needed long-term effort."[17] By degrees, the possibility of spin-offs of commodities from academic research became one of the facts of life for science and for industry.

In the 1950s, for example, Professors Joseph C. Muhler, Harry G. Day, and William Nebergall of Indiana University–Bloomington worked on ways to combine stannous fluoride with abrasive materials in a toothpaste, and tested their experimental creations on Bloomington, Indiana, schoolchildren. It had long been known that fluoride could help prevent tooth decay, but getting it into a usable form was difficult. Indiana University's Department of Chemistry was supported in the project by Proctor and Gamble, based in nearby Cincinnati. The final result was Crest toothpaste, which was put on the market in 1956. On the evidence of further testing by Indiana, Crest received an endorsement from the American Dental Association—an approval that was critical in its becoming the leading dentifrice of the 1960s and '70s.[18] Although the scientists who did the research prospered, they apparently never became fabulously wealthy. The university owned the patent and continued to enjoy benefits from its agreement to license "fluoristan" for toothpaste exclusively to P&G.

As a member of the faculty who arrived on the Indiana campus almost a decade after the Crest success, I was vaguely aware that I was in an institution basking in the revenues from the toothpaste I used. The commercial arrangement seemed innocuous to me, actually, and I was reassured whenever I saw Harry Day on campus or in the Faculty Council. He was a solid citizen who not only studied the toothpaste from a nutritional angle but went on to perform other research and to chair the university's chemistry department. Nevertheless, as an ordinary English professor, I had always been aware of—accepted as a fact of life for humanities professors—the relatively bounteous salaries and plush accommodations accorded to my colleagues in the hard sciences (and in economics departments and business schools). It was only when I became an arts and sciences associate dean, working with deans from chemistry, physics, and economics, that I began to appreciate the importance of "overhead" in the campus budget. I had never realized that there was a fee system for scientific research grants, and that the whole campus as well as science departments depended on them. Without such fees, labs could not be retrofitted, graduate positions might not be fully funded, and the entire academic enterprise would suffer. I also began to realize that the publication of science papers was richly subsidized by page publication costs embedded in grants. I tried not to feel left out because English never enjoyed such financial benefits, but I can recall a dawning recognition that the life of even a moderately productive scientist had many hidden benefits. Those might be hard to resist.

The commercial success of Crest toothpaste was a minor result of the new nexus of funding that began to raise the standard of living for scientists in the last quarter of the twentieth century. We will see that today, when the requirement for outside funding has become the sine qua non for much academic science, the research payoffs for universities are far more complicated than they were in the days when fluoride was just beginning to become a standard prophylaxis for dental caries. Academic science is now very often big business, with all the attendant features and problems. At the same time, it is accompanied by science-specific worries. Thus, even before Crest, there was a great deal of anxiety about fluoridation of water by evildoing scientists. That anxiety continued, and it indeed ties into the plot of Stanley Kubrick's *Dr. Strangelove,* which revolves around the efforts of an unhinged military officer to launch an atomic attack against the Soviet development of a "doomsday machine" in the Russian Arctic. The officer believes that Russian science is conspiring "to sap and impurify all of our precious bodily fluids." The blend of physics and biology in this prophetic satire prefigures the ways in which environmental and medical experimentation joined nuclear research as sources of public mystification about the results of science in daily lives.

From the 1950s through the 1980s academic science moved beyond occasional collaborations with industry for research and development—with the signal achievements of such companies as IBM, Eli Lilly, and Bell Labs—into an even wider spectrum of possibilities. University experimental facilities in chemistry, engineering, agriculture, nutrition, biotechnology, and all the branches of medicine provided companies with opportunities that they could hardly afford to pursue on their own and that government science was unlikely to sponsor. The University of Virginia Patent Foundation lists twenty-seven inventions from American universities alone between 1879 and 1979, and the variety is astonishing. For example, saccharin was invented by Constantin Fahlberg when he was visiting Johns Hopkins in 1879 (he patented it independently because Ira Remsen, his German adviser, was against patenting academic discoveries). And the list goes on, from the Drunk-O-Meter at Indiana in the 1930s to the Salk vaccine at Pitt in 1955, the pacemaker at Minnesota in 1958, Gatorade at Florida in 1966, the LCD at Kent State in 1967, "Tif" grasses (Bermuda hybrids) for golf courses at Georgia in the 1960s, the CAT scan at Georgetown in 1973, the MRI at SUNY's Downstate Medical Center in 1977, and the canine parvovirus vaccine at Cornell in 1979.[19]

The list of moneymaking discoveries by academic science denotes continuing progress in the alliances joining government, industry, and the universities, even in times of some public doubt about the ability of the scientific establishment to work for the common good. In fact, widespread public awareness of the sometimes deleterious effects of science grew out of the environmental movement of the 1960s. One milestone was the publication of Rachel Carson's *Silent Spring* in 1962. Carson's study reached a broad audience with its message that there was more to worry about in modern science than nuclear fallout— that the uses of scientific discovery in everyday life, as in the potent insecticide DDT, could have effects on the air and water and on birds and beasts in uncalculated ways. Carson was a scientist with the federal government rather than in a university, but her discoveries were accepted by the academy and helped lead to specializations in environmental studies there. There was an additional disturbance in the positive relations between science and the public good in the late 1960s, stemming from the Vietnam War. The universities' cooperation with companies like Dow Chemical to develop ever more lethal chemical and other weapons agitated students and antiwar activists. And indeed, questions about the effects of such inventions as the toxic defoliant Agent Orange troubled even supporters of the war. More significantly, academic science came to be viewed as extremely vulnerable, liable to be shaped not only by pressure from outside forces but by willing accommodation from within.

After Vietnam, controversy about academic science seemed to subside, though there has always been a grain of suspicion about America's weapons of mass destruction. Post-1980 discoveries on the Virginia Patent Foundation list are concentrated among very high-tech medical and pharmaceutical categories—advances that were foreshadowed by the recombinant DNA technology patented at the University of California–San Francisco and Stanford in

1974. Such medical miracles enhanced public belief in the power and reliability of science. And the rewards were very high; the California schools involved in developing DNA procedures founded Genentech and have since received huge sums in licensing fees. In their personal statements on the Genentech Web site, the present leaders of that company—both former professors at California and Stanford—claim an academic culture, reversing the direction of exchange between industry and university. Richard Sheller explains: "I was initially drawn to Genentech because its culture lies somewhere between academic and corporate and comprises the best of both worlds. Like a university, Genentech values research and individual creativity tremendously, with its scientists publishing many important papers in prestigious journals." And Marc Tessier-Lavigne agrees: "We have the best of both the academic and the corporate worlds here: we have the satisfaction of working on the development of novel therapeutics while we continue to elucidate basic biological processes."[20] Clearly, academic science had come a long way from a century earlier when a scientist would reject the idea of reaping profit from the laboratory. And industry is now eager to reward the ingenuity of academic science with the profits of applied development.

In our own time, profitability tends to create public trust. Academic science since 1980 has benefited from the economic returns on two epoch-making sources of discoveries: computer technology and genetic engineering. The developments in these fields have been marked by public fascination, the making of astonishing individual fortunes, and the inflows of enormous amounts of money to the academy. On the whole, enchanted by the power and brilliance of these scientific breakthroughs, the public has not been interested in the details; instead, it takes refuge in reliance on scientific infallibility validated by the universal penetration of the Internet and news of the cures derived from biomedical research.

Yet this ascendance of information technology and molecular biology has created some problems for academic science. First, although these enterprises may have set up the kinds of research communities praised by the Genentech executives, they may also have diverted faculty in universities from their teaching roles. Second, they have tended to subsume traditional academic governance and values under the mandates of managerial commercialism. Third, in too many cases they have substituted contractual clauses about the commercial uses of intellectual property for the traditional academic commitment to individual autonomy in pursuing research and freedom in publishing results.

And fourth, where academic science enters the marketplace, it often finds itself pressured by political and religious ideologies to constrain its unbridled openness. Academic science has come a long way from Project Chariot, but it has also encountered ever more insistent temptations to stray from the principles that inspired the heroes of that episode.

❧   ❧   ❧

In earlier chapters, I have dwelled on the changes that the market mentality and managerial style have wrought upon teaching in the university. I have illustrated these in areas as disparate as the campus as a whole—its gyms, its classrooms, its technology, and its faculty recruitment and retention. I will forbear analyzing each of the ways in which this market mentality has changed academic science as well. The entrepreneurial competition for funding and its implications for science have already been brilliantly laid out in *Academic Capitalism: Politics, Policies, and the Entrepreneurial University* by Sheila Slaughter and Larry Leslie. They have marshaled evidence to show the deleterious effect of commercial impulses on the teaching of science. I will focus here on two areas of teaching in which the almost total preoccupation with outside funding has made such inroads that alarms have been sounded from within science itself. One is, of course, the diversion of attention and energy away from introductory and general undergraduate classes, especially in research universities and in those that aspire to research status. The other is the sometimes catch-as-catch-can clinical training of medical students. Although these represent different teaching situations, their problems derive from a common predicament: resources and prestige flow to product rather than process throughout our system of higher education, and especially in our science departments. And teaching is a process.

Any analysis of the shift in resources for universities under the pressures of national and global academic capitalism will confirm that funds for research in the sciences have managed to hold their ground and even increase over time. But it is also true that funding for research goes to *research,* not to *teaching.* Outside funding may free up moneys for research assistants or adjuncts, but direct graduate student support funds them mainly to work in project labs and field stations. Thus the instructional budgets of most research departments are as stretched to airy thinness as those in other departments. The TAs in Berkeley's big intro chemistry course, for example, are generally first-year grad students with little experience as teachers.[21]

Under these conditions, science departments have to cope with extreme enrollment pressures as more and more students see their futures in technology. And of course, as a feature of liberal education, most schools require some mix of basic science courses for all undergrads. Given this universally accepted mandate to give college students some familiarity in math and the biological and physical sciences, the faculties of the departments, together with their administrative leaders, have to struggle to meet student needs even as they maintain the grant income that may pay part of basic faculty salaries, support recruitment of excellent graduate students by offering them appealing work in active labs, and promise an occasional windfall. In this mix of pressures, it is no surprise that the dependence on outside funding has installed in science departments a layer of managerial professionals—grants managers and proposal writers who rarely teach and have little connection with core research activities. In addition, each science department is likely to have a group of teaching staff who have been trained in the field but carry no research program and have no access to tenure. Although they are poorly paid, usually from the university budget rather than grants, these staff do run important courses and may do some other teaching and research. In addition, science departments frequently employ academic counselors to help place majors in graduate programs or medical schools. For some, the task of providing recommendations for students to use in applications is a genuine logistical problem. That process has perforce become streamlined and somewhat impersonal. UC Berkeley's Biology 1A syllabus for spring 2005 advises: "It is probably better for you to obtain letters from upper division classes, in the future, but we are willing to write letters. Your GSI [graduate student instructor] will write an initial draft of the letter (they know you the best). The Course Coordinator will edit the letter and a faculty member will sign the edited letter. The course coordinator will then forward your letter to the Placement center. This takes time—at least two weeks."[22]

Thus undergraduate science classes have become massive, with multiple sections, in most departments where research is a mandate. And even in non-research departments, science classes are usually larger than classes in other disciplines. In my own undergraduate experience the required biology and psychology classes were lectures, with smaller labs. But that meant no more than fifty or seventy-five souls in the hall. Today the classes may be twice that size. In a quick survey of colleagues around the country, I have found this generalization to hold true. Science colleagues from Appalachian State, Wooster College, Mills, and Baylor tell me that their introductory classes are lectures—not only because of the numbers of students but because so much material must be presented in a highly organized manner if students are to get a clear enough view of the basic landscape to begin to think about the subject intelligently.

In larger schools the introductory courses present more than one puzzle for undergraduates to solve. Berkeley's Biology 1A course mentioned above offered forty-two lectures presented by three faculty researchers and twenty discussion labs; scheduled weekly office hours totaled nine and one-half by faculty during the weeks they were lecturing, three by the course coordinator, and twenty by graduate student instructors (between 10:00 A.M. and 2:00 P.M.). That setup presented students with a plethora of variables as they tried to navigate the course. Thus the online syllabus is largely taken up with these logistics; for example, it sternly warns that if the lecture attendance drops below 80 percent, the webcast lectures will be dropped. But such services show why those classes are likely to have the best technological facilities. Indeed, they are laboratories for experimentation in whether or not PowerPoint, simulcasts, and elaborate visuals can replace the presence of the faculty.[23] Nevertheless, the chatter and hum of learning communities in science departments are usually heard in the research offices and labs, where gifted undergraduate students may penetrate (sometimes as "peer tutors") but where most of the excitement lies in interactions with graduate students.

There are very dedicated teaching faculty in science departments, of course, though they may be torn between the classroom and their labs. Some of them have reached a hiatus in their research and are happy to be out of that competition, even if their salaries can hardly match those of colleagues who have active, supported labs, and perhaps patents or royalties. And many notable scientists actually enjoy teaching, finding it not only a relief from the pressure of always thinking up new things but a spur to creativity. Thus Richard Feynman once remarked, "If you're teaching a class, you can think about the elementary things that you know very well. These things are kind of fun and delightful. It doesn't do any harm to think them over again. Is there a better way to present them? The elementary things are *easy* to think about; if you can't think of a new thought, no harm done; what you thought about it before is good enough for the class. If you *do* think of something new, you're rather pleased that you have a new way of looking at it."[24] Jasper Rine, one of the faculty instructors in Berkeley's Biology 1A and a distinguished geneticist, has won teaching awards and the honor of having his best lectures called "Rinestones" by students. Like

Feynman he emphasizes the fun in the work as part of what he teaches: "The Berkeley faculty as a whole are extremely hard working and are burdened, because of their success, with countless other local, national, and international responsibilities. Thus many of us run about with a harried demeanor, despite the fact that we fundamentally love our jobs. If the students never see that we love our jobs, I worry that our fields will be starved of an influx of fresh talent, and will eventually die. When in front of a large lecture class, I shed my self-consciousness, and throw as much energy, passion, and drama into the exchange as I can."[25]

I don't think these attitudes about teaching are unusual in science departments, but they cannot entirely overcome the situational deficiencies of trying to carry out both education and sponsored research there. No matter how dedicated and sincere, the faculty in introductory classes must appear to students as a minimal presence—even if it is the faculty who have organized the course and its materials. Students' main one-to-one contacts are with graduate instructors, and although they may also be eager to help, many of them are focused mainly on their own work. In some cases they are not well monitored, and frequently their language skills are less than optimal or even a positive impediment to the ordinary American student's understanding. It is one of the most telling signs of the nation's deficit in science education that so many of its undergraduates are taught the basics in math and the sciences by graduate students from Asia or Europe. I was struck in a professional trip to St. Petersburg, Russia, in December 2004, by a sly question posed for my group by a bright student at St. Petersburg University's School of International Relations. "Is it true," he asked us, "that although the United States leads the world in technology, American students learn their math from graduate students from Russia?" The controversy over nonnative TAs in science classes has been in the news a number of times, and responses have varied from providing better English classes and qualifying exams for foreign students to blaming U.S. students for their insularity. But the major problem does not lie in the language deficiencies of either undergrads or TAs; it lies in the failure of our educational system, from bottom to top, to take science training seriously enough.

I do not think that the answer is to suspend outside research, but I do think that there should be a tax on such research, and the moneys garnered thereby should be spent on hiring teaching faculty on the tenure track. There are signs that the science crisis has penetrated industry, as a matter of fact, for on September 16, 2005, IBM announced a program to support their own employees who had science backgrounds to acquire the training that would help them move into teaching during their retirements.[26] More funding for college science teaching from corporations and state and federal governments is certainly needed. But such funding will make it necessary for science departments to devise ways to assess undergraduate teaching as a prime criterion for tenure. If such a move were to institutionalize a dual-track faculty, so be it. For at the present time, no matter how hard a major science department tries to integrate its teaching with its research, there is no question as to which value will win out.

Since a large percentage of the most serious undergraduate students enrolled in biology and chemistry courses intend to go on to graduate work in the health professions, the relation between the science teaching crisis and the situation of teaching in medical schools must be studied as well. An important 2002 report from the Commonwealth Fund on "training future doctors" repeats the description familiar to anyone who has looked at undergraduate teaching in the sciences: "The new prototype of a faculty member is a star researcher or, less commonly, a world-class clinical specialist. Tenure committees place most emphasis on research productivity in their deliberations, but will also consider excellence in clinical service. The message regarding education has been clear: it is less important than research and patient care. In part because of the perceived lack of academic reward associated with education, deans report increased difficulty recruiting clinical faculty to teach preclinical courses."[27] Compounding the problem of teaching in medical schools, much of the training after the first two years of basic science requires the time and attention of clinicians. Students begin their round of specializations in their third year, and from then on through internships and residencies, their education is conceived as learning through doing. It is not research alone that interferes with the necessary interchange between teachers and learners in this expectation, however. The other constraint is the continuing squeeze on costs within the academic health centers where most training of future doctors takes place.

Fifteen years ago Medicare funding and other government provisions helped underwrite the extra costs of clinical teaching. As managed care schemes proliferated and competition for welfare fees from private medical enterprises grew, much of the educational funding dried up. Further, clinical physicians found themselves so pressured to treat large numbers of patients that there was hardly time for stopping the clinical day to take stock with students. And students themselves—interns and residents—found their time and energy ravaged by the need to meet patients' needs, in many cases to practice medicine as students, at minimal pay for long, demanding hours. Their efforts to organize for a better deal may have been frowned on by their professors because success would mean increased costs to an already faltering system. But the argument that the education they received through their work was partial payment lost plausibility as it became clear that clinical years spent as "first responders" in caring for sick people were all too often unsupervised by overstressed clinical faculty.

In his farewell speech in 2005 after ten years as president of the National Academy of Sciences, Bruce Alberts delivered a studied emphasis on scientific education: "If we really care about creating a 'scientific temper' for the United States, we will need to completely rethink most of our introductory college courses—both to make them more inquiry based and to focus them on the goal of conveying an understanding and appreciation of science, and its relation to society, to all students."[28] Like other leaders of the scientific and medical establishment, Alberts calls on his colleagues to find a way to balance the excitement and material rewards of research with a need that has become more pressing even as science has been making its extraordinary discoveries. That need is to provide the public with an attitude of understanding—a "temper"—that is informed enough about science to be able to interpret its findings, judging both their value and their threats. The Harvard curriculum review articulates just this goal for Harvard's introductory science courses: "Every Harvard College student should be educated in the sciences in a manner that is as deep and as broadly shared, as has traditionally been the case in the humanities and the social sciences."[29]

❧ ❧ ❧

The failure of scientific training designed to help college graduates understand scientific principles well enough to be skeptical of their commercialization and suspicious of the deforming influence of ideology on them is one feature of the most pressing problem for academic freedom in academic science in our day. It may be that another loss incurred by the emphasis on research in academic science is the scarcity of trained scientists who can speak to the general public. Lisa Randall, a professor of physics at Harvard, has made this point in an opinion piece in the *New York Times*. Analyzing some of the main mistakes that nonscientists can make because of a misunderstanding of scientific procedures and vocabulary, she concludes, "When advances are subtle or complicated, scientists should be willing to go the extra distance to give proper explanations and the public should be more patient about the truth."[30] In an earlier day, when scientists banded together to warn against nuclear warfare and environmental contamination, the effort to educate the public proceeded freely both inside and outside the academy. I am not sure that there were more heroes of scientific integrity then—such researchers as Pruitt, Viereck, and Foote—but I do believe that academic science today is beset with more complicated temptations than those men had to resist. There are similarities, though. Once again there is a concerted effort of political and ideological agents to rewrite the conclusions of research. One recent case involves editorial ministrations by Philip A. Cooney on a government climate research report titled "Our Changing Planet." Cooney, whose objectivity was called into doubt by his former position as a lobbyist for a major oil company, persistently softened the predictions about the effects of global warning. For example, he justified the deletion of one passage that warned of likely deleterious effects by noting in the margin that the scientists' conclusions were "straying from research strategy into speculative findings here."[31] Cooney resigned from his government job under the glare of negative publicity, but efforts to emend, if not negate, the findings of science are evident in many other places.

Perhaps the most extraordinary of these has involved federal, state, or municipal efforts to dislodge the accepted evolutionary explanations of natural phenomena by sponsoring alternate ones from the backers of intelligent design or of the Old Testament story of creation. Thus the bookstore managed by the National Park Service at the Grand Canyon now sells a popular account of the formation of the canyon by a biblical flood rather than by the work of the Colorado River over millions of years. According to a group called Public Employees for Environmental Responsibility, "In a series of recent decisions, the National Park Service has approved the display of religious symbols and Bible verses, as well as the sale of creationist books giving a biblical explanation for the Grand Canyon and other natural wonders."[32] Even more bizarre was a quickly withdrawn effort by some city fathers and zoo directors of the Tulsa, Oklahoma, Zoo to "balance its evolution science exhibit with a display extolling the Genesis account of God's creating the universe from nothing in six days."[33] No matter how silly such resistance to the judgments of science may be, it manifests a contemporary notion of truth that is even more insidious than Edward Teller's salesmanship for atomic testing.

This "public epistemology," backed strongly by anti-intellectual forces in politics, religion, and the media, ignores scientific conclusions as presenting merely one side of any argument. There has to be another side, and it could legitimately consist of intuitive belief, sacred scriptural interpretations, or poll data. To use the motto of Fox News, media offerings need present only "fair and balanced" arguments rather than the basic findings on which any judgment should be made. By this standard, any view can be taken seriously, providing that at least one critic has been given equal time to point out its idiocy. This substitution of opinion for fact is so menacing that it has put the national science community on alert as never before. Thus Bruce Alberts warily celebrates the reports of the National Academy of Sciences for steering clear of policy conclusions:

> Our review processes remove all non-scientifically based conclusions and recommendations from our reports, so we cannot be discredited for going beyond the science. I like to use our reports, on *Climate Change Science* and on *Arsenic in Drinking Water*, both published in 2001, to make an important general point. These reports do not tell our government exactly what it should *do* about carbon-dioxide emissions or about establishing appropriate limits on arsenic levels. Instead, what we say to government is, "If you decide to allow arsenic concentrations of five, 10, or 20 parts per billion, these are the effects that you are likely to see decades from now." We take pride in simply telling the truth—the scientific truth—to power.[34]

Many observers have noted that our society's ignorance about science will eventually undermine American leadership in discovery. Already our students are taught by instructors from other countries, and our labs and medical facilities are places of cultural exchange. All this is to the good, but the failure of the rest of our population to engage with science will also weaken our ability to enter into informed policy discussions of such issues as global warming and arsenic in our water. Since science has become so complex that it often requires assessment by trained minds, moreover, faculty from all fields in the academy must commit to understanding enough of the scientific method and principles to join their colleagues in dialogue about the broad range of ethical concerns that scientific discoveries give rise to. The university must be a place for such discussions to take place and for creditable conclusions to be drawn. I use the word *creditable* here advisedly, because I am aware that the truths of science itself have been modified by changes in philosophical thought in the late twentieth century. Even in the midst of scientific achievement, the historians of science have raised questions about the possibility of utter security in scientific discovery. Einstein's theory of relativity is now thought to be off by a very small margin. In an essay on academic freedom, Nicholas Wolterstorff has offered a helpful summary of this issue:

> Around thirty years ago, a group of scholars trained as natural scientists, philosophers, and historians began to study episodes from the history of modern Western natural science to compare the dominant self-understanding of natural science with actual practice. Thomas Kuhn became the most famous of these scholars. What they bumped up against over and over were reputable, even admirable, episodes that simply did not fit the self-understanding of natural science as a classically foundationalist enterprise. One outcome of these discoveries was the breakup of the old hierarchy of the disciplines, which had been based on judgments about the degree to which a discipline exhibited the logic of well-formed *Wissenschaft.* Now there was no longer consensus on whether there was even such a thing as *the* logic, let alone on what it might be.[35]

It is ironic that the simplistic substitution of opinion for truth may have derived from such epistemological discoveries in the postmodern period. To be sure, constructionist critiques have helped instill a judicious skepticism toward accepting traditional judgments that were taken as absolute facts before a more probing historicist understanding investigated them. But the extension of those critical approaches into the sophistry that counts all judgment as rhetoric is self-defeating. And it has been adapted by partisans on the right as well as the left.

Despite the findings of scholars like Thomas Kuhn, scientists tend to brush off the application of cultural critique to what they can prove through observation and experimentation with material reality. The results are self-evident, and the possibility that there have been some unseemly biases in getting there is negligible in the long run. The discourse of science may be opaque, but its findings are finally unassailable because they work. The infamous "Sokal hoax," in which Alan Sokal, a physicist at NYU, trapped some of his humanist colleagues into publishing an article that undermined the "reality" of gravity, has been taken to prove that the social constructionists of the humanities have gotten what they deserve from science. But the hoax also shows that science has its own jargon, that its failure to explain the complexity of its findings clearly may undercut the power of intellectuals outside science to sort them out.[36]

Science departments should therefore provide opportunities for faculty lectures that are not so technical as to bewilder colleagues. Medical schools, for example, have tended to become isolated in their separate buildings and pursuits. Yet the stem cell and cloning debates make clear that it is time for intense dialogues with colleagues in the humanities and social sciences. Indeed, it is time for scholars in those fields to engage in interdisciplinary studies of science and technology far more seriously than they now do. I know that useful communications among advanced academic scientists and their peers—and the general public—can lead to a deeper understanding of what we know and what we do not, for I had the privilege to attend the White House Millennium Evening on informatics and genomics in the fall of 1999. In that ultimate political setting, a couple of extremely articulate scientists, Vinton Cerf and Eric Lander, spent two hours helping to explain the intersection of their fields and human welfare in language that even an English professor could follow. What I learned that evening has stayed with me as a marker for understanding the progress and problems of science during the many public controversies I have encountered since.[37] As I suggested in my earlier discussion of teaching, the absence of senior scientists from many classrooms reduces science literacy among college graduates. It is clear that science faculty need to recognize that the problem is theirs. Further, it might be that more work with undergraduates could remind research faculty of the need for scientific truth telling, or even complexity telling, to nonscientists. The academy often suspects a scientist who "goes public" of oversimplification, but in these ignorant days, those science faculty who can speak effectively to the public should be encouraged to do so. As a British white paper on science in the twenty-first century has remarked, "science is too important to be left only to scientists."[38]

Meanwhile, in Alaska, there is still controversy over the continuing legacy of Edward Teller in the uses of academic science and academic facilities for testing modern armaments. Although Dan O'Neill, the historian of the firecracker boys, agrees that the Poker Flats facility owned by the University of Alaska should be used for testing,[39] a series of his columns in the *Fairbanks News Miner* in 2002 questioned the government's secrecy in its experiments with Scud missiles as well as the university's policies on classified research. Dan O'Neill's columns were suspended in 2003 when he was fired by the paper's corporate owners.[40]

CHAPTER EIGHT

The Disposable Faculty

Tenure Now

In an unusual editorial column titled "Okay, We Give Up," editors of the April 2005 *Scientific American* addressed current controversies about the validity of scientific conclusions. The column opened with a description of the state of relations between the journal and some of its critics brought on by their objections to its injection of politics into science: "For years, helpful letter writers told us to stick to science. They pointed out that science and politics don't mix. They said we should be more balanced in our presentation of such issues as creationism, missile defense and global warming. We resisted their advice and pretended not to be stung by the accusations that the magazine should be renamed *Unscientific American,* or even *Unscientific Unamerican.*" Promising to respond by adhering to popular notions of journalistic integrity, the editors agree that they've been too certain about the principles of evolution, global warming, and the like. They close the column with a promise to pursue more "balance": "We owe it to our readers to present everybody's ideas equally and not to ignore or discredit theories simply because they lack scientifically credible arguments or facts."[1] Of course, the editorial turned out to be an April fool's joke, but the joke is not so funny in the light of the current public epistemology, which seems to have taken comfort in postmodern notions that "truth" is inevitably, somehow, in the eye of the observer.

It is true that the American public, or any public, has a tendency to be credulous. But the current public credulity is especially dangerous because it has forced one of the country's most respected science journals into a defensive posture, even if under the cover of satire. As we have seen in the previous chapter, the effort to draw a line between scientific data and conclusions is nothing especially new. But when the scientific community—the American Academy of Sciences and the American Association for the Advancement of Science as well as the Union of Concerned Scientists—issues public warnings about tampering with research findings, we must conclude that there is a perilous national misunderstanding about knowledge.[2] As the *Scientific American* satire suggests, in some sectors ideas are now taken to be "un-American" if they are inconvenient politically. If all conclusions are matters of opinion, then every citizen can claim the intellectual standing of the undergraduate English student who proclaims that any corrective of his or her interpretation by a professor is "only *your* opinion."

The question of the status of scientific knowledge, or any knowledge, is a question of trust, and it obviously bears on the scholarly profession's claim to establish and maintain a structure of secular trust for the public. It is from that claim that the necessity for a system of tenure was extrapolated in the early twentieth century, and has been upheld by tradition and by legal precedent during the past ninety or so years. The question of intellectual credibility is therefore also a question about tenure, and so this chapter explores the university's responsibility to maintain its promise. In doing so, the chapter will take some time to examine the role of the faculty in promulgating knowledge. This examination inevitably looks at the founding of the American Association of University Professors in 1915, reengaging in the reasoning through which the need for tenure was initially derived.

Then the chapter will analyze recent efforts to justify substitutes for tenure, laying out some features of a project titled "New Pathways: Faculty Careers and Employment in the 21st Century," which was launched by the American Association of Higher Education in 1994. That project began by issuing a panoply of arguments for dismantling tenure as a central feature of faculty careers. When the project moved into a second stage in 1996, lodged in the Project on Faculty Appointments at Harvard led by Richard P. Chait, it continued to "target issues identified as points of leverage in the academic career that can make individual faculty careers more vital and resilient and provide institutions with the flexibility needed to anticipate and respond to a rapidly changing educational environment."[3] Although the talk about vitality and resiliency was attractive, the mention of institutional "flexibility" could signify only one thing—fiddling with tenure. Thus New Pathways gave support—perhaps involuntarily—to an animus against tenured faculty that has long been strongly held by the corporate establishment.

Finally, however, this chapter will argue that the status of the professoriate as a source of public trust has been far less damaged by frontal attacks on tenure than by the growth of non-tenure-track and part-time faculty in the past two decades. The replacement of permanent by contingent faculty has undercut faculty authority in dealing with the major problems discussed in this book—campus commercialization, pedagogical reform, curricular revision, competition in hiring and peer review, participation in university governance, and control of research. The drift of our institutions away from permanent faculty has created a hole in the traditional governance system, for example, depopulating faculty senates and putting managerial "experts" in positions to make decisions that should be guided by the insights of classroom teachers. Most significantly, the drift away from tenure has put academic freedom under stress in the many college classes taught by faculty who do not have full liberty in their teaching. Thus American faculty has become disposable—outsourced, unbundled, and de-professionalized to such an extent that its members will have to struggle mightily, just as they did almost a hundred years ago, to regain the power to make choices about their own future.

❧   ❧   ❧

The crisis of knowledge signaled by the *Scientific American* spoof is part of a credibility crisis that now seems to engulf all areas of our national life. At one time a variety of fields had a number of accepted structures of assurance about their truth claims. Science was one of these structures, of course: it formed an island of relatively secure, measurable data in a world of floating opinion. Given the evident intellectual power involved in scientific discoveries and the miracles wrought by them, science seemed self-validating.[4] Each of the other structures of credibility for the public similarly derived power from the expertise of its proponents and the palpable good it did in society. The courts once led among these structures. Even though partisan politics could enter into their election or appointment, judges—at the federal level, at least—were on the whole trusted to render reliable judgments. Impartiality and fairness were deemed so intrinsic to their professional self-definition, in fact, that they were granted lifetime appointments to reinforce their independence. The notion of a professional identity that could transcend self-interest and political or sectarian ideology once gave credibility to the judgments required in other sectors of society as well—medicine, law, religion, journalism, and even accounting. The norms for these callings may have been violated, grossly and notoriously, on some occasions, but in a more innocent day, the public was encouraged by national leaders and the media to grant their professional conclusions the benefit of the doubt. Without this kind of trust, they could hardly perform the work of their core practices.

The university has been another center of credibility, of course. Although its individual faculty members could be criticized, its faculty's successful claim to the singular protections of tenure allied the maintenance of their authority as arbiters of knowledge and judgment with that of the judiciary. Indeed, as Louis Menand has pointed out in *The Metaphysical Club,* the notion of academic freedom as the ultimate source of validation for ideas in a democracy has been a defining development in secular American thought—a strategy for finding legitimacy in a world of shifting phenomena when it has rejected "hereditary authority and tradition."[5] The alternative to absolute certitude for those seminal thinkers who created the nation's philosophical tradition, especially John Dewey and Oliver Wendell Holmes, Sr., were the procedures of the academic disciplines—procedures which emphasized that the source of authority would lie in rigorous approaches to thinking rather than predetermined conclusions. Menand defines one of the major problems for this pragmatic approach to knowledge as the issue of trusting "the claim that a particular state of affairs is legitimate." Thinkers such as Dewey and Holmes and other progressive intellectuals decided to approach the problem sideways: "The solution has been to shift the totem of legitimacy from premises to procedures. We know an outcome is right not only because it was derived from immutable principles, but because it was reached by following the correct procedures. Science became modern when it was conceived not as an empirical confirmation of truths derived from an independent source, divine revelation, but as simply whatever followed from the pursuit of scientific methods of inquiry."[6]

The thinkers that Menand has studied as progenitors of the American idea of academic freedom were not only philosophical pragmatists but pragmatic actors in society as well. They therefore understood that a secure working environment would be a bedrock condition for enabling the exercise of free judgment and choice. It is not surprising, then, that John Dewey was a cofounder, with A. O. Lovejoy, of the American Association of University Professors.

Dewey, Lovejoy, and the others who established the Association articulated the principles upon which trust in the professoriate should be based in the

"1915 Declaration of Principles on Academic Freedom and Academic Tenure."[7] In that statement, they wrestled with the problem of fostering an open "marketplace of ideas"[8] while advocating the kind of coherence and confidence that advanced study should inspire. Who would arbitrate among the ideas? How could one be judged as superior to another? Should any be suppressed because of its inanity or pernicious tendency? In short, AAUP's founders confronted the same questions we must answer in an equally contentious time in our own national life, for as the 1915 Declaration maintained, "Public opinion is at once the chief safeguard of a democracy, and the chief menace to the real liberty of the individual."[9]

A. O. Lovejoy is often neglected in accounts of the founding of AAUP, though he was in fact more active in the Association than Dewey was. He conducted its first investigation of a violation of academic freedom and was vitally involved in the work of the Association for the rest of his life.[10] It should also be remembered that he was the founder of the study of the history of ideas and therefore well aware of the connections between cultural predispositions and the dominance of one or another system of truth and value throughout history. His great book, *The Great Chain of Being* (1936), is a magisterial study of the intellectual power of one cosmology that can seem to the modern reader an emanation of the fantasy of J. R. R. Tolkien. Thus the early proponents of academic freedom were fully conscious of shifting certainties in worldviews. And so it might seem that the philosophical foundations of academic freedom would be consonant with the impulse to give credence to all sides on any question—scientific, moral, aesthetic, or political.[11]

For such thinkers as Lovejoy, the defining barrier against such a philosophical free-for-all was the conviction that the pursuit of truth required not only adherence to the procedures set up by the relevant discipline but also dispassion. It was in his study of the history of ideas that Lovejoy coined the phrase "metaphysical pathos" to convey the notion that an idea can carry an emotional charge as well as intellectual substance. Probably no body of ideas can totally escape such pathos—even mathematicians become elated over the beauty of a formula—but the scholar had a special mandate to discipline subjective responses while exploring nature, society, art, or religion. Menand points out that the American pragmatic tradition was deeply suspicious of ideological rigidity and commercial self-interest, both in teaching and in politics. Not to rob ideas of their cogency, however, early thinkers about academic freedom stipulated that the mandate for disinterestedness did not carry an expectation that scholars would subdue all conviction in their research and teaching. "The university teacher, in giving instruction upon controversial matters, while he is under no obligation to hide his own opinion under a mountain of equivocal verbiage, should, if he is fit for his position, be a person of fair and judicial mind."[12]

Thus what remains credible in knowledge beyond the personal is the rationality with which it is discovered and framed: its pursuit must be conducted with the rigor of tested procedures, and its presentation must be made with the equanimity of reasoned argument. In defending academic freedom, then, thinkers such as Lovejoy and Dewey and their colleagues in the founding of AAUP saw that the greatest danger to scholarship lay in its manipulation by those for whom ideas are only instruments for the furtherance of some particular, emotionally held doctrine. For them, sentimentality was a universal target.

Embedded in the 1915 Declaration is a sweeping claim that the dispassionate discovery and transmission of knowledge are intrinsic and necessary features of a democracy. The work of the university was not the simple chore of providing a service to the nation's young people. It was the "wresting from nature of her intimate secrets,"[13] as well as the furthering of essential exploration in social science and philosophy and religion. Given the scope of such pursuits in the modern university, the faculty could not do their proper work at the mercy of public opinion. Since their mission is to educate that opinion, professors must inspire trust through the discipline of their extensive training, the rigor with which they lead a life of study and research, and the responsibility with which they articulate their hypotheses, findings, conclusions, and recommendations. Thus their practice of scholarship and teaching is a matter of public good, not commercial exigency. The 1915 Declaration designated the faculty member as more than an employee for hiring, and firing, at will. Each tenured faculty member was an "officer" of the university, deeply implicated in all of its workings. That claim was surely the origin of the faculty member's rebuke of President Eisenhower for addressing the Columbia faculty as "employees." Furthermore, the identity of the profession derives from the essential service it renders to society above any allegiance to a particular employer.

The 1915 statement expressed special concerns about the temptations of commercialization in the work of the university, because so many of the violations of academic freedom at that time turned on disagreements with boards and administrators about economic policies and social theories. Nevertheless, scholars were material creatures and had to live; given that American scholars were rarely independently wealthy, the argument for tenure was also based on material reality. They must receive enough support to pursue their professional lives in economic freedom, though not necessarily in luxury. The trade-off for security and autonomy would be modest but sufficient maintenance for a career of selfless thinking and teaching: "It is not, in our opinion, desirable that men should be drawn into this profession by the magnitude of the economic rewards which it offers; but it is for this reason the more needful that men of high gift and character should be drawn into it by assurance of an honorable and secure position, and freedom to perform honestly and according to their own consciences the distinctive and important function which the nature of the profession lays upon them."[14] Such a description sought to be realistic about the likelihood of modest faculty remuneration while assigning a touch of monkish renunciation to the vocation of college and university work.

The history of tenure in American higher education from the founding of AAUP until the present day can be viewed through the lens of the principles laid down in the 1915 Declaration. Especially influential have been the statement's "Practical Proposals," which laid out basic requirements for "faculty committees on reappointments," "tenure of office," "grounds for dismissal," and "judicial hearings before dismissal."[15] Other elaborations defining conditions for tenure followed from time to time over the years, culminating in the 1940 "Statement of Principles on Academic Freedom and Tenure."[16] The 1940 statement repeated the main ideas expressed in 1915, but more succinctly and with a list of specific recruitment and retention procedures necessary to retain academic freedom for individual faculty members. Those procedures have been further refined in statements issued since 1940.[17]

The astonishing thing about the AAUP's stand on academic freedom and tenure is that it took hold. Through the force of the AAUP's arguments, the ideal of academic freedom, ensured by faculty tenure, eventually became the norm for personnel practices in the academy. For example, it has been recognized by the courts as a vital feature of the free exchange of ideas.[18] It has also been embedded in faculty handbooks on almost every campus in the nation. Finally, the statement has been endorsed by a majority of the scholarly and faculty associations in the nation; currently the AAUP Web site lists 187 of these.[19] In short, during the twentieth century, academic freedom based on the security of its individual professors became intrinsic to the nation's intellectual culture, and its procedures still guide human resources practice in most colleges and universities.

To measure the force of the idea of academic freedom as a professional requirement, one has only to think about journalists' *lack* of free speech. It is true that the publishers of newspapers and owners of media claim the freedom of the press promised in the First Amendment. But individual reporters are protected only through their publishers. They can be fired without recourse except when questions of speech are involved. Even then, they must resort to personal litigation—which is costly and frequently unavailing. Whereas violations of freedom of the press must be pursued through the courts, academic freedom is usually adjudicated at the campus level through an appeal to a system of peer review first described in 1915.[20]

🍃   🍃   🍃

It is no surprise that tenure has had critics since its first declaration in 1915 and its definitive formulation in 1940. There have always been schools that seek substitutes for it, as well as schools that defy its guidelines in recruiting, reappointing, and promoting faculty members. The AAUP's investigation of and reports on these defiances, continuing annually since Lovejoy undertook the first in 1916, have further strengthened the tenure system by alerting faculty to violations beyond their campuses, thereby warning new faculty recruits away from those institutions that suppress teaching and research and make no pretense of shared governance. This censure practice has generated intense antagonism in some administrative circles.

But administrative resistance is not the only source of animus against tenure. It is also true that the tenure system can be transformed from a tool for safeguarding faculty freedom to an instrument that merely protects the status quo and thus thwarts the spontaneous growth and development of new ideas. And it can be extremely harsh in application: "publish or perish" is a saying that has been around for a long time, and a number of scholars and teachers have been so scarred by their encounters with the tenure system that they have turned against it. Peer review sounds good—but when self-selected peers make decisions based on narrow or biased criteria, the tenure system itself can undercut the faculty's claims for its positive influence on openness and spontaneity of thinking. Thus complaints from outside the academy and from academics who have suffered as a result of the tenure system have gathered force over time. And recently there has been a concentrated attack from within higher education launched by critics who believe that tenure may have served its purpose and should be reformed, cut back, or abolished.

This criticism of the past decade is notable in its departure from previous tenure reforms that focused on trying to mend the system. Ernest L. Boyer's thoughtful *Scholarship Reconsidered: Priorities of the Professoriate* was one signal example of the earlier kind of critique. There Boyer, president of the Carnegie Foundation for the Advancement of Teaching, issued an eloquent and informed call for redefining the kinds of intellectual power on which tenure judgments should be made. Concerned about the drift away from earlier democratic notions of the professorial life, Boyer made a convincing case that scholarship should involve a spectrum of abilities; he categorized these as the integration, application, and teaching of knowledge as well as its discovery. In thereby providing new categories of excellence that broadened the conventional notions of "scholarship," Boyer and his colleagues were making a determined effort to influence presidents and faculty to come together to wrench the "research" reward system free from narrow definitions of worth and fixations on institutional status.[21] In 1990 Boyer's call for more wise and generous standards for tenure was hopeful. He believed that the decade to come would provide an opening of employment for "a new generation of scholars"; the replacement of a whole cohort of retiring faculty from the 1960s would provide an opportunity to reform the system.[22] What Boyer did not predict, however, was that retirements in the '90s would provoke wholesale cashing in of tenure lines, to be replaced with part-time and non-tenure appointments. He died before the results of such short-term hiring practices were fully apparent, but his suggestions remain useful as keys to some of the changes that might refresh the tenure system.

Yet it has become dismally clear in research universities, at least, that while the Boyer Report was greeted with reverence, the research-above-all value system was deeply entrenched not only among the faculty but also within administrations and boards. And the squeeze on personnel budgets intensified the competition for that one good hire that would define a department or program. In my time as a professor, I have heard many deans and presidents talk enthusiastically about the value of teaching and service while failing to support a tenure case in which teaching is vigorous and creative but research reviews do not promise bragging rights.[23] It is perhaps because the system seems so resistant to change that some reformers after Boyer began to argue that the end of tenure should be embraced, at least in part, rather than resisted.

A primary source of such thinking was a broad-ranging project initiated by the American Association of Higher Education in 1995. The New Pathways Project: Faculty Careers and Employment in the 21st Century deserves close scrutiny here because several of its sponsors worked closely with Boyer and believed that they were carrying on his work. The project also had a substantial effect in instigating discussions of tenure. Its series of "inquiries" were read widely in educational circles and were released with fanfare to the national press. Since the project was funded amply by the Pew Foundation (which also funded its "Phase II" at Harvard), it could easily promulgate its findings by circulating position papers, sponsoring speakers for national conferences, and so on. Thus New Pathways has had greater reach than any other recent criticisms of tenure. An analysis of its main arguments can therefore shed some light on the situation of tenure now.

The philosophical justification for the New Pathways Project was expressed in the first "inquiry," "Making a Place for the New American Scholar," by Eugene R. Rice, director of the AAHE's Forum on Faculty Roles and Rewards. Rice's meditation embodied anxieties about trends in faculty careers that began to predominate after Boyer's 1990s efforts to redefine scholarship. These included many that I have addressed in this book—overspecialization, excessive emphasis on research, flight from the undergraduate classroom, and a reluctance to engage in the total life of a college or university campus. Rice was an adviser to Boyer on *Scholarship Reconsidered* in 1990 and promised an essay on the "new American scholar" to follow as a companion piece. By 1995, however, Rice seems to have become less optimistic about possibilities for reform of tenure standards: "I am becoming increasingly persuaded that it is time to take a transformative approach to the way we think about faculty work and the structure of the academic career."[24] He seems to have concluded that the only way to continue the movement that Boyer started might be to argue for the near abandonment of tenure itself—the call for amelioration of tenure's rigidity having made little difference.

Despite its invocation of an independent, "new" American scholar, Rice's introduction to the New Pathways Project was also attuned to the mood of the general public—beset by downsizing, forced career shifts, and layoffs. The preamble of his inquiry made this clear: "Much of the campus debate and the vigorous activity surrounding faculty responsibilities and rewards are externally driven. They are responses to the calls for accountability from legislators and trustees, new developments in information technology, and the very real financial constraints and demographic shifts confronting our institutions. And respond we must" (p. 1). Here was a note of determined sympathy with public objections to the culture of tenure. Rice's conclusion invoked the shadow of corporate "downsizing with a vengeance" and called on the professoriate to offer better explanations of tenure as a social good if it hoped to survive the public's resentment (p. 32).

In addition to being aware of criticism from outside, Rice was alert to anxieties about tenure inside the academy. His interviews with junior faculty in his project on faculty roles and rewards had revealed that the demanding process of achieving tenure can demoralize new faculty members—transform them into embittered enemies of their institutions, their colleagues, and even their students by the time it's all over.[25] Rice's efforts to establish more flexible norms in his faculty roles and rewards program were admirable, and they informed his vision of the faculty career as needing room to grow over a span of many years. Nevertheless, while his distrust of the tenure system as a whole may have given some consolation to junior faculty, he didn't seem to realize that what they really needed was more tenure, not less. No matter how anxious the struggle for tenure could make them, the prospect of spending a career as a "contingent"[26] faculty member was much more dispiriting.

Thus Rice's introductory inquiry put a gloss on a project that was not inclined to open up professional independence for the new scholars he sought to help. For example, New Pathways made no all-out effort to argue in favor of *salvaging* faculty job security; rather, its papers tended to accept the practice of hiring non-tenure-track faculty as inevitable and therefore inarguable. And so "The New American Scholar" echoed Emersonian idealism in its advocacy of new modes of learning freed from the external worries that so preoccupy faculty on the tenure track. Their work would be strategically guided by institutional goals rather than personal ambition. And their new order would exert the pressure of a freshly liberated civic spirit on the complexities of faculty choices in pedagogy, specialization, and disciplinary ambition. While the innovations in faculty appointments imagined by Rice would embody a vivid concern for teaching and service, they would also serve institutions by enabling them to shift and change professorial careers to accommodate ever new mission statements. In this new model the faculty assumption about eventually earning a continuing career in higher education would shift from "dependence" to "resilience" (p. 21).

Rereading Emerson, however, one might reach a different conclusion—that his call for a peculiarly "American" reliance on the radical *individuality* of intellect is actually at odds with Rice's vision. Emerson calls on the American "Man Thinking" to break out of the mass with singular new ideas, while Rice imagines colleagues coming together to facilitate the common insights of eager students in classes where no one claims superior knowledge.[27] Actually, I like Rice's emphasis on collaboration in the academy better than Emerson's heroic individualism, but the discrepancy between the two views suggests that the communitarian rhetoric of Rice's New Pathways argument might in fact conflict with the constraints on individual freedom embedded in its proposed tenure reforms. Emerson's call to such freedom was a submerged inspiration for AAUP's philosopher-founders when they insisted that the only sure protection for *academic* freedom must be the security of tenure for individual scholars.

In the working papers on tenure subsequent to inquiry #1, the New Pathways Project sought to avoid rehashing the old philosophical debates about tenure, according to Russell Edgerton, then president of the American Association for Higher Education. Instead, the immediate need was to provide answers to such practical questions as "What career paths are appropriate for the 21st century professoriate?" and "What employment arrangements [are] necessary to one's tenure *per se*?"[28] And so there were studies and surveys of a number of ancillary issues—colleges with contract systems for faculty, measures of college financial stability, faculty work and family issues, retirement options, and post-tenure review programs—as well as possible modifications within the tenure system and models for contracts outside the system. Despite its preference for the kind of "hard research" (statistical details, structured interviews, and on-campus survey visits) included in these papers, however, the New Pathways Project needed to say something further about the theory of tenure and its relation to academic freedom.

That argument was staged in the fifth inquiry, "Academic Freedom without Tenure?" by J. Peter Byrne, a Georgetown professor of law and a respected commentator on academic freedom. Byrne set up his essay as a thought experiment—making an effort to imagine a school in which academic freedom could be exercised *without* a tenure system. Perhaps most striking about his effort was its need to labor mightily to imagine ways in which academic freedom could be "uncoupled" from tenure. In suggesting that there might be a possibility for non-tenure systems "to adopt procedures that will still provide legal and practical substance to academic freedom for . . . faculty,"[29] Byrne eventually confronted the fact that the evaluation of faculty would require some kind of independence for the evaluators themselves: "In our hypothetical tenureless college, these [evaluating] professors would themselves not be tenured. Their continued employment would rest to some extent on some of the very institutional decision makers whose actions they are reviewing. They simply cannot enjoy the independence of decision making that tenured professors would be able to enjoy. . . . At a minimum, professors serving on such a committee must explicitly be protected against retaliation by the institution; perhaps longer-term contracts *or even tenure* would be desirable, to give them adequate independence" (emphasis added).[30]

Byrne's difficulty in imagining a tenureless system thus revolved around the philosophical issue of peer review for hard cases. While Rice and his colleagues worried about the narrowness of peer review, Byrne could see no alternative to it. The crux of tenure in practice is its dependence on a reliable system of "quality control" effected by the rigorous evaluation of intellectual and disciplinary expertise by a community of colleagues who are free to decide. As we have seen, AAUP's founders had based their claims for tenure on the importance of peer review not only to assess faculty work but to protect that expertise from outside or "lay" interference. Without such collective judgments, knowledge and interpretation become prey to a variety of pressures—commercial, political, ideological. Byrne acknowledged the continuing validity of this argument when he concluded his New Pathways paper with a warning about the risks of abandoning a culture of tenure: "it is more difficult without tenure to construct alternative procedures that ensure more subtle aspects of academic freedom. Tenure has preserved the preeminence of peer review in faculty evaluation, and that is a powerful safeguard for free inquiry and discussion, as well as a support of intellectual values in higher education."[31]

Peter Byrne's paper made the best imaginable brief for managing faculty freedom in the absence of tenure in higher education, but his reservations were nearly insurmountable—despite the positive spin put on his arguments by some members of the project. Indeed, a misuse of his thinking about academic freedom was passionately rejected by Byrne himself when a Virginia district court miscited his views in the case of *Urofsky v. Gilmore* in 2000. Rejecting the court's claim that in matters of access to sexually explicit materials on the Internet, academic freedom applies not to state employees (i.e., professors at state schools) but to their employers, Byrne spoke for the philosophical freedom of the faculty as—now more than ever—required to ward off threats from public opinion: "The distinctive needs and values of the intellectual life of a university have sunk from judicial view, as legal doctrines fashioned for the streets and the market are applied to the classroom or the admission process without nuanced consideration of how the operations and purposes of higher education are different, and how that difference benefits society."[32]

In unpacking two of the most important theoretical working papers of the New Pathways Project, it is important to compare several of their arguments against tenure with arguments made in favor of it by the founders of the American Association of University Professors. The latter recognized very clearly that a tenure system would be a difficult institution to administer and sustain. The conclusion of their 1915 statement contained a warning that is still relevant: "It is conceivable that our profession may prove unworthy of its high calling, and unfit to exercise the responsibilities that belong to it."[33] Nevertheless, seeing no "evidence of such unfitness" at the time, they moved ahead with concrete proposals to enable the American professoriate to exercise its responsibilities within a system of review that installed faculty peers in both hiring and tenure committees and in grievance mechanisms designed to make sure that their decisions would be as fair as possible. These proposals were eventually adapted across higher education. They ensured not just freedom but the growth of a diverse professoriate that would be united, from one school to the next, in a network of professional security and of commitment to maintaining public trust in the value of the pursuit of knowledge. Once the members of this network are considered to be disposable by means other than the serious judgments of peers within their fields, the trust embedded in its procedures must wither.

❧ ❧ ❧

In addition to the offerings by Rice and Lynch, twelve other New Pathways working papers tried to "reframe" the debate about tenure under several headings. Their authors sought balance in analyzing important issues in the tenure system, and they presented very useful statistical and opinion research. Yet many of them were evidently biased against the current tenure system, though the project claimed to present only the facts, with proposals that accommodated them. Faculty resistance to such conclusions clearly put New Pathways on the defensive, and some of the papers complained about the faculty's irrationality in arguing about issues when the project merely sought to clarify them. Still, the final essay in the series left no doubt that a major goal of the project was to rationalize the erosion of tenure through the hiring of disposable faculty. Consider how David W. Breneman, former dean of the School of Education at the University of Virginia, opened "Alternatives to Tenure for the Next Generation of Academics":

> The premise of this essay is that academic tenure in higher education is, if not a doomed institution, one that is likely to play a diminishing role in the employment relationship of college and university professors in coming generations. Indeed, aspects of this future are already apparent, as the number of full-time, nontenure-track faculty increases yearly, reaching more than 110,000. . . . One can anticipate an acceleration of this trend toward a more diverse pattern of employment relationships, better suited to the circumstances facing institutions but also to the needs and concerns of potential academics. . . . The view espoused in this paper is that tenure may have made sense in the 1920's, or in the 1960's, but may not make sense as the dominant employment relationship in the 1990's or in decades beyond.[34]

The key to Breneman's argument is his emphasis on the "employment relationship," for that terminology accents his assumption that tenure is about nothing more than employment contracts. Breneman is all facts and numbers, and so his interpretation of "tenure through the eyes of a young academic" presupposes that tenure is a "property right" that ought to "have a price" (p. 6). Further, since the university is an increasingly entrepreneurial institution that is beset by economic woes, it must deal with its employees as other enterprises have done through "privatization, limited government, productivity, assessment, outcomes, and efficiency" (p. 2). As for academic freedom, Breneman believes it is no longer an issue, mistakenly citing Peter Byrne's very tentative conclusion as part of his rationale (p. 5).

Breneman envisions the disappearance of uniform personnel policies in higher education. Academic employment relationships would differ from school to school and even from department to department, depending on the labor market. In such a system, especially in its transition away from the current one, prospective faculty members would bargain either for higher salary or for tenure. Breneman's expectation is that superior faculty candidates—that is, those who could get jobs elsewhere—would inevitably opt for salary over security. Those who didn't would be, self-evidently, either in noncompetitive arts and sciences fields or personally noncompetitive: "Any candidate who places a high value on tenure is one that an institution might wisely avoid hiring, for the candidate may be signaling a need for job security not warranted by ability" (p. 10).

Breneman understands that such a change would differentiate American colleges and universities from one another, dividing the haves and the have-nots. As they bid for top-flight faculty, for example, schools that maintained tenure would be able to offer good salaries *plus* tenure. On the one hand he suggests that these are facts of life, and on the other he calls for better treatment for nontenured faculty in salaries and workload and benefits. He does mention some drawbacks. One would be the possible loss of tenure's instrumentality in assessing faculty performance. But Breneman declares that stringent reviews of nontenured, long-term faculty would not be sacrificed. The system would remain intact: "I see no reason why the resources and energy of the college should not be available for a review as demanding as that done for tenure. The practices and tradition are already in place and need not be invented" (p. 12).

In "a concluding comment" to his inquiry, Breneman judges disapprovingly the faculty activism that emerged when tenure was threatened at the University of Minnesota. There, he notes, the "faculty response to review of the tenure code (and to a proposal that faculty believed would curtail faculty rights or undermine the tenure system) was to begin organizing a union, an outcome that many fear would be the logical response of a threatened faculty." Opining that this reaction has "tainted" the debates about tenure because of its emotional nature, Breneman adds, "I personally have no desire to see the spread of faculty unionization, and believe that a thoughtful discussion of alternatives to tenure for the incoming generation of academics need not veer into this unattractive path" (pp. 15–16). During the tenure debates of the past decade, it has been quite obvious that the educational establishment does not want to hear about the possibility of formal collective action by the faculty. Indeed, my mentioning such a development at the AAHE panel that introduced the New Pathways Project in March 1995 in Washington, D.C., was greeted with silence, and I was later told that my mention of unionization had been taken as a threat.

Nevertheless, the faculty impulse to defend tenure by moving to collective bargaining cannot be ignored. Not only does it reveal the political problems with abolishing tenure, but it emphasizes one fact about tenure that the New Pathways initiative never seems to have understood clearly: tenure does more than protect academic freedom. It has also established a system of self-management that binds faculty together in a broad range of work in managing the university. It encompasses a series of active responsibilities at the most basic level of faculty labor; because of its requirements, faculty traditionally choose their immediate supervisors—chairs and deans—who perform the essential work of the institution. Without its promise, very few faculty would willingly take on its managerial chores—on hiring and tenure and curriculum committees, for example. Thus its absence would create problems not just at the level of academic freedom but at the level of basic, day-to-day management of staffing classes and deciding their content as well as of personnel.

The turn to unionism would therefore be a natural solution for a faculty whose management prerogatives are no longer intrinsic to their professional status. Far from presenting an "unattractive path" in the absence of tenure, I think that unionization would be an inevitable response. Ironically, the alternative status that Breneman posits—one in which faculty would serve as contractors rather than autonomous and self-governing professionals—is the very at-will status that might make them eligible for collective bargaining rights in many schools where their "managerial" status now prohibits their forming unions.

The faculty urge to unionize in the tenureless state thus emphasizes the managerial and economic bargain that tenure provides for running the complex operations of colleges or universities. Its governance facet prepares faculty to manage their own affairs; without its guarantees of autonomy, an additional layer of management would be needed. Tenure has also provided the economic trade-off of stability for salary level, and thus given many schools access to extremely smart and talented people who might command higher pay in business or industry. The idea that these benefits could be retained without a tenure system is less practical than it might seem at first.

Aside from prospects of the faculty without tenure acting in collective opposition to management, what Breneman and other critics of tenure have left out of their alternative models are exactly the qualities of a communal concern for teaching and service that Rice's "New American Scholar" essay envisioned— the collaborative work of equals, the inventive exploration of interdisciplinary study, the connection of learning with society, and, most of all, each faculty member's sense of "connectedness" with the other. The best features of any job are continuity of commitment and the respect of the culture. Emerson could afford those; even Thoreau could afford them. As AAUP's founding thinkers realized, the ideal of devotion to scholarship in American education, writ in individual lives through the institutional guarantee of continuing employment for responsible work, should not be limited to a select few but should spread to schools across the nation. In a scientific age, when secular knowledge must undergird secular understanding, independent scholar-teachers are more critical than ever before. When they and their training are redefined as dispensable, valued only for their instrumentality in the competitive arena of vocational skill training, academic freedom becomes a privilege of powerful universities and status-laden faculty. Everyone else would be disposable, and a disposable faculty would not speak truth to power, but rather do its bidding.

🐝   🐝   🐝

Despite their theoretical arguments against the traditional tenure system and their efforts to present alternatives, the New Pathways Project essays make it clear that tenure is threatened less by such theorizing than by the growing numbers of disposable faculty, both full-time and part-time. Two significant New Pathways "inquiries" dealt specifically with these untenured faculty. They present a picture that is more telling about the current realities of faculty instability than any of the other publications in the project. The experts on non-tenure-track faculty who wrote for New Pathways in the 1990s were Judith Gappa, a longtime academic administrator and researcher, and David Leslie, a noted professor of higher education. Their work first appeared in a 1993 study titled *The Invisible Faculty: Improving the Status of Part-Timers in Higher Education,* much of which informed the 1997 New Pathways papers, especially their "Two Faculties or One? The Conundrum of Part-Timers in a Bifurcated Workforce."[35]

The studies by Gappa and Leslie depended greatly on on-site surveys of administrators and faculty at selected representative schools, but their summaries of findings about attitudes toward contingent faculty tend to be less reliable than their marshaling of statistics. Though the evidence of persistent discontent among contingent faculty is strong, Gappa and Leslie tend to dismiss such negativity as minority views. They focus on contract faculty who have other high-status jobs and so are not much bothered by their situation; such instructors take time from their "regular" jobs to teach, or they come back from retirement to keep a hand in and to enjoy campus life. Of course, they are not unhappy with their lot; it gives them added income and the prestige of an academic connection. About these part-time and non-tenure-track workers, AAUP takes a tolerant view, even as it points to the plight of the bulk of contingent faculty who are not so fortunate:

> A small percentage of part-time faculty bring the benefit of expertise in a narrow specialty to add depth or specificity to the course offerings otherwise available at

an institution. Another small percentage are practitioners of a profession such as law, architecture, or business and bring their direct experience into the classroom in a class or two each week. While many individuals with such appointments may find the conditions of part-time academic employment acceptable, their situation is the exception rather than the norm, and therefore should not serve as the primary model for a policy discussion. The vast majority of non-tenure-track faculty, part- and full-time, do not have professional careers outside of academe, and most teach basic core courses rather than narrow specialties.[36]

The New Pathways view of contingent faculty not only assumes that they are relatively happy in their jobs but sees no real solution to their displacement of continuing faculty in most colleges and universities. Since this conclusion has the force of numbers and the tight academic job market behind it, Gappa and Leslie encourage faculty to think of the growth of contingent faculty as adding flexibility for institutions rather than as exploiting colleagues whose choices have been greatly diminished. Many faculty have not been so patient, however. The disciplinary associations for the humanities and social sciences have seen the growth of non-tenure-track hires as a direct threat to the integrity of their fields. And so they have collaborated to study the problem and recommend ways to hold back the tide of non-tenure-track faculty who threaten to swamp the professoriate in all but the technology and vocational areas.

In 1997, a group of associations from the humanities joined together in the Coalition on the Academic Workforce (CAW) to advise both faculty and departmental chairs on how to respond to the crisis, noting that "Over reliance on contingent faculty members also puts institutions at a disadvantage. The immediate cost savings that institutions realize from their use are often offset by the lack of program coherence and reduced faculty involvement with students and student learning. Permanent faculty members must be present in sufficient numbers to develop courses, research new trends, set requirements, [and] design general education courses, majors, minors, and graduate programs."[37] The work of this coalition influenced the thinking of the Modern Language Association, which made a concerted push in the late 1990s to update the Gappa-Leslie statistics on part-timers. Contingent faculty in English and the foreign languages had become powerful lobbies within the MLA. There was also pressure from TAs, who were serving as long-term apprentices at research universities without any real prospects for finding tenured jobs at the end of their training. Striking at the heart of the faculty's sense of scholarship and teaching, contingency had become a burden that could not be lightened by appeals to self-reliance or institutions' flexibility. And in increasing numbers, contingent faculty have decided to go down the path of unionization.

To be fair, Judith Gappa and her colleagues were not deaf to signs of discontent among the faculty without tenure whom they interviewed. But their project seemed to be geared more toward amelioration than reform; the possibility of unionization is barely mentioned—perhaps because the movement had only begun to make its demands known in the mid-1990s. Thus the New Pathways' calls for fairer treatment of part-time and adjunct faculty—such as long-term contracts, access to fringe benefits, and participation in faculty governance at some appropriate level—seem out of touch with faculty anger. By contrast, the disciplinary associations are advocating more specific measures—including approval of collective bargaining efforts, attention to the production of PhDs by graduate schools, and mentoring students out of the profession when there are no permanent positions for them in college humanities departments.

Most of the remedies for the exploitation of the contingent academic labor force have been directed to institutions under pressure from contingent faculty themselves. Nevertheless, a more intense resistance to the current trends has been mounted by tenured as well as non-tenure-track faculty. There are several reasons for this collaboration. For one thing, faculty are increasingly aware of a tendency in the reform movement to solve the problem of casual academic workers by eliminating tenure altogether. For another, they understand that the initiative and power in the kinds of employment relationships posited by the New Pathways remedies would inevitably belong to the employer. The recurrent complaint of nontenured faculty is that they are defined as contractors rather than autonomous professionals. And in the Gappa-Leslie interviews, even the most secure of them commented that they must continually worry about the next contract. Equally dangerous, in the eyes of the faculty, is that entrepreneurial contracting would inevitably divide the professoriate along a spectrum of oppositions—the researchers against the teachers, the professional schools against arts and sciences, those who depend on the academy for a living and those who have other sources of income (Breneman includes "family wealth" among these),[38] and a handful of "successes" against a mass of "failures." Faculty, as well as administrators from the faculty, are aware that such bifurcations would undermine the notion that American higher education should be diverse, both to embody and to further equality.

Finally, one of the most telling criticisms of schemes to do away with tenure is that they would end up treating continuing faculty the same way that the present non-tenure system treats contingent faculty. The present system is extremely unsystematic, as a matter of fact. Faculty are hired at the last minute without much review of their qualifications and with little feedback about their work. In practical terms, de-tenuring regular faculty by normalizing part-time teaching would remove such oversight from the entire academic work-force. Some tough-minded educational administrators do not want to see the very effective system of personnel management under tenure come undone. Contrary to Breneman's optimism, they know that they could not count on continuing practices and traditions that are already in place, and that new systems to manage the faculty would indeed "have to be invented." Although some institutions have engaged law firms in efforts to design a new system, the results tend to look like the old one when all is said in done—except with legalese that further alienates the faculty.

The departmental unit, frequently criticized though it has been, has actually been both the foundation for faculty tenure and the academic unit that is most efficient in responding to change and in keeping faculty communities cohesive. As Henry Rosovsky has remarked, "departments are our main instruments of quality control, and also the disciplines and specializations are—certainly in the last century—the main engines of scholarly quality."[39] In short, the tenure system at the core of academic departments has also become key to organizing personnel in higher education. In institutions of every variety and complexity, it not only sets up rules but monitors their implementation. Neither the New Pathways Project nor other schemes for displacing tenure in higher education fully appreciate these facts—until the faculty threatens to unionize.

🙞 🙞 🙞

And so, finally, who needs academic freedom and tenure? In the mid-1990s, it seemed plausible to brush away that question as no longer relevant. After the terrorist attacks of 2001, its relevance has returned with a vengeance. As we have seen, both scientific researchers and teachers of science need academic freedom and tenure. Not only has trust in their findings been challenged or simply cast aside by popular opinion, but they are now being asked to teach in ways that are at variance with their training and disciplinary principles. Professors in Middle Eastern studies need academic freedom and tenure. Many of them have been called to task in places like the "Campus Watch" Web page (www.campus-watch.org), which invites students and other readers to submit names of suspect scholars in the field. Demanding teachers who refuse an administrative order to give grades that reflect student effort rather than mastery need tenure. And college and university faculty members in the humanities and social sciences, under suspicion for any number of transgressions in these uneasy times, need academic freedom and tenure.

The stupefying destruction of 9/11, and the fanaticism that brought it about, presented a concerted challenge to the kind of thinking that goes on in universities. Some faculty responded with comments that were thoughtless, to be sure, but most acted in the best tradition of what universities do. They examined the contexts of the attacks and the motives of the attackers, considering the possibility that different American policies might have mitigated their hatred. Such discussions aroused conservative critics' suspicion of the professoriate, which was already simmering, as I have noted elsewhere. It also incited a round of passionate condemnation and a call for more public scrutiny not only of the faculty as a whole but of specified individual faculty members.

Those in the Academic Bill of Rights movement have led this scrutiny, using evidence of the political affiliations of faculty in the humanities and social sciences to intimate that all faculty think alike and try to influence their students to do the same. In a shrewd invocation of AAUP's founding principles, proponents have sought federal and state legislative measures to oversee processes of hiring and tenuring with special attention to the politics of candidates for tenure-track jobs. The mechanics of this oversight are vague in the legislative language, but there are more specific measures outlined on the "Students for Academic Freedom" Web page.[40] One of the most important strategies is to encourage students to report incidents of faculty liberal bias to the campus administration, the Web page, and the local student or town newspapers. The first of these actions is sometimes warranted, of course, and indeed several of the accounts by students make clear that faculty who egregiously violated their responsibility were dealt with by their institutions. While no administration wants to set up a witch hunt, none wants to indoctrinate students either. But these critics seem unimpressed with administrative remediation. Instead, they want to publicize all accusations so as to drive home to the entire country their contention that the tenured faculty generally oppress conservative students.

Such determinedly punitive movements have reminded the faculty and the educational establishment that there is still a need for tenure. The rhetoric of academic freedom is easy to summon, and projects like the Academic Bill of Rights usually make a nod toward it. But the rhetoric does not come near to the reality of classrooms that lack academic freedom. To my mind, the most telling description of such privation comes from a faculty member who taught without tenure in her native land at a time when the whole society was succumbing to pressure from the presiding ideology; her account of surveillance became a surprise best-selling book in 2003. In *Reading Lolita in Tehran,* Azar Nafisi describes the habitual behavior of a member of the Muslim Student Association in her class on modern fiction. Here is what she confronted every day: "As I talk, my gaze involuntarily shifts to the last chair by the wall in the last row. Since the beginning of the semester, I have been both irritated and amused by the antics emerging from this corner of the room. Usually, midway through the lecture, the tall, lanky occupant of that chair . . . would lift himself up halfway, and, without waiting to rise fully or for me to give him permission to speak, begin to enumerate his objections. It was always objections—of this I could be certain."[41]

Nafisi's book details what happens to a university, and a culture, when its professoriate has been deprived of the kind of personal security that is necessary for genuine teaching and research. Her story also makes clear the devastation brought to any scholarly dialogue when it is subject to endless objections that are beside the point. She tries to engage her Revolutionary Guard students in "teachable moments," but their minds are at once clouded by passion and illuminated by assurances of divine revelation. Her training and knowledge cannot reach them. Indeed, her narrative should be enough to caution the current supporters of state and student surveillance on our campuses that the damage that they can do exceeds the gains from identifying incidental cases of abuse. Nafisi's ultimate inability to teach in Iran also shows the vulnerability of faculty members who cannot appeal to a tradition of systematic protection for their classroom speech.

In answer to the Academic Bill of Rights movement, the AAUP's Committee on Academic Freedom asserts: "Skepticism of professional knowledge, such as that which underlies the Academic Bill of Rights, is deep and corrosive. This is well illustrated by its requirement that 'academic institutions . . . maintain a posture of organizational neutrality with respect to the substantive disagreements that divide researchers on questions within . . . their fields of inquiry.'"[42] Teaching *Lolita,* or any other text, in a country that equates all judgments, no matter how well informed, with political bias will lead to surveillance, paranoia, and betrayal.

That is why we need tenure now.

CHAPTER NINE

Staging a Comeback

Exemplary Cases

I have written this book mainly as a faculty member in the humanities, but in the hopes of reaching other members of the higher education community as well. Starting with the question in my title, I have also criticized the way the faculty live now. Though there have been many criticisms like my own in the past decade, few remedies beyond small remediations or wholesale demolition have been offered. Bill Readings, a brilliant analyst from a younger generation than mine in English, believed that the demolition has already occurred, leaving "the university in ruins." He called for a new kind of pragmatism: "Such a pragmatism, I shall argue, requires that we accept that the modern University is a *ruined* institution. Those ruins must not be the object of a romantic nostalgia for a lost wholeness but the site of an attempt to transvalue the fact that the University no longer inhabits a continuous history of progress, of the progressive revelation of a unifying idea."[1] Readings's picture of the contemporary university as inhabiting a De Chirico landscape clearly differs from the celebratory panorama of campuses with which I began this book. Perhaps the homage to Brueghel in my own rendition of our reality is a form of romantic nostalgia, but my pragmatism must go beyond Readings's prescription that we observe the cognitive dissonances of our present setting and analyze their ironies without much hope of changing them. My effort to imagine the faculty as more than ghostly presences on our campuses is less a romantic dream than a conviction that faculty still have the power to make choices that can resist the deterministic sense that all is lost.

Of course, I believe that the best remedy would be for everyone in higher education to undergo a change of heart. Trustees, administrators, faculty should throw away ambition, forget competitive advantage, renounce status and rankings, and concentrate on their research and on teaching the students who sit in their classrooms. Since rejecting the entrepreneurial spirit may be taken as unpatriotic, however, and since changes of heart are rarely available en masse, I will opt for describing hopeful changes by giving examples. For it is true that there are some exemplary cases which show that faculty can actually make a comeback. In most instances, their activism has been a matter of using the continuing tradition of governance on their campuses to focus on recurrent problems. In other instances, faculty energies have been rekindled by crisis, inspiring more militant strategies. In almost every case I will mention here, faculty success has not been achieved without allies. The restoration of faculty as genuine actors in our colleges and universities has inevitably required the participation of administrators and boards—and sometimes public opinion. There have been some failures, of course, but in the anthology of case histories I've chosen to present, I have seen faculty make the specific, strategic choices that have brought renewed authority to their roles in their institutions. I have tried to be helpful in the presentation of my cases by providing a checklist for faculty after each one.

🙚   🙚   🙚

Before getting down to cases, however, I want to emphasize the importance of faculty governance in every one of them. Indeed, that is the main arena in which faculty influence has been most severely tested. If the faculty wish to assert their right to provide oversight for higher education, they must make some hard choices, and make them together. The responsibility for such choices falls most heavily on tenured faculty, for they are, on most campuses, the only cadre of academics who have been accorded the structural authority to participate in institutional planning. It is tenured faculty who have decisive influence at the departmental and substantial force at the institutional level, especially when they are working in concert with one another. Their values tend to be enacted in the hiring of new faculty, in the provision of courses relevant to the general curriculum, and in the supervision of teaching and research. Their suspicion of the motives of politics and commerce can help steady the institution as a whole, taking a longer view of its short-term choices and checking its excesses.

Over and over, I have asked in this book why such faculty power has atrophied. The easy answer has been that forces acting from outside higher education have squeezed the life out of faculty decision making. One such force is the competitive force that overrides institutional identities by indulging in institutional envy. Another is a managerial culture that replaces faculty investments in institutional continuity with the insertion of contingent labor both in the classroom and in administrative offices. And yet another is a determined political effort to bend the academy to its particular view of knowledge and of the social good.

But such pressures on the tenured faculty are not the entire story in the dissipation of their power. I have insisted that there are deeper sources of their malaise within their own culture. In many ways my colleagues have internalized some of the values that they so strongly criticize in the world outside their campuses. The incessant struggle for money and status, the failure to participate in communal efforts outside their sphere of interest, laziness about doing the work of curricular reform, and a narrow view of the needs of undergraduates—none of these can be shrugged off as results of the external oppression of the faculty. I believe that they are outcomes of exasperation with the complexity of our educational institutions and fear of discovering that time spent on fixing them is time wasted.

Comparing the dire situation of professors to that of physicians, Martin Finkelstein has mentioned the power of the American Medical Association as an "external rudder" to help guide change in the new world of health care. Just so, he suggests that in the academy, "the system's radical decentralization requires that individual institutions and constituencies assume an especially critical responsibility for self-consciously steering their own responses to the transformation with a view toward the future of both their own institution and the system itself."[2] If the faculty is to steer, it must also turn to its own levers of collective power to help restore the status of its profession. The professoriate has no AMA, of course, but it does have national associations of faculty—among them the American Association of University Professors and faculty unions such as the American Federation of Teachers and the National Education Association. Unions can be problematic when they substitute their own entrenched bureaucracies for grassroots activism; but when they are run by the faculty themselves, unions are one hope for the wise use of faculty influence. Another resource for faculty is their disciplinary associations. Although organizations such as the American Council of Learned Societies and the Modern Language

Association are hesitant to use their influence for causes that might be labeled "political," they have the freedom to speak for their members, most especially on the crisis of excess reliance on contingent faculty.

Finally, the faculty must find more effective ways to convey to the general public the value of what it does. Many faculty discussions of the situation turn to the notion of getting on the op-ed pages, taking out ads, running spots on radio and television. I am not automatically averse to such spin, but I believe it should be based on the faculty's more active participation in areas where it can make a difference to the public—primarily in working as colleagues with educators in primary and secondary education. I have also seen the value of faculty efforts to work with their communities in other areas and talk to ordinary citizens about the benefits of liberal education as conducted by trained and committed scholars. Nevertheless, in some ways, the faculty (especially in English departments) suffer from their own public self-criticism. Given the impulse of academics to give words to their discontent and their sense of the ridiculous, the collective psyche of the academy has been on full display in comic novels, including Don DeLillo's *White Noise,* Jane Smiley's *Moo,* and Richard Russo's *Straight Man.* We would not want to be without these mordant portrayals of the academy, but we need not leave our work as a blank page to be inscribed by others.

ಶ೭   ಶ೭   ಶ೭

    Case #1. The faculty at Francis Marion University in Florence, South Carolina, greeted their new president in early 1993 with eager anticipation. Many of them had taught South Carolina students in this moderately sized comprehensive institution for many years, and they had great loyalty to the school. The honeymoon was soon over: the president began to assert total power over the faculty and showed an acute sensitivity to any resistance. When faculty members objected through their senate, he and the board abolished the senate. The faculty leaders—many of the most distinguished professors among them—scrambled. They sought help from any outside source they could think of, which included the NEA and AAUP. They also consulted friends in state government about their sense that the school's finances should be investigated. At long last, an audit of expenditures by the president was conducted. It was this latter exercise that brought release from an administration that had grown isolated and programmatically authoritarian. The audit found irregularities in matters like the remodeling of the president's house, and local members of the board became upset with arbitrary treatment of loyal faculty. In the end, the faculty senate was restored, the president was dismissed, and Luther F. "Fred" Carter was installed as his successor.

The new president had been a professor and chair of political science at the College of Charleston, but he was also executive director of the South Carolina Budget and Control Board during the 1990s. He left his position in state government to become president of Francis Marion, and he was greeted by the faculty as a savior. When I visited the campus for meetings with the president and faculty leaders in 1999, the change in faculty morale was palpable, and in our discussions I noticed that it was the president who insisted most strongly on openness and mutuality in governing the university. After the old regime, it was necessary for the school to begin treating faculty it had hired with full respect and attention to due process. I felt certain that there would be malice toward none as the school recovered its equanimity. The president gave us all dinner in the president's house, and he confided to me privately that he was trying to get the faculty to believe that they were welcome to park in the back of his house and come right in. The dinner was extremely friendly. Faculty members took me aside to point out the fabulously expensive refrigerator that had been a cause for scandal in the audit. And the new president of the board assured everyone there of his respect for the faculty as constituting the heart of the university. Nowadays the school seems to be thriving. Its Web site (www.fmarion.edu) shows a rich array of activities among faculty and students—and the president. And it hired twenty-one new faculty members in the 2005–6 school year.

When a campus is led by sensible academic deans, provosts, and presidents who follow clear procedures, faculty governance tends to fall asleep. The senate becomes a debating club, the junior faculty decline to stand for election to the senate, and submerged issues are left alone. Some of these submerged issues include grade inflation, the moribund curriculum, the increase of non-tenure-track faculty in introductory courses, and inequity in apportionment of workload, salary, or special awards. When any one of these rises to the level of scandal, it may be too late to take care of the problem without extraordinary and debilitating strife. For some time, Francis Marion had been in those straits. The restoration of the faculty senate under the leadership of a president who understood by training and by experience in government the need for faculty participation helped not just to please the faculty but to revive the entire institution.

There remains the question, however, of how to keep faculty governance awake when things are going well. I offer the following list of principles to guide faculty and administrations:

1. Every educational institution must have a faculty senate or other instrument of faculty governance. Most representatives in this body should be elected rather than appointed, and its membership should be organized so as to give its faculty members the majority vote. The body should be supported by the institution with secretarial help and release time for its faculty leader.

2. Faculty governing bodies should have programs for orienting faculty to participation in governance. Such orientation should include introductions to the history of the campus—its mission and how it evolved, a review of the faculty handbook (or contract), an analysis of issues before the senate, and a review of *Robert's Rules of Order.*

3. All new faculty should be introduced to campus administrators, leaders of campus governance bodies, and leaders of faculty organizations such as the faculty union or AAUP.

4. Senior faculty should join chairs and deans in presenting orientation sessions on campus tenure and promotion procedures. The campus legal office might be involved in such sessions, but the procedures should emphasize traditional professional standards rather than litigation. These sessions should explain the campus provisions for due process—including explanations of grievance procedures.

5. Faculty senate leaders should have a schedule of regular meetings with the president and designated opportunities to meet with members of the board of trustees.

6. The faculty senate should have access to vital campus data. Such data should include an annual census—including race and gender—of tenured and nontenured faculty, replacement information for professors who have retired, salary averages by department, the entering student demographics, and information about student grade distribution and student retention. A faculty budgetary affairs committee should have access to the institution's budget and administrative help in understanding it. (It is important for the faculty to appoint at least one of their number from business or finance to this committee.)

7. Initiatives from the administration or board should be presented in such a way as to allow time for thorough faculty discussion. Critical

administrative changes should not be enacted during summer or other times when the faculty is not present on campus.

8. Faculty should be appointed to administrative search and screen committees. And they should be consulted systematically in reviews of major administrators.

☙ ☙ ☙

Case #2. Like the faculty at Francis Marion University, the faculty at Adelphi University in Garden City, New York, welcomed their new president, Peter Diamandopoulos, when he arrived in 1985. Although he had arrived with some bad press from the faculty at Sonoma State in California, he brought a sense of excitement and the energy of an educational ideologue. He planned to put Adelphi on the map as a center for the core values of traditional liberal arts education. His origins were Greek, and he held out the inspiration of the Greek *paideia* for this working-class institution that had its roots in a mission to train women for careers in nursing. When his board convened, it brought together a number of conservative thinkers, including Hilton Kramer, William Simon, and John Silber. Diamandopoulos treated them well, and they treated him well in return. By 1995, his salary was revealed to be the second highest of any university president in the United States. Meanwhile, student enrollment at Adelphi had slipped and faculty relations with the president and board were dismal. In retaliation, Diamandopoulos filed to decertify the AAUP union—a holdover from the days before the Yeshiva decision (discussed in chapter 5).

The Diamandopoulos regime was characterized by extremes. For example, in 1994 the president convened the board in Greece and hosted the Greek World Cup soccer team on Long Island. In preparation, he ordered new campus signage in Greek. On the other hand, to punish the union in 1996, he cut off electricity to the campus AAUP office and withdrew parking privileges from its director. In response to the entire situation, the AAUP chapter at Adelphi formed the Committee to Save Adelphi, which attracted alumni, colleagues from elsewhere, and friends of the university. Under its aegis, the union petitioned the New York State Board of Regents to investigate the administration. As a result of that investigation, the Board of Regents dismissed all but one Adelphi board member. The new board then immediately fired Diamandopoulos, who responded by demanding that his position in the philosophy department be honored, arguing that he had tenure there. He eventually left Adelphi to serve as a consultant to John Silber at Boston University. When an interim president was appointed, he recruited Gayle Insler, president of the AAUP chapter during the time of troubles, to become dean of the College of Liberal Arts at Adelphi.

This case, typifying what happens when there is a demise of faculty governance at a university, has also been glossed as an illustration of corporate greed as well as corporate mismanagement.[3] In addition, the Adelphi case demonstrates the imperial aspirations of a kind of curricular program that seeks to impose its own vision of "the canon" on every school. Adelphi was a working-class school that had traditionally prepared local students for careers in nursing and social work. While it had also paid attention to core courses in the arts and sciences, its faculty had no illusions about its student population. Many of them needed remedial courses, for example. The faculty understood that they were not as well prepared for college as students at other kinds of schools, but the Adelphi professors were committed to the needs of their students. They tried to explain this to the president and the board, but Diamandopoulos plunged ahead in 1995 with his plan to establish an honors college that would add verisimilitude to his favorite advertising ploy—touting Harvard as "the Adelphi of Massachusetts" in Boston publications; the text proclaimed, "There are three things everyone should read before entering college: Plato's *Republic,* the complete works of Aristotle, and this ad."[4] In short, because of his ambitions curricular committees were overridden, faculty were displaced, "star" conservative faculty were hired outside the traditional faculty process, student tuition increased, and enrollments decreased.

The faculty's response, after a period of long suffering and under threat of dissolution of their union—was to go public. They were aided by the publicity about their president's salary and perks. And with the help of the AAUP national office, unions in New York State, and an outraged public, they found a way to involve the governance structure of New York's educational system. Some criticism was levied at the state for taking such a decisive role in a private institution, but that seems to have been incidental. There was no doubt that the faculty had managed to save Adelphi not only from an imperial and wasteful presidency but also from a wrong-headed effort to usurp faculty direction in defining its educational mission and designing its curriculum. There are still problems at Adelphi these days. Budgets remain tight, a condition exacerbated by the deficit left in the wake of Diamandopoulos's reign; the full-time faculty are overworked; and there are too many part-time and non-tenure-track fac-

ulty (though 50 percent of the full-time faculty have tenure).[5] Nevertheless the
university is viable, and Adelphi's School of Nursing, which was temporarily
closed under Diamandopoulos, now thrives.

The Adelphi case illustrates the importance of curriculum in preserving the
identity and mission of an institution. Given the canon wars of the past two
decades, faculty are surely aware of the controversies by now. Nevertheless,
they have tended to manage both the curriculum and the educational mission
of their schools one course or program at a time. Calls for curricular review are
not, however, unreasonable; they challenge faculty to rethink important features of their teaching. Given the rapid change in student populations, information technology, and interdisciplinary possibilities, all faculties should
undertake curricular reviews on a regular basis (every five to seven years). Here
is a checklist for such reviews:

1. What is the preparation level of the student body? How many stu-
    dents need remedial courses? Who teaches the remedial courses? Are
    faculty who teach such courses represented on the review committee?
2. Is there an identifiable rationale for the courses required for all under-
    graduates? Do courses that meet those requirements take pains to
    represent their importance to general education in their catalogue
    descriptions or their introductory materials?
3. Who teaches core courses? What is the average size of core classes in
    each of the disciplines involved? Do undergraduates have an opportu-
    nity to enroll in faculty-taught introductory courses? in introductory
    courses of fewer than thirty-five students?
4. Is it possible for undergraduates to pursue the core curriculum in
    sequence? If not, are core courses arranged so that they do not require
    sequential planning?
5. Are there ancillary programs to help teaching and learning in core
    courses? Are there training and mentoring programs for TAs? adjunct
    faculty? Is the teaching center well organized and used? What about
    the writing center? Does the math department offer tutorials?
6. Have the core courses been designed to include segments on Internet
    research and citation as well as provisions for dealing with Internet
    plagiarism?

These are significant questions for curriculum review. They cover pedagogy as well as content. If the faculty on the campus are not thinking about them cooperatively, their complacency may be undermining not just undergraduate education but public confidence in their own commitment to it.

ও৪ ও৪ ও৪

Case #3. The faculty at the San Francisco Art Institute are practicing artists who have never expected much support from the school. Although the institute has a wonderful building, a mural by Diego Rivera, a location on Russian Hill, and a history of distinguished faculty and alumni, it has survived hand to mouth for many years. It has been especially notable in the development of photography: Ansel Adams was on the faculty and founded the first school of photography there in 1946, and Annie Leibovitz was a student there in 1968. When I first visited in the mid-1990s, the school had a small AAUP chapter that was attempting to negotiate for faculty standing and benefits even though most faculty seemed unused to thinking of such matters. In speaking to the AAUP president, I discovered that there were no retirement benefits and that his salary, after many years at SFAI, had not yet gone above $30,000. When I asked him how he had managed to live on this, to raise his daughter and send her to college, he replied with some serenity that he did some work on the side and that his family lived simply. They had spent years finishing their house in San Rafael by hand. He also sympathized with the school's struggles to stay afloat, and he loved teaching there.

In the late 1990s, a staff member from the AAUP office in Berkeley became interested in advising the Art Institute faculty group. Helped by his expertise, the chapter signed an initial contract in 2002. Although the terms would seem minimal to many faculty on unionized campuses, they were transforming for SFAI faculty. There were no raises promised, but medical benefits were specified, and the administration agreed to a gradual increase of contributions to a retirement plan, starting at 1.5 percent and increasing over five years to 8 percent. Then in 2004, with the change of administrations and growth of the faculty chapter, a new contract was drawn up that gave a 1.5 percent raise to all ranks and committed to an 8 percent retirement contribution by 2006— moving the institution's maximum contribution ahead by a year. Most important, the new contract negotiated tenure for "resident" (continuing) faculty. Thus despite all the publicity about the disappearance of tenure, one of the smallest and most vulnerable faculties in the country managed to work with the administration to put it in place in the twenty-first century.

Tenure has become a given for faculty who have it and a nuisance to those who lack it. Unionization may also seem too legalistic to serve a profession that needs autonomy to implement its creative ideas. The change in the lives of faculty at SFAI should cause colleagues who harbor such sentiments to take a second look. It should also inspire administrators who have concluded that tenure is too expensive to take another view. The negotiated benefits in the SFAI contract are exceedingly, almost painfully modest. Nevertheless, they give the faculty the assurance of professional status and the administration a personnel system that clarifies relationships and promotes continuity.

In advocating for reasonable accommodations in terms of wages and benefits—the basic components of their professional lives—faculty must be aware of basic employment expectations, even in a period when all expectations have been sacrificed to the bottom line. They need rudimentary information to assess the institution's ability to meet these expectations. The requirements for such assessment include

1. Access to budgetary data and planning projections for the institution.
2. Access to institutional data on the status of faculty—including tenure/non-tenure ratios, departmental course loads, and salary averages and medians. The faculty should be aware of the annual AAUP salary survey (in the March–April issue of *Academe*) and its usefulness for comparisons with compensation in peer institutions.
3. Clear estimates of costs for health care and retirement plans, including provision for consulting experts in these fields and allowances for canvassing faculty sentiments on the available choices.
4. Outlines of institutional policies and procedures for granting sick leave, child care, research leaves, and the like.
5. Access to expert professional advice on practices and laws governing human resource decisions, employment law, faculty handbook language, unionization, and the process of collective bargaining.

ℰℰ ℰℰ ℰℰ

Case #4. The AAUP union at Western Michigan University in Kalamazoo was more "mature" than the chapter at the San Francisco Art Institute, and that is why in its bargaining for a new contract in 2002 it managed to achieve the promise of tenure for non-tenure-track faculty who had never been able to achieve that status before. AAUP's statement on contingent faculty summarizes how this change was made within reasonable budgetary limits: "At Western Michigan University, the faculty successfully bargained for a contract that offered tenurable positions to a group of 'faculty specialists' including health specialists and teachers in the College of Aviation. Because the faculty union and the institution had moved incrementally toward this step, first regularizing the positions by adopting job descriptions and promotional ranks and agreeing on some due process provisions, and then offering job security with four-year reviews, the cost of the transition to the tenure track was negligible."[6] The AAUP description accurately defines the achievement, but it gives little sense of the complexity of the negotiations or the flavor of the debate among the faculty that preceded the contract's ratification.

The complexity is important because it signifies two capacities that faculty who really want to address the issue of contingency have to cultivate to be successful. The first is an understanding of the dimensions of the problem and its ramifications in undermining their own professional status. This capacity must include a commitment to maintaining solidarity with other academics on their campus as well as to understanding the dimensions of the problem on their campus. The second is the expertise to imagine solutions that must call on detailed understanding of budgets, fringe benefits, personnel practices, and strategic institutional planning. The Western Michigan negotiating team possessed these characteristics because its members had been forced to think about the university as a whole by virtue of their belonging to a faculty union with a tradition of rank-and-file faculty participation in conducting its bargaining. This tradition helped ensure the presence of a cadre of knowledgeable people who could work with the administration to find acceptable solutions to the faculty's problems in the trenches.

But coming to contract terms with the administration was only part of the achievement of the WMU faculty. Persuading colleagues to vote for the contract was another. The faculty's discussion of the status of non-tenure-track faculty uncovered issues of "regular" faculty interests that are usually submerged by protestations of goodwill. The account in the Western Michigan AAUP newsletter of the "feisty" debate before the 2002 contract vote gives a good sense of fears among the tenured faculty when confronted with admitting non-research-oriented academics to status and a say in governance, especially at the departmental level. Ariel Anderson, the contract administrator for the chapter, described the arguments:

> Statements were made to the effect that without a Ph.D. and engagement in significant research it is impossible to do good teaching. Voices were raised over the issue of second class citizenry. Some proclaimed that to extend tenure to faculty specialists would serve to lower the quality of the institution overall. Others voiced certainty that without a cap on the number of faculty specialists permitted in the bargaining unit, Western's administration would move to do away with all "traditionally-ranked faculty," and to simply staff the institution with faculty specialist types. It was asserted that to approve this contract would make "us" vulnerable to the administration essentially turning the institution into a community college.[7]

Despite these anxieties, the faculty ratified the contract by a vote of 285 to 183. The leadership of the chapter promised to revise the contract if problems were encountered. And there was a significant change on the issue of "faculty specialists" in the new contract, negotiated in 2005. To wit: "Persons holding this appointment shall be fully participating faculty members in the academic community; however, departments, through their Department Policy Statements, may limit the participation of faculty specialists in tenure and promotion reviews of traditionally-ranked faculty."[8] This new contract was ratified overwhelmingly on September 14, 2005, by a vote of 433 to 82 with 60 percent of the WMU faculty voting. The transition from non-tenure to tenure for a significant number of academics seems to have taken hold, and faculty fears of institutional decline at Western have not materialized.

Problems in the overuse and exploitation of contingent faculty have been debated widely in the past decade and a half. The root cause seems to lie in the supply-demand equation, reinforced by the discovery that there are no longer any real restraints on hiring part-timers from accreditation bodies, from students, or from budget-squeezed faculty administrators. Some observers in the disciplinary associations most affected have sought to head off the trouble at its source by advocating changes in graduate education. These remedies have included recommendations to close down marginal graduate programs and cap enrollments in successful ones, to mandate a return of tenured faculty to undergraduate course instruction, and to peg pay and benefits for contingent faculty at levels that would make them too expensive to choose over tenure-track faculty.

None of these approaches has really worked. The supply still exceeds the demand. Contingent faculty have been normalized by institutional design, personal economic circumstance, and their own ardency about being part of the academy. Faculty choices must therefore center on finding ways to accept contingent faculty as colleagues and on working effectively to remediate their treatment. The Western Michigan case shows that making such reforms happen requires a lot of thought, and some soul-searching. Here are some basic questions for tenure-track and non-tenure-track faculty in working through to mutual understanding.

Tenure-Track Faculty

1. Do you know how many contingent faculty teach in your department or program? in your institution?
2. Do you know the names of your contingent colleagues? Do you know where their offices are?
3. Do you know how much your department pays part-timers per course? Do you know the course load for contingent faculty?
4. Have you ever observed the teaching of such a colleague? read her work? included him in a lunch invitation?
5. Have you helped a part-time faculty member look for a tenured job? Does your institution have a job placement program for such faculty?
6. Do you know what happened to your department's tenure lines from ten or twenty years ago?

Contingent Faculty

Because part-time and non-tenure-track faculty are so exploited, they are often imagined as the blameless beneficiaries of any reform that comes along. But the oversupply of academics who are willing to join the ranks of contingent faculty is part of the problem. Those who participate in this supply should be self-critical in considering their own situation. The following checklist attempts to summarize the main issues for them:

1. Are you contingent because you got weary of the dissertation and decided not to finish? If so, do you expect to go on a tenure track with only a master's degree?

2. Have you prepared a professional résumé that includes an explanation of how your experience might substitute for a terminal degree if your position became tenurable?
3. Are you willing to undergo the kind of probation and review that tenure-track faculty face?
4. If you don't want to "do research," are you nevertheless an active student of developments in your field?
5. If you were offered tenure, would you be willing to take on the committee assignments as well as other responsibilities in the department?

ᏂᏃ   ᏂᏃ   ᏂᏃ

Case #5. Calvin College in Grand Rapids, Michigan, is an educational institution of the Christian Reformed Church. Its tradition of religious commitment is both serious and unabashed. Within the exception for doctrinal orthodoxy that is clearly stated in its faculty handbook and faculty contracts, Calvin is a strong defender of academic freedom.[9] I first learned about Calvin College at the AAUP Conference on Academic Freedom in Religiously Affiliated Schools held in Chicago in 1997. The Association invited the dean of the college, David Hoekema, to speak, and he gave a stirring explanation of the way that Calvin's Christian mission meshed with its concept of academic freedom. I was impressed not only with Hoekema's statement but also with the various Calvin College faculty who attended that meeting and remained loyal members of the Calvin AAUP chapter. It became clear to me that the protection of academic freedom at any college or university depends on the consent of faculty and administration to a set of common purposes, guided by a vision that sees the world of study and students as needing them and their variety of talents and ideas. The religious element, then, is liberating rather than confining. Hoekema so contends in his AAUP address: "The differences between institutions in matters of academic freedom are . . . differences of degree and extent, not differences between freedom and its absence."[10]

All of this seemed nice to me, and although I found my faculty colleagues from Calvin to be convincing, I wondered what the campus was *really* like in terms of academic freedom. I believe that a definitive answer came in the form of an open letter in May 2005, when Calvin hosted President George W. Bush as its commencement speaker. The letter was signed by 100 members of the faculty (about a third) and some 40 staff members and emeriti faculty. It dissented from the president's views in the most courteous tone, explaining academic freedom along the way: "We seek open and honest dialogue about the Christian faith and how it is best expressed in the political sphere. While recognizing God as sovereign over individuals and institutions alike, we understand that no single political position should be identified with God's will, and we are conscious that this applies to our own views as well as those of others. At the same time we see conflicts between our understanding of what Christians are called to do and many of the policies of your administration."[11]

I offer Calvin College as my last exemplar because its faculty have so effectively exercised their academic freedom as a matter of common practice and educational mission. The collective action of a group of them in going public regarding their concerns about national policy was considered and shrewd, even as it braved the possible risks. The open letter received national publicity, and although the Calvin administration couldn't have been totally pleased with it, there were no retaliations. Most important, the pedagogy of the Calvin College faculty is revealed as passionate without hostility: "We ask you, Mr. President, to re-examine your policies in light of our God-given duty to pursue justice with mercy, and we pray for wisdom for you and all world leaders."

Faculty at other schools might well consider some of the guidelines suggested by the Calvin College efforts to engage in public utterance about the state of the nation:

1. The statement was worked on and agreed to by a sizable number of faculty members. They consulted one another and assented to its content and tone by adding their signatures to it.
2. The tone of the statement was civil—its seriousness underlined by its restraint and its appeal to fully articulated principle.
3. The statement admitted the existence of contradictory views and of their possible legitimacy.
4. The statement avoided ad hominem implications, addressing policies rather than personalities.
5. The statement included an effort to work together for a better outcome.

❧   ❧   ❧

The cases I've outlined here illustrate the power of some faculty communities to "come back" in a number of the arenas in which other faculties have given ground. In each case, these colleagues repossessed their responsibilities, and their sense of possibility, by acting together. Their cases point to some solutions for problems I've discussed throughout this book. At Francis Marion it was the senior faculty who insisted on restoring faculty governance, at Adelphi the tenured faculty resisted superstardom and an ideological appropriation of the curriculum, at the San Francisco Art Institute they negotiated tenure where none had been imagined before, at Western Michigan University tenured faculty included contingent faculty in their contract, and at Calvin College they made a public assertion of academic freedom that was notable for its eloquent civility. There are other encouraging examples, of course, and not only among faculty who are allied with AAUP. I have mentioned some of these in preceding pages—the University of Oregon, the University of Minnesota, and Harvard (despite all the attendant publicity), for instance.

The future of higher education will challenge the professoriate to welcome innovations, revive institutional and professional loyalties, and even adjust some traditional definitions and practices. The moral power of faculty colleagues coming together under these challenges recalls other eras when America's academics outlasted the incursions of politics, managerial authoritarianism, or even their own inertia to preserve the academy's essential commitment to academic freedom and mutuality in governance. To some observers, life on American campuses today may seem already ruined—pursuing unworthy purposes, devoid of intellectual energy, and unconvinced of its own necessity. I have written this book in another mood, however. After working with committed colleagues among the faculty and within academic administrations over the past forty years, I have confidence that their skill, cunning, and idealism will continue to animate higher education, defending it from its enemies without. And from its enemies within.

Notes

Introduction

1. Stephen Watt, the present chair of the Indiana English department, has recently deplored the inflation of letters of recommendation in an online essay co-authored with Cary Nelson, "Tenure and Promotion Goes Crazy," *Inside Higher Education,* May 2005, www.insidehighered.com/views/2005/05/11/nelson (accessed June 2005).

ONE: Bricks and Mortar

1. Sir John S. Daniel, "Why Universities Need Technology Strategies," *Change,* July–August 1997, pp. 11–17; quotation, p. 13.

2. The United States Open University failed to obtain sufficient backing to continue. Like several other highly touted ventures, it simply didn't take hold (see chapter 4).

3. Sir John Daniel, "The University of the Future and the Future of Universities," keynote address at Improving University Learning and Teaching: 25th International Conference, Frankfurt, July 18, 2000; available at www.open.ac.uk/johndanielspeeches/FrankfurtJuly2000.htm (accessed March 2005).

4. For the most concise statement of these ideas in the context of the college "moratorium," see Erik Erikson, "Late Adolescence," in *A Way of Looking at Things: Selected Papers from 1930 to 1980,* ed. Stephen Schlein (New York: Norton, 1987), pp. 631–43.

5. Ibid., p. 635.

6. For a historical account, see John and Virginia Demos, "Adolescence in Historical Perspective," *Journal of Marriage and the Family* 31 (1969): 632–38. See also John Demos's study of early American childhood and adolescence in his classic *A Little Commonwealth: Family Life in Plymouth Colony* (New York: Oxford University Press, 1970).

7. See Craig Swenson, "Customers and Markets: The Cuss Words of Academe," *Change,* September–October 1998, pp. 34–39, for the typical distance ed argument that faculty must accept market terminology based on the needs of this new class of academic customer; for quotation, see p. 34.

8. Swenson (ibid.) cites the WGU as a fine case of breaking free of campuses. The reluctance to support campuses is not a phenomenon in budget-strapped states only in the Southwest: it can also be seen in the recurrent budgetary problems in states like New York. See also chapter 4, "Distance Makes the Heart Grow Colder."

9. Of course, our culture's other structure for the initiation of late adolescents is its armed forces. Since the first G.I. Bill expanded opportunities for ordinary soldiers to go to college, one of the motivations for young people to join up has been to finance a

college education. The exchange seemed fair in peacetime; in a time of war, it seems unsupportable. In the present situation, in effect, college graduates do not fight for the country in proportion to their numbers. I have always regretted the abolition of the draft and think it should be restored.

10. For a study that makes a plea for restoring attention to campus cultural rituals, see Kathleen Manning, *Rituals, Ceremonies, and Cultural Meaning in Higher Education* (Westport, Conn.: Bergin and Garvey, 2000).

11. Robert D. Putnam, *Bowling Alone: The Collapse and Revival of American Community* (New York: Simon and Schuster, 2000), p. 19.

12. See "Primary Documents in American History: Morrill Act," www.loc.gov/rr/program/bib/ourdocs/Morrill.html (accessed March 2006).

13. Thomas Hardy, *Jude the Obscure,* ed. Norman Page (New York: Norton, 1999), p. 64.

14. Allan Bloom, *The Closing of the American Mind: How Higher Education Has Failed Democracy and Impoverished the Souls of Today's Students* (New York: Simon and Schuster, 1987), p. 243.

15. See Audrey Williams June, "As It Seeks More Room, Columbia Treads Carefully," *Chronicle of Higher Education,* October 1, 2004, A29.

16. See "The Morrow Plots: A Landmark for Agriculture," http://agronomyday.cropsci.uiuc.edu/2001/morrow-plots/ (accessed October 2004).

17. I haven't listed the most memorable school mascot I've encountered—the real, live "Leo" the lion at Northern Alabama University—out of respect for his memory, as he died several years ago. I have recently been told by a resident of Florence, Ala., that after several years of searching, NAU obtained two lions—Leo III (male) and Una (female)—from a Texas circus, and now provides an environmentally correct "lion habitat" for them (see www.roarlions.com/Lion_Tradition/Mascots_Leo_UNA/index.html; accessed March 2006). They can be seen by video at http://lioncam.una.edu/.

18. "Harvard University, Department of Molecular and Cellular Biology: Overview," www.mcb.harvard.edu/Overview/Intro.html; "Virtual Tour," http://golgi.harvard.edu/Overview/Tour/Tour20.html (accessed October 2004).

19. Some students objected to Washington University's demolition of Eliot Tower in the fall of 2003, bemoaning the loss of its value as a source of group bonding. According to one senior, "even though it was tall and big and sometimes the elevators were broken, I didn't mind walking up the 11 flights of stairs because I loved it so much. It brings back fond memories, and I'm so sad to see it go" (Bernell Dorrough, "Demolished! Eliot Comes Down" in *Student Life: The Independent Newspaper of Washington University,* July 25, 2003, http://media.www.studlife.com/media/paper337/news/2003/07/25/News/Demolished.Eliot.Comes.Down-448580.shtml?sourcedomain=www.studlife.com&MIIHost=media.collegepublisher.com (accessed March 2006).

20. Faculty and administrators may disagree on the intensity of the arms race in athletics, but even though a recent study for the NCAA downplays the expenditures, Myles Brand believes that they must be "closely monitored" (Welch Suggs, "Building Boom in Big-Time College Sports Is Not Proof of an 'Arms Race,' Report Says," *Chronicle of Higher Education,* May 2, 2005, A37).

21. Among several excellent studies, I would recommend James L. Shulman and William G. Bowen, *The Game of Life: College Sports and Educational Values* (Princeton: Princeton University Press, 2001); Murray Sperber, *Beer and Circus: How Big-Time*

Sports Is Crippling Undergraduate Education (New York: Henry Holt, 2000); and John R. Thelin, *Games Colleges Play: Scandal and Reform in Intercollegiate Athletics* (Baltimore: Johns Hopkins University Press, 1994).

22. James W. Earl, "The Faculty's Role in Reforming College Sports," *Academe,* August–September 2004, pp. 53–57; quotation, p. 54.

23. Ibid., p. 54.

24. University of Oregon, official athletic site, "Facilities," at http://goducks.com/ (accessed February 2005).

25. John Biaggio, *NCAA News and Comment,* September 11, 2000, www.ncaa.org/ news/2000/2000091/comment.html (accessed November 2004).

26. Arnold S. Relman and Marcia Angell, "America's Other Drug Problem," *New Republic,* December 16, 2002, p. 33.

27. See, for example, AAUP's investigative report on the fiasco resulting from the reorganization of the Medical College of Pennsylvania's Hahnemann School with the Allegheny Health, Education, and Research Foundation, "Termination of Tenured Appointments: MCP Hahnemann School of Medicine (Pennsylvania)," *Academe,* May–June 2000, pp. 42–58. See also Michael M. Whitcomb, MD, "Major New Challenges for Academic Medicine," *Academic Medicine* 78 (2003): 1077–78.

28. See David L. Kirp and Patrick S. Roberts, "Mr. Jefferson's University Breaks Up," *Public Interest,* Summer 2002, pp. 70–80. This article is incorporated in Kirp's recent book on the corporatization of American higher education, *Shakespeare, Einstein, and the Bottom Line: The Marketing of Higher Education* (Cambridge, Mass.: Harvard University Press, 2003).

29. Such signage can come to be embarrassing. When I visited Baylor after the Enron collapse in late 2001, one of my faculty colleagues there told me that some students were upset about having the name of Arthur Anderson, Enron's accounting agency, carved over the portal to a campus building. For further information on the "branding problem," see Ron Alsop, "B-School Naming Rights: A Peek at the Price Tag," *CollegeJournal* (from the *Wall Street Journal*), September 20, 2004, at www.collegejournal.com/ mbacenter/mbatrack/20040920-alsop.html (accessed January 2005).

30. One singular, and very successful, alternative to this outsourcing of food services has been sponsored by Graham Spanier, the president of Penn State. I once heard him remark (at a meeting of faculty leaders from the Big Ten and Chicago) that when he came to University Park as president, the current managerial wisdom advised getting rid of the campus food service. Instead, he fostered the university's food operation on the basis of its inclusion of faculty research, training for students, and employment for members of the community. One beneficial result is the continuation of Penn State's Creamery, one of the best ice cream and dairy shops on any campus in the country, serving customers "Peachy Paterno" as one of its signature flavors. See "University Creamery at Penn State," www.creamery.psu.edu (accessed November 2004).

T W O : The Myth of the Bloviating Professor

1. Margaret A. Miller, "New Ideas about Campus Architecture," *Change,* September–October 2004, p. 6.

2. The phrase seems to have originated in the title of a pedagogical article published

by Alison King, "From Sage on the Stage to Guide on the Side," *College Teaching* 41, no. 1 (1993): 30–35.

3. Larry D. Spence, "The Case against Teaching," *Change,* November–December 2001, p. 18.

4. I have tested the following survey with visits to several classroom buildings on the University of California–Berkeley campus, at Cal State Fresno, at Mills College, and at the University of Santa Clara. At the latter, I was mainly in a new building, and so my generalizations would not hold there.

5. Billie Moorehead, "Physics Hall Bids Farewell to Original Wooden Seats," *Iowa State Daily,* October 22, 2003.

6. *Creightonian Online,* April 12, 2002, http://press.creighton.edu/ (accessed October 2004).

7. A Google search for "syllabi, cell phones" yields more than 454,000 hits, of which approximately 95 percent warn against cell phones in class. For a survey of cell phone prohibitions in economics classes, see "The Grapevine," in *The Teaching Economist,* ed. William A. McEachern, no. 28 (Spring 2005), www.swlearning.com/economics/mceachern/teachingeconomist/wam28.html#grapevine (accessed February 2005).

8. See Paula Krebs, "The Faculty-Staff Divide," *Chronicle of Higher Education,* November 14, 2003, B5.

9. Diane Harley, Michael Maher, Jonathan Henke, and Shannon Lawrence, "An Analysis of Technology Enhancements in a Large Lecture Course," *Educause Quarterly,* 26, no. 3 (2003): 27.

10. See Alan E. Guskin, "Reducing Student Costs and Enhancing Student Learning, Part II, Restructuring the Role of Faculty," *Change,* September–October 1994, pp. 16–25.

11. AAUP, "Statement on Faculty Workload with Interpretive Comments," in *Policy Documents & Reports,* ed. B. Robert Kreiser, 9th ed. (Washington, D.C.: The Association, 2001), p. 154.

12. Howard Mancing, "Teaching, Research, Service: The Concept of Faculty Workload," *ADFL Bulletin* 22, no. 3 (Spring 1991): 47.

13. David Lodge, *Small World: An Academic Romance* (London: Secker and Warburg, 1984), pp. 151–52.

14. These statistics are based on the fall 2004 U.S. Office of Education report, provided by John Curtis, director of research for the American Association of University Professors (personal communication, summer 2005).

15. See Harold E. Yuker, *Faculty Workload: Research, Theory, and Interpretation* (Washington, D.C.: Association for the Study of Higher Education, 1984); the crisis in teaching science is discussed in chapter 7 of the present volume.

16. See "Small Class Sizes," on the Central Oregon Community College home page, www.cocc.edu/ (accessed October 2004).

17. On the rise of the "knowledge society," see Peter F. Drucker, *Post-Capitalist Society* (New York: HarperBusiness, 1993), pp. 19–47.

18. Hewlett-Packard's hiring of a hard-driving but noncollaborative CEO like Carley Fiorino indicates both how easily management may drop the ideal of the "learning corporation" in favor of strong leadership and how badly top-down decisions may misfire.

19. As a corollary to this change, the American Association of Higher Education simultaneously initiated a project designed to "reimagine" the status of faculty and,

notably, to suggest that the institution of tenure was as outdated as the faculty's notions of teaching. See my analysis of the New Pathways Project in chapter 8. But see also a cautionary presentation made by K. Patricia Cross at a 1998 conference and published in March 2005 as an occasional paper by the University of California Center for Studies in Higher Education: "What Do We Know about Students' Learning and How Do We Know It?" (available at http://cshe.berkeley.edu; accessed April 2005).

20. Robert B. Barr and John Tagg, "From Teaching to Learning: A New Paradigm for Undergraduate Education," *Change*, November–December 1995, pp. 12–25; quotation, 16.

21. Ibid., p. 17.

22. Ibid., pp. 13–14; the second quotation cites Guskin, "Reducing Student Costs and Enhancing Student Learning," p. 20.

23. See Kevin Mattson, "The Managed University," *Academe*, January–February 2005, pp. 12 (quotation), 23–26.

24. See, for example, Ken Bain, *What the Best College Teachers Do* (Cambridge, Mass.: Harvard University Press, 2004). Bain's survey of good teachers starts off by posing the battle between the lecture and the "discussion" camps as both prevalent and beside the point.

25. I choose this phrase from the work of D. W. Winnicott, who advocated "good enough mothering" in part to ease the burden of expectations that threaten to turn parenting into an impossible challenge for ordinary mothers and fathers. It has now entered common parlance. Although most faculty would like to imitate those teachers described by Bain in *What the Best College Teachers Do*, the sheer size of his inventory of good practices would be daunting to them as a single model.

26. "World's 'Oldest University' Unearthed in Egypt," DiscussAnything.com, May 26, 2004, www.discussanything.com/forums/showthread.php?t=60779 (accessed March 2006); "Ancient Classrooms Discovered in Alexandria," Science/Tech, OIL, at www.iol.co.za, May 27, 2004 (accessed March 2006).

27. Jeanne L. Narum, "Science Spaces for Students of the 21st Century," *Change*, September–October 2004, p. 10.

28. Steven Pinker, *How the Mind Works* (New York: Norton, 1997), pp. 341–42.

29. Personal communication from Dan Maki, professor of mathematics at Indiana University–Bloomington and member of the Committee on the Undergraduate Program in Mathematics of the Mathematical Association of America.

30. See Oliver Sacks, *The Man Who Mistook His Wife for a Hat and Other Clinical Tales* (New York: Summit Books, 1985), and *Awakenings* (Garden City, N.Y.: Doubleday, 1974).

31. See Primo Levi, *The Periodic Table*, trans. Raymond Rosenthal (New York: Knopf, 1996), and Oliver Sacks, *Uncle Tungsten: Memories of a Chemical Boyhood* (New York: Knopf, 2001).

32. See *The Pleasure of Finding Things Out: The Best Short Works of Richard P. Feynman*, ed. Jeffrey Robbins (Cambridge, Mass.: Perseus Books, 1999).

33. Barry Kroll, *Teaching Hearts and Minds: College Students Reflect on the Vietnam War in Literature* (Carbondale: Southern Illinois University Press, 1992), pp. 16–17.

34. "International Hoof-Care Summit Succeeds with Innovative Format"; while the release is no longer available at *Horsecity.com*, where I first read it, it may be found at

Horse Tack Review, February 28, 2004, www.horsetackreview.com/article-display/209 .html (accessed March 2006).

35. Thomas Kuhn has made the point that teaching the paradigms—both old and new—is critical to the progress of science; see *The Structure of Scientific Revolutions,* 2nd ed. (Chicago: University of Chicago Press, 1970), pp. 165–66.

36. Robert Scholes, "Learning and Teaching," in *Profession 2004* (New York: MLA, 2004), p. 124.

37. Garfield reportedly made this statement at a Williams College alumni dinner in 1871 in response to criticisms of the college's dilapidated classrooms. For an invocation of Mark Hopkins's log that envisions its use in information technology, see Michael S. McPherson and Morton Owen Shapiro, "Mark Hopkins and the Log-on," *Educause Review,* May–June 2002, pp. 10–11.

THREE: Getting the "Liberal" Out of Education

1. Commission on General Education in the 21st Century, "A Survey of Related Initiatives in General Education," http://cshe.berkeley.edu/gec/pdf/survey_of_related_ inititatives.pdf (accessed April 2005).

2. "A Report on the Harvard College Curricular Review: Summary of Principal Recommendations," available at www.fas.harvard.edu/curriculum-review/HCCR_Report .pdf (accessed April 2005).

3. Dean William C. Kirby, letter to the Harvard faculty, March 1, 2006; available at www.fas.harvard.edu/home/administration/kirby/letter_faculty_03012006.pdf (accessed March 2006).

4. Robin Wilson, "The Power of Professors," *Chronicle of Higher Education,* March 3, 2006, A12.

5. See Bettina J. Huber, "What's Being Read in Survey Courses? Findings from a 1990–91 MLA Survey of English Departments," *ADE Bulletin,* no. 110 (Spring 1995): 40–48; see also Huber's "Today's Literature Classroom: Findings from the MLA 1990 Survey of Upper-Division Courses," *ADE Bulletin,* no. 101 (Spring 1992): 36–60.

6. Gerald Graff, *Beyond the Culture Wars: How Teaching the Conflicts Can Revitalize American Education* (New York: Norton, 1992).

7. The full commission included members from the ranks of college presidents, such as Nathan M. Pusey (Harvard), Eric Ashby (Cambridge University), Katherine McBride (Bryn Mawr), and Theodore M. Hesburgh (Notre Dame), as well as such academics as Carl Kaysen (Princeton's Institute for Advanced Studies) and David Riesman (Harvard).

8. Carnegie Commission on Higher Education, *Reform on Campus: Changing Students, Changing Academic Programs* (New York: McGraw-Hill, 1972), p. 67. This report is hereafter cited parenthetically in the text.

9. I have spoken with Martin Trow, the primary author for the Carnegie survey, and he does not remember the commission as having any particular ideological motivation in its use of the data gathered by his team.

10. Saul Bellow, introduction to *The Closing of the American Mind: How Higher Education Has Failed Democracy and Impoverished the Souls of Today's Students,* by Allan Bloom (New York: Simon and Schuster, 1987), p. 13.

11. For an account of the book's reception, see George Anastaplo, "In re Allan Bloom:

A Respectful Dissent," in *Essays on "The Closing of the American Mind,"* ed. Robert L. Stone (Chicago: Chicago Review Press, 1989), pp. 267–84.

12. National Foundation on the Arts and the Humanities Act of 1965 (P.L. 89–209); the text of the legislation is available on the NEH Web site, www.neh.gov/whoweare/legislation.html (accessed March 2006).

13. William J. Bennett, *To Reclaim a Legacy: A Report on the Humanities in Higher Education* (Washington: National Endowment for the Humanities, 1984), p. 19.

14. There were other screeds against the academy in the late 1980s, and Charles Sykes's *ProfScam: Professors and the Demise of Higher Education* (New York: St. Martin's Press, 1988) was especially vicious. But Bloom's was the most serious critique of them all.

15. Lynne V. Cheney, *American Memory: A Report on the Humanities in the Nation's Public Schools* ([Washington, D.C.]: National Endowment for the Humanities, 1987), [p. v]; *Humanities in America: A Report to the President, the Congress, and the American People* (Washington, D.C.: National Endowment for the Humanities, [1988]), [p. v]; *50 Hours: A Core Curriculum for College Students* (Washington, D.C.: National Endowment for the Humanities, [1989]), [p. v].

16. Lynne V. Cheney, *Tyrannical Machines: A Report on Educational Practices Gone Wrong and Our Best Hopes for Setting Them Right* (Washington, D.C.: National Endowment for the Humanities, 1990), pp. [v], 2; this work is hereafter cited parenthetically in the text.

17. See Cheney, *American Memory,* p. 10; she wrote her PhD dissertation on Matthew Arnold when she was at the University of Wisconsin–Madison.

18. Cheney admitted that she turned back some projects; see Lynne V. Cheney, *Telling the Truth: Why Our Culture and Our Country Have Stopped Making Sense, and What We Can Do about It* (New York: Simon and Schuster, 1995), p. 13.

19. Ibid.

20. Cheney was joined by Senator Joseph Lieberman (D-Conn.) in founding ACTA.

21. See Carol Innerst, "'Teach-In' Goes All-Out in Hailing Shakespeare: Shunned Bard Has Support on U.S. Campuses," *Washington Times,* May 1, 1996.

22. For a summary of the political effects of such a project in New York, see "Through His Trustees, Pataki Leaves Big Imprint on State University System," *New York Times,* March 24, 2005.

23. One notable exception was John Ellis's *Against Deconstruction* (Princeton, N.J.: Princeton University Press, 1989). Unhappily, his lucid exposition branded him a conservative and his objections to an unofficial AAUP statement against critics of speech codes helped alienate him from liberal colleagues in the academy. He elaborated on this alienation in a question he posed to me when I spoke at a meeting of the National Association of Scholars in Washington, D.C., on May 3, 1996. For Pierre Bourdieu, see *Distinction: A Social Critique of the Judgement of Sense,* trans. Richard Nice (Cambridge, Mass.: Harvard University Press, 1989).

24. Jerry L. Martin and Anne D. Neal, "Defending Civilization: How Our Universities Are Failing America and What Can Be Done About It," first published November 2001, revised and expanded February 2002, pp. 1, 3; available at www.goacta.org/publications/Reports/defciv.pdf (accessed March 2006).

25. F. R. Leavis, *The Great Tradition: George Eliot, Henry James, Joseph Conrad* (London: Chatto and Windus, 1948), p. 1.

26. Leavis did include an appendix on Dickens's *Hard Times* in *The Great Tradition*, and he and his wife, Q. D. Leavis, restored Dickens to the tradition in *Dickens the Novelist* (London: Chatto and Windus, 1970).

27. Margaret Drabble, "An Interview with Margaret Drabble," conducted by Scherrey Cardwell, Margery Kingsley, and Von Underwood on April 16, 2000, *Oklahoma Review* 1, no. 2 (Fall 2000), at www.cameron.edu/okreview/vol1_2/drabble3.html (accessed March 2006).

28. See, for example, Lorrie Moore and Katrina Kenison, eds., *The Best American Short Stories 2004* (Boston: Houghton Mifflin, 2004), and Lyn Hejinian, ed., *The Best American Poetry 2004* (New York: Scribner, 2004).

29. Pierre Bourdieu, quoted in John Guillory, *Cultural Capital: The Problem of Literary Canon Formation* (Chicago: University of Chicago Press, 1993), p. 325.

30. See Guillory's *Cultural Capital.*

31. Bennett, *To Reclaim a Legacy*, p. 11.

32. E. D. Hirsch, Jr., *Cultural Literacy: What Every American Needs to Know* (Boston: Houghton Mifflin, 1987), p. 107.

33. David Lodge, *Changing Places: A Tale of Two Campuses* (New York: Penguin, 1978), pp. 135–36.

34. See John Frank, "UNC Makes Summer Reading Selection," *Daily Tar Heel*, February 25, 2004, www.dailytarheel.com/media/paper885/news/2004/02/25/Investigative/Unc-Makes.Summer.Reading.Selection-1358034.shtml?norewrite200603212120&sourcedomain=www.dailytarheel.com (accessed April 2006). The books involved were Michael Sells, *Approaching the Qur'an: The Early Revelations*, (Ashland, Ore.: White Cloud Press, 1999); Barbara Ehrenreich, *Nickel and Dimed: On (Not) Getting By in America* (New York: Metropolitan Books, 2001); and David Lipsky, *Absolutely American: Four Years at West Point* (Boston: Houghton Mifflin, 2003).

35. See Graff, *Beyond the Culture Wars.*

36. Emily Eakin, "Into the Dazzling Light," *The Observer*, November 11, 2001. For an overview record of the controversy, see "A Book, an Author, and a Talk Show Host," *Complete Review* 3, no. 1 (February 2002), at www.complete-review.com/quarterly/vol3/issue1/oprah3.htm (accessed March 2006).

37. I have written more extensively about Bennett's work in "Virtues and Vices: The Lists," *Academe*, January–February 2001, p. 87.

38. Hillel Italie, "More Colleges Embrace Freshman Reading Programs," *Indystar.com*, August 30, 2005, www.indystar.com/apps/pbcs.dll/article?AID=/20050830/LIVING/508300344/1007/LIVING (accessed March 2006).

FOUR: Distance Makes the Heart Grow Colder

1. See the discussion of bricks and mortar in chapter 1. This chapter grew out of a keynote address to "Digital Diploma Mills," a conference arranged by David Noble in April 1998. For an extremely accurate account of this signal event, see Langdon Winner's "Report from the Digital Diploma Mills Conference," in the online *Tech Knowledge Review* 1.1, in *Netfuture*, no. 72 (June 2, 1998), at www.netfuture.org (accessed March 2006). Noble's book *Digital Diploma Mills: The Automation of Higher Education* (New York: Monthly Review Press, 2001) is an essential document in the controversy about technology in the classroom.

2. See, for example, Greg Winter, "Behind the Bush Budget: A Pell-Perkins Switcheroo," *New York Times,* April 24, 2005, *Education Life,* p. 8.

3. Cited by Michelle Rodino in "Corporate Fantasy and the 'Brave New World of Digital Education,'" *Workplace: A Journal for Academic Labor* 5, no. 1 (October 2002), at www.louisville.edu/journal/workplace/issue5p1/5p1.html (accessed March 2006), from the 1996 WGU Web page at www.wgu.edu (no longer available). Rodino's article offers a shrewd analysis of corporate influence in the establishment of online education.

4. University 21 Web language as of March 30, 2005, at www.u21global.com/cgi-bin/corp.dll/portal/ep/programViewPrint.do?programId=32. This language no longer appears on a revised page.

5. A press release in 2001 announced yet another reorganization under U21Global. See "U21Global Establishes in Singapore," www.universitas21.com/news/press3.pdf (accessed November 2005).

6. See U21Global's home page, www.u21global.com/cgi-bin/corp.dll/portal/ep/home.do (accessed March 2006).

7. In 2000 Universitas 21's Web address was www.universitas.edu.au. By 2005 the enterprise had changed its name to UNext and given up its "edu" designation. Now (March 2006) www.unext.com brings up Cerdean Learning Group. Earlier Web pages have disappeared from the Net.

8. "U21Global Establishes in Singapore."

9. Goldie Blumenstyk, "Company That Sells Duke's Online MBA Courses Files for Bankruptcy," *Chronicle Daily News* (online), June 1, 2001, chronicle.com/free/2001/06/200106010u.htm (accessed June 2001).

10. See Q3/A3, "The Duke MBA—Global Executive: Frequently Asked Questions," www.fuqua.duke.edu/mba/executive/global/faqs (accessed November 2004).

11. See Michael L. Sandler, "The Emerging Education Industry: The First Decade," White Paper for the Education Industry Leadership Board, April 2002, www.educationindustry.org/eilb/media/EmergingEducation.pdf (accessed November 2005).

12. The enthusiasm of the majority of the members of this commission can be seen in the exclamatory subheadings of its final report. See *The Power of the Internet for Learning: Final Report of Web-Based Education Commission,* December 2000, available at www.ed.gov/offices/AC/WBEC/FinalReport/index.html (accessed November 2004).

13. See "United States Open University Announces Plan to Cease Operations," *Higher Education/Daily News,* February 6, 2002, at Distance-Educator.com, www.distance-educator.com/dnews/modules.php?op=modload&name=News&filr=article&sid=6109 (accessed September 2004).

14. This citation was taken from the Apollo Group Web page in 2002. Its language has now been supplanted by less "industrial" locutions, and its philosophy is now tied to the biography of John Sperling, its founder: "As an institution, University of Phoenix is unique in its single-minded commitment to the educational needs of working adults. This focus informs the University's teaching and learning model, approach to designing and providing student services, and academic and administrative structure. It also guides the institution as it plans and prepares to meet the needs of working adult students" ("History of the Apollo Group," www.apollogrp.edu/History.aspx; accessed March 2005).

15. The Sloan Foundation has been especially active in sponsoring distance learning initiatives under the aegis of one of its officers, Frank Mayadas, who once worked

at IBM. According to its own Web site, "The purpose of the Sloan Consortium (Sloan-C) is to help learning organizations continually improve the quality, scale, and breadth of their online programs according to their own distinctive missions, so that education will become a part of everyday life, accessible and affordable for anyone, anywhere, at any time, in a wide variety of disciplines" ("Our Mission," www.sloan-c.org; accessed April 2005).

16. Christopher Shea, "The Gap," *Washington Post.com: Education Review,* April 11, 1999, www.washingtonpost.com/wp-srv/local/edureview/higher2.htm (accessed April 2005).

17. Jorge Klor de Alva, "Remaking the Academy in the Age of Information," *Issues in Science and Technology Online,* Winter 1999, www.issues.org/16.2/klor_de_alva.htm (accessed March 2005).

18. Laura Palmer Noone and Craig Swenson, "5 Dirty Little Secrets in Higher Education," *Educause Review,* November–December 2001, pp. 20–31. When I discussed this broadside with colleagues at an AAUP seminar the following summer, they were distressed and so drew up a response to the attack. See Mary Burgan and Susan Meisenhelder, "An AAUP Response to 'Dirty Little Secrets,'" *Educause Review,* November–December 2002, pp. 48–50.

19. It is difficult to assess such claims, because Phoenix courses are also the sole possession of the corporation; when an AAUP delegation visited the home office in the late 1990s, the members were told that they could not have copies of course materials because they were "trade secrets."

20. For example, see Craig Swenson's "Customers and Markets: The Cuss Words of Academe," *Change,* September–October 1998, pp. 34–39.

21. For a full discussion of educational lobbying, with an emphasis on the Apollo group in the George W. Bush administration, see Brian Pusser and David A. Wolcott, "Politics, Lobbyists, and the Transformation of Postsecondary Education," University of Virginia, draft, April 2003, pp. 15–22; prepared for the conference "Markets, Profits, and the Future of Higher Education," National Center for the Study of Privatization in Education, New York, May 2, 2003, available at www.ncspe.org/publications_files/PusserWolcott1.pdf (accessed March 2006).

22. Under the Clinton administration, the position of assistant secretary for postsecondary education was held by David A. Longanecker, who was also friendly to technological approaches in higher education. Longanecker is now executive director of the Western Interstate Commission for Higher Education—a nonprofit governmental organization. Like the Western Governor's Association, which initiated the Western Governor's University described at the beginning of this chapter, WICHE favors distance education as one method of meeting the needs of higher education in its member states—Alaska, Arizona, California, Colorado, Hawaii, Idaho, Montana, Nevada, New Mexico, North Dakota, Oregon, South Dakota, Utah, Washington, and Wyoming.

23. Ruth Flower, "Measuring Education," *Academe,* November–December 2002, p. 88.

24. For a full description of 1992 amendments to the Higher Education Act that imposed rules intended to limit fraud in student aid for distance ed programs, see Patricia A. Wood, "The U.S. Department of Education and Student Financial Aid for Distance Education: An Update. ERIC Digest," ERIC Identifier: ED457762 (2001-00-00) at www.ericdigests.org/2002-2/distance.htm (accessed March 2006). See also the AAUP

brochure, "The Higher Education Act: A Faculty Perspective" (n.d.), available at www.aaup.org/govrel/hea/HEAFinal.pdf (accessed March 2006).

25. Sally Stroup, quoted in Diana Jean Schemo, "Major Education Official Is Quitting House Post," *New York Times,* March, 21, 2006, A11. See also Sam Dillon, "Online Colleges Receive a Boost from Congress," *New York Times,* March 1, 2006, A1, 17.

26. See Goldie Blumenstyk and Shailaja Neelakantan, "U. of Phoenix Uses Pressure in Recruiting, Report Says," *Chronicle of Higher Education,* October 8, 2004, A1.

27. "Boards & Commissions: National Advisory Committee on Institutional Quality and Integrity," *Ed.gov,* www.ed.gov/about/bdscomm/list/naciqi.html#mission (accessed April 2005).

28. For the way these aims have been articulated for the Department of Education, see the University of Phoenix wish list for reauthorization of the Higher Education Act conveyed by Noone to the deputy assistant secretary for policy, planning, and innovation on February 28, 2003: "Boards & Commissions: Reauthorization of the Higher Education Act of 1965," *Ed.gov,* www.ed.gov/policy/highered/reg/hearulemaking/2002/reauthhearing/f-robert-collins.html (accessed April 2005).

29. Flower, "Measuring Education," p. 88.

30. See the American Bar Association's foreword to its "Standards for Approval of Law Schools and Interpretations 2005–06," at www.abanet.org/legaled/standards/foreword.html (accessed April 2005).

31. New Jersey City University sold rights to its library to Phoenix to enable it to apply for a license in the state. The New Jersey Commission of Higher Education finally approved its application in 2003, and Phoenix opened a Jersey City campus in 2005. See "University of Phoenix Campus Perfect Fit for Working Students," *Courier News,* January 8, 2005; available at the Jersey City Economic Development Corporation Web site, www.jcedc.org/new/phoenix010805.html (accessed April 2005).

32. "Online Learning: Student Experience," University of Phoenix, www.phoenix.edu/online_learning/student_experience/ (accessed March 2006).

33. For commentary on dropout rates, see R. Phipps and J. Merisotis, "What's the Difference? A Review of Contemporary Research on the Effectiveness of Distance Learning in Higher Education" (1999), Institute for Higher Education Policy, Washington, D.C.

34. Kris Frieswick, "The Online Option: It's Cheaper, Faster, and Easier to Distribute Than Live Classes. But Is It Effective?" *CFO Magazine,* December 1, 1999, available at www.cfo.com/printable/article.cfm/2989693?f=options (accessed April 2005).

35. See Diane Harley, Michael Maher, Jonathan Henke, and Shannon Lawrence, "An Analysis of Technology Enhancements in a Large Lecture Course," *Educause Quarterly* 26, no. 3 (2003): 26–33.

36. Carol Francis, Richard Pumerantz, and James Caplan, "Planning for Technology: What You Thought You Knew Could Lead You Astray," *Change,* July–August 1999, pp. 22–25.

37. For a thorough review of research on e-learning, see "Current Research on Quality in Distance Learning," the Western Cooperative for Educational Telecommunications (WCET), www.wcet.info/resources/research/ (accessed April 2006). This Web site is sponsored by WICHE, the Western Interstate Commission for Higher Education. Many of the articles abstracted in the WCET review take as their point of departure Phipps and Merisotis's 1999 article "What's the Difference?" In their efforts to define

the problems and benefits in distance education, most emphasize that more mature and focused students are most likely to succeed, that course designers and instructors must stress the interactive features of the course, and that the technology must be compatible with student resources and not subject to glitches or breakdowns. For a useful case study that leads to such findings, see Herbert E. Muse, "At-Risk Factors for the Community College Web-based Student," presented at the 20th Annual Conference on Distance Teaching and Learning held at Madison, Wis., August 2004 (accessed April 2006).

38. Kimberly S. Young, "Internet Addiction: A New Clinical Phenomenon and Its Consequences," *American Behavioral Scientist* 48 (2004): 408.

39. See George P. Landow, *Hyper/Text/Theory* (Baltimore: Johns Hopkins University Press, 1994).

40. Edward R. Tufte, "PowerPoint Is Evil: Power Corrupts. PowerPoint Corrupts Absolutely," *Wired* 11, no. 9 (September 2003), at www.wired.com/wired/archive/11.09/ppt2.html (accessed March 2006). Tufte's monograph is titled *The Cognitive Style of PowerPoint,* 2nd ed. (Cheshire, Conn.: Graphics Press, 2002).

41. John Seely Brown, "Growing Up Digital: How the Web Changes Work, Education, and the Ways People Learn," *Change,* March–April 2000, p. 13. For a view that is more aware of student cognitive development and its needs, see Ed Neal, "Distance Education: Prospects and Problems," *National Journal: The Phi Kappa Phi Journal,* Winter 1999, pp. 40–43.

42. Brown, "Growing Up Digital," p. 19.

43. Ibid., p. 17.

44. For an overview of this problem, see Edward Tenner, "Searching for Dummies," *New York Times,* March 26, 2006, sec. 4, p. 12.

45. See the Purdue Writing Center help page for an excellent example of the uses of technology in writing instruction, "The OWL at Purdue," http://owl.english.purdue.edu/owl/ (accessed April 2005).

46. See Robert Kraut, Vicki Lundmark, Michael Patterson, Sara Kiesler, Tridas Mukopadhyay, and William Scherlis, "Internet Paradox: A Social Technology That Reduces Social Involvement and Psychological Well-Being?" *American Psychologist* 53 (1998): 1017–31.

47. Gary Rhoades, *Managed Professionals: Unionized Faculty and Restructuring Academic Labor* (Albany: State University of New York Press, 1998), pp. 179–86.

FIVE: A More Perfect Union

1. This chapter derives, in part, from a presentation on governance at the Association for the Study of Higher Education meeting of November 2002, in Sacramento, California, and my preface to *Competing Conceptions of Academic Governance: Negotiating the Perfect Storm,* William G. Tierney (Baltimore: Johns Hopkins University Press, 1999), pp. vii–xiv.

2. *Renewing the Academic Presidency: Stronger Leadership for Tougher Times* (Washington, D.C.: Association of Governing Boards of Universities and Colleges, 1996).

3. Albert J. Dunlap, with Bob Andelman, *Mean Business: How I Save Bad Companies and Make Good Companies Great* (New York: Times Business, 1996); Jack Welch,

with John A. Byrne, *Jack: Straight from the Gut* (New York: Warner Business Books, 2001).

4. In 2002, an editorial in *Business Week* noted that CEO compensation, increasingly disconnected to performance, has gotten "out of hand": "In 1980, CEO compensation was 42 times that of the average worker. In 2000, it was 531 times" ("CEOs: Why They're So Unloved," *Business Week,* April 22, 2002, p. 118).

5. Roger Bowen and Jane L. Buck, "College Presidents Are Hard-Working, Talented, and Vastly Overpaid," *Chronicle of Higher Education,* May 5, 2004, B24.

6. Stephen R. Covey, *The Seven Habits of Highly Effective People: Restoring the Character Ethic* (New York: Fireside Books, 1990), and *The 8th Habit: From Effectiveness to Greatness* (New York: Free Press, 2005); Michael Masterson, *Automatic Wealth: The Six Steps to Financial Independence* (Hoboken, N.J.: Wiley, 2005); Joe Vitale, *The Attractor Factor: 5 Easy Steps for Creating Wealth (or Anything Else) from the Inside Out* (Hoboken, N.J.: Wiley, 2005); Patrick Lencioni, *The Five Dysfunctions of a Team: A Leadership Fable* (San Francisco: Jossey-Bass, 2002); and Peter S. Pande, Robert P. Neuman, and Roland R. Cavanagh, *The Six Sigma Way: How GE, Motorola, and Other Top Companies Are Honing Their Performance* (New York: McGraw-Hill, 2000).

7. Michael Hammer and James Champy, *Reengineering the Corporation: A Manifesto for Business Revolution* (New York: HarperBusiness, 1993); see Art Kleiner, "Revisiting Engineering," *strategy + business,* 3rd quarter 2000, pp. 27–31.

8. The most revealing exposé of Enron's failure is Kurt Eichenwald's *Conspiracy of Fools* (New York: Broadway, 2005). See also Bethany McLean and Peter Elkind, *The Smartest Guys in the Room: The Amazing Rise and Scandalous Fall of Enron* (New York: Penguin, 2003).

9. One recent manifestation of this problem can be seen in the controversy over the appointment of John Bolton as U.S. ambassador to the United Nations, which grew out of the accusation that he tried to have a CIA agent fired for insisting on information counter to Bolton's desired outcome. There have been similar stories of retaliation in the Justice Department, the Food and Drug Administration, and NASA.

10. Alan Greenspan, "Corporate Governance," remarks at the Stern School of Business, New York University, New York, New York, March 26, 2002; available at www.federalreserve.gov/boarddocs/speeches/2002/200203262/default.htm (accessed April 2005).

11. It is no surprise that one of the comic productions of the managerial ethos is Scott Adams's cartoon, *Dilbert.* Trapped in a cubicle in an enterprise run by a stupid boss who has read all the management literature, Dilbert registers the existential absurdities of a workplace that has been drained of collective common sense by the recitation of managerial mantras. See Adams, *The Dilbert Principle: A Cubicle's-Eye View of Bosses, Meetings, Management Fads & Other Workplace Afflictions* (New York: HarperBusiness, 1996).

12. Peter Drucker, the prolific, and sometimes self-repeating, writer on management, is largely unknown to humanities faculty. I rely heavily on *Post-Capitalist Society* (New York: HarperBusiness, 1993) and *Managing in Turbulent Times* (New York: HarperBusiness, 1980), here quoting p. 133 of the latter.

13. For a short, handy guide to the main issues in government, see *Academic Governance: Charting a New Course,* a special issue of the Association of American Colleges and Universities' publication *Peer Review* (3, no. 3 [Spring 2001]), especially Ann S. Fer-

ren, William R. Kennan, and Stephen H. Lerch, "Reconciling Corporate and Academic Cultures," pp. 9–11.

14. James J. Duderstadt, *A University for the 21st Century* (Ann Arbor: University of Michigan Press, 2000), p. 240.

15. For a full study of management incursions into higher education, see Robert Birnbaum, *Management Fads in Higher Education: Where They Come From, What They Do, Why They Fail* (San Francisco: Jossey-Bass, 2001). On fads generally, see Joel Best, *Flavors of the Month: Why Smart People Fall for Fads* (Berkeley: University of California Press, 2006). And for *Forbes'* list of the top best-sellers of the "long boom," see Dan Ackman, "The 20 Most Influential Business Books," *Forbes.com,* September 30, 2002, www.forbes.com/2002/09/30/0930booksintro_2.html (accessed April 2005). Finally, an excellent analysis of management theory can be found in John Micklethwait and Adrian Wooldridge's *The Witch Doctors: Making Sense of the Management Gurus* (New York: Times Books, 1996).

16. See "Academic Freedom and Tenure: Bennington College," *Academe,* March–April 1995, pp. 91–103. See also Richard Chait, "Thawing the Cold War over Tenure: Why Academe Needs More Employment Options," *Chronicle of Higher Education,* February 7, 1997, B4.

17. Hammer and Champy used the success of their book to aid the fortunes of their now defunct consulting firm, CSC Index, though they are still featured on the speaking circuits for associations. The manipulation of the business best-seller market by their colleagues, Michael Treacy and Fred Wiersema, was revealed by *Business Week* in 1995. See Willy Stern, "Did Dirty Tricks Create a Best Seller?" *Business Week,* August 7, 1995, pp. 22–25.

18. For a short, contemporaneous (1996) description of this crisis from a faculty point of view, see Kinley Brauer (then chair of Minnesota's history department), "The Tenure Crisis at Minnesota," *OAH Newsletter,* www.oah.org/pubs/nl/96nov/brauer1196 .html (accessed April 2005). Gary Engstrand, administrative assistant for the Faculty Consultative Committee at Minnesota, has compiled a voluminous unpublished document that quotes every important memo, news article, and actor in this episode: "It Is from Small Missteps that Great Tragedies Grow: Tenure and the Drive for Collective Bargaining at the University of Minnesota—Events, Commentaries, and Lessons."

19. For a full account of the Bennington situation, both the initial episode and later events, see "Academic Freedom and Tenure: Bennington College"; "Bennington College: A Supplementary Report on a Censured Administration," *Academe,* January–February 1998, pp. 70–75; and "AAUP Protests Curbs on Academic Freedom at Bennington College," *Academe,* July–August 2000, pp. 17–19.

20. My informant was Carolyn Williams, professor in the School of Public Health and a member of the Academic Health Center at Minnesota. It was she who suddenly appeared in my Washington office one day in 1995, pulled out a copy of *Reengineering the Corporation,* and said, "Read this!" Although Carolyn could not vote in the union election that was held later—the Academic Health Center was not in the defined bargaining unit—she was a leading figure in analyzing the forces at work in the Minnesota crisis.

21. See Sheila Slaughter and Larry L. Leslie, *Academic Capitalism: Politics, Policies, and the Entrepreneurial University* (Baltimore: Johns Hopkins University Press, 1997).

22. David Kirp, *Shakespeare, Einstein, and the Bottom Line: The Marketing of Higher Education* (Cambridge, Mass.: Harvard University Press, 2003).

23. Slaughter and Leslie, *Academic Capitalism*, pp. 228–31, 241.

24. Quoted in "Report of the ADE Ad Hoc Committee on Governance," *ADE Bulletin*, no. 129 (Fall 2001): 4–13. See also Charles B. Harris, "The Downsizing of the American Mind: Academic Citizenship and the Current Crisis," *ADE Bulletin*, no. 121 (Winter 1998): 25–28.

25. See "AGB Statement on Institutional Governance" in *AGB Statement on Institutional Governance and Governing in the Public Trust: External Influences on Colleges and Universities* (Washington, D.C.: Association of Governing Boards of Universities and Colleges, 2003), pp. 1–13. For the MLA report, see "Report of the ADE Ad Hoc Committee on Governance."

26. The Modern Language Association and the American Association of University Professors have collaborated in writing and publishing a volume on collective bargaining in the academy—Ernst Benjamin and Michael Mauer, eds., *Academic Collective Bargaining* (Washington, D.C.: AAUP; New York: MLA, 2006)—for which I have written an introduction; see especially the essays by Patricia Gumport, Ernst Benjamin, and Gary Rhoades.

27. There is, however, an annual conference held at the Hunter College campus of CUNY where members of academic management and labor—mostly from the highly unionized northeastern states—meet to discuss issues of mutual concern. The National Center for the Study of Collective Bargaining in Higher Education and the Professions publishes an annual anthology of papers presented at this conference. For an excellent example of administrative appreciation of "mature" union activity in governance, see Daniel J. Julius, "Making Collective Bargaining Work," in ibid., pp. 196–212.

28. See Gary Rhoades, *Managed Professionals: Unionized Faculty and Restructuring Academic Labor* (Albany: State University of New York Press, 1998), p. 15.

29. "AGB Statement on Institutional Governance," p. 10.

30. Rhoades, *Managed Professionals*, p. 131.

s i x : Superstars and Rookies of the Year

1. This chapter derives in part from essays that have appeared in publications of the Modern Language Association, the Association of Departments of English, and the American Association of University Professors.

2. "UA Leads Nation with Six Students Named to USA Today's All-USA College Academic Team," February 15, 2006, available at www.ua.edu (accessed March 2006). The criteria for the *USA Today* contest, not made clear by the University of Alabama Web page, center on students' ability to describe their contributions; see "All-USA College Academic Team: About and Advice," USAToday.com, updated September 23, 2005, www.usatoday.com/news/education/2004-08-12-2005-colllege-team_x.htm (accessed March 2006).

3. Robert H. Frank and Philip J. Cook, *The Winner-Take-All Society: Why the Few at the Top Get So Much More Than the Rest of Us* (1995; reprint, New York: Penguin, 1996), p. 24. This work is hereafter cited parenthetically in the text.

4. National Commission on the Cost of Higher Education, *Straight Talk about College Costs and Prices: Report of the National Commission on the Cost of Higher Education* (Phoenix: Oryx Press, 1998), p. 14.

5. See the annual salary reports published by the American Association of University Professors in *Academe*'s March–April issue.

6. National Commission on the Cost of Higher Education, *Straight Talk about College Costs and Prices*, p. 24.

7. For an excellent analysis of the relations between college costs, cutting faculty, and competing for research standing, with convincing numbers, see William C. Symonds, "College in Crisis," *Business Week Online*, April 28, 2003, www.businessweek.com (accessed February 2005).

8. As we will see in more detail in chapter 7, Sheila Slaughter and Larry L. Leslie argue in *Academic Capitalism: Politics, Policies, and the Entrepreneurial University* (Baltimore: Johns Hopkins University Press, 1997) that the competitive research drive, "academic capitalism," derives more from "resource dependence." In the removal of federal and state funding from higher education, faculty have had to seek alternatives. See especially pp. 234–35.

9. Stephen J. Dubner, "Toward a Unified Theory of Black America," *New York Times Magazine*, March 20, 2005, pp. 54–59.

10. Thomas Kuhn, *The Structure of Scientific Revolutions*, 2nd ed. (Chicago: University of Chicago Press, 1970).

11. See Brenda Maddox, "The Double Helix and the 'Wronged Heroine,'" *Nature* 421 (January 23, 2003): 407–8; see also James D. Watson, *The Double Helix: A Personal Account of the Discovery of the Structure of DNA* (London: Weidenfeld and Nicolson, 1968).

12. MLA Ad Hoc Committee on the Future of Scholarly Publishing, "The Future of Scholarly Publishing," in *Profession 2002* (New York: MLA, 2002), pp. 172–86. See, especially, "Recommendations for Departments," p. 183.

13. The Center for Higher Education Studies at the University of California, Berkeley, has launched a special project on scholarly communication that has generated excellent discussions of the economic crisis in scholarly publication affecting schools, libraries, and faculty. Behind the discussions that I have attended, there lurks the question of how journals are used to "credential" the work of faculty on the hiring and retention market. When this process spawns expensive publications, owned by global conglomerates, many experts advise organized resistance from disciplinary groups, faculty, and universities, though none has advocated unilateral disarmament in the scholarly race. See "The Future of Scholarly Communication," http://cshe.berkeley .edu/projects/scholarlycomm/index.html (accessed March 2005).

14. "Carnegie Foundation Changes Richmond's Classification," *Richmond Matters*, December 1, 2004, http://oncampus.richmond.edu/news/ricmat/volume7/708a.html (accessed March 2005).

15. See John Lombardi, "How Classifications Can Help Colleges," *Chronicle of Higher Education*, September 8, 2000, B24.

16. I use this term advisedly for John Lombardi, who has had a successful administrative career in higher education, with some controversy along the way. I first knew him as a faculty colleague; and when he was my dean at Indiana, I found his clear views and methods refreshing and fair.

17. See John Gravois, "Holding Pattern in the Humanities," *Chronicle of Higher Education*, March 11, 2005, A10–12.

18. Leon Fink, "The Unbearable Heaviness of Being Harvard," *Chronicle of Higher*

Education, April 1, 2005, B5. The "Summers" reforms of the undergraduate curriculum at Harvard include the recommendation that the institution pledge itself to hiring and retaining junior faculty.

SEVEN: The Case of the Firecracker Boys

1. The health of peer review has been the subject of much debate, especially after the criticisms of current practices leveled by Arnold S. Relman, then editor of the *New England Journal of Medicine,* in the early 1990s. For a more current summary of issues, see Merrill Goozner, "Unrevealed: Non-Disclosure of Conflicts of Interest in Four Leading Medical and Scientific Journals," July 12, 2004, Center for Science and the Public Interest, Washington, D.C., www.cspinet.org/new/pdf/unrevealed_final.pdf (accessed July 2005).

2. Government oversight of standards should be equally trustworthy, but the controversies of the past ten years suggest that government scientists may now be at risk if they render views that conflict with one interest or another. Recent efforts to deny civil service protections to government employees point to a further diminution of the authority of these scientists. So does the practice of giving supervisory positions to political appointees and of appointing members of review committees according to their political leanings. The American Association for the Advancement of Science has issued a statement identifying and condemning these developments: see "AAAS Resolution Regarding Membership on Federal Advisory Committees," March 3, 2003, www.aaas.org/news/releases/2003/0305fair2.shtml (accessed July 2005).

3. Stephen H. Balch, president of the National Association of Scholars, made this point in an article titled "The Antidote to Academic Orthodoxy" in the *Chronicle of Higher Education* (April 23, 2004, B7): "The first step to reform, then, is to admit the differences that exist among divergent fields of inquiry. In some, the classic paradigm of scientific investigation is largely realized, and internalized checks can be more or less relied upon to keep things on the straight and narrow. In others, rationalist aspirations are too clouded by passion and prejudice to prevail long without extra reinforcement."

4. There is some question about Teller's motives and whether this project was really a cover for continuing work on nuclear bombs during Eisenhower's negotiations with the Soviet Union for a moratorium on testing. See Dan O'Neill, *The Firecracker Boys* (New York: St. Martin's Press, 1994), pp. 48–51; my account draws extensively on this book.

5. O'Neill points out that the description of the Livermore and AEC publicists as "firecracker boys" was coined by a fisheries teacher named Tom English, who was one of the early skeptics about the project among the University of Alaska faculty (ibid., p. 69).

6. See ibid., pp. 51ff.

7. William Pruitt, quoted in ibid., p. 82.

8. O'Neill, *The Firecracker Boys,* p. 162.

9. William R. Wood, quoted in ibid., p. 177.

10. Professor Pruitt has expressed to me his belief that if Johnson had been present, things might have gone differently (telephone conversation, June 21, 2005).

11. Pruitt, quoted in O'Neill, *The Firecracker Boys,* p. 197.

12. Ibid., p. 259 (also phone conversation with Pruitt).

13. Donna Demac, *Liberty Denied: The Current Rise of Censorship in America* (New Brunswick, N.J.: Rutgers University Press, 1990), p. 93.

14. Richard Feynman, *The Pleasure of Finding Things Out: The Best Short Works of Richard P. Feynman*, ed. Jeffrey Robbins (Cambridge, Mass.: Perseus Books, 1999), pp. 168–69.

15. The administration at Washington University has won AAUP's Alexander Meiklejohn Award for Academic Freedom two times. The first award was given to Chancellor Ethan A. H. Shepley in 1959, on the basis of a nomination written by Barry Commoner. The second went to former chancellor William Danforth in 2000 on the basis of a nomination written by Michael Friedlander.

16. In *Academic Capitalism,* Sheila Slaughter and Larry Leslie suggest that the most significant shifts in university dependence on the marketplace, especially the global marketplace, began in the 1980s (*Academic Capitalism: Politics, Policies, and the Entrepreneurial University* [Baltimore: Johns Hopkins University Press, 1997], p. 5). Slaughter and Leslie's book is an essential study based on data concerning the shifts of academic science to a market orientation, and I owe a major debt to their work.

17. The comment is quoted in Neil Tudiver, *Universities for Sale: Resisting Corporate Control over Canadian Higher Education,* CAUT Series (Toronto: James Lorimer, 1999), p. 145. Slaughter and Leslie offer evidence in *Academic Capitalism* (p. 17) that Canadian universities have been more resistant to changes caused by the globalization of "Western" universities than those in Australia, the United Kingdom, and the United States.

18. See Peter Miskell, "How Crest Made Business History," *Harvard Business School Working Knowledge,* electronic newsletter, January 17, 2005, http://hbswk.hbs.edu/item.jhtml?id=4574&t=innovation (accessed July 2005).

19. See "University Inventions That Changed the World," University of Virginia Patent Foundation, www.uvapf.org/index.cfm/fuseaction/viewpage/page_id/115 (accessed July 2005).

20. "Genentech: Researcher Profiles, Richard Scheller," www.gene.com/gene/research/sci-profiles/research/scheller/index.jsp, "Genentech: Researcher Profiles: Marc Tessier-Lavigne," www.gene.com/gene/research/sci-profiles/research/t-lavigne/index.jsp (accessed July 2005).

21. Diane Harley, Michael Maher, Jonathan Henke, and Shannon Lawrence, "An Analysis of Technology Enhancements in a Large Lecture Course," *Educause Quarterly* 26, no. 3 (2003): 28.

22. "Biology 1A: UC Berkeley, Spring Semester 2005," http://mcb.berkeley.edu/courses/bio1a/Spring2005/Intro_SP05.html (accessed July 2005).

23. For an interesting and suggestive study of this issue in a large science classroom, see Harley et al., "An Analysis of Technology Enhancements," pp. 32–33.

24. Richard Feynman, as told to Ralph Leighton, *"Surely You're Joking, Mr. Feynman!" Adventures of a Curious Character,* ed. Edward Hutchings (New York: Bantam Books, 1986), p. 166.

25. Jasper Rine, quoted in "University of California, Berkeley, Distinguished Teaching Awards 1997: Jasper Rine," April 3, 1997, http://teaching.berkeley.edu/dta97/rine.html (accessed March 2005).

26. See "News and Highlights: IBM Launches 'Transition to Teaching' Program," September 19, 2005, www.ibm.com/ibm/ibmgives/news/transition_to_teaching.shtml (accessed March 2005).

27. David Blumenthal, "Training Tomorrow's Doctors: The Medical Education Mission of Academic Health Centers," The Commonwealth Fund, April 2002, p. 30, available at www.cmwf.org/publications/publications_show.htm?doc_id=221258 (accessed March 2005).

28. Bruce Alberts, "Summing Up: Creating a Scientific Temper for the World," president's address at the 142nd Annual Meeting of the National Academy of Sciences, Washington, D.C., May 2, 2005, p. 9, available at www.nasonline.org/site/DocServer/speech2005.pdf?docID=741 (accessed July 2005).

29. "A Report on the Harvard College Curricular Review: Summary of Principle Recommendations," p. 1, available at www.fas.harvard.edu/curriculum-review/report.html (accessed March 2005).

30. Lisa Randall, "Dangling Particles," op-ed, *New York Times*, September 18, 2005.

31. See Andrew C. Revkin, "Bush Aide Edited Climate Reports," *New York Times*, June 8, 2005.

32. See "Faith-Based Parks," Public Employees for Environmental Responsibility, www.peer.org/campaigns/faith-based/index.php (accessed July 2005).

33. "It's All Happening at the Tulsa Zoo," editorial, *New York Times*, July, 10, 2005.

34. Alberts, "Summing Up," pp. 2–3.

35. Nicholas Wolterstorff, "Ivory Tower or Holy Mountain? Faith and Academic Freedom," *Academe*, January–February 2001, pp. 19–20.

36. The details of the Sokal controversy were published in *Lingua Franca*. The reactions to it have varied from a dismissive brush-off from the left to glee on the right. David Kirp reads the controversy as a sign of divisions and power struggles within NYU; see *Shakespeare, Einstein, and the Bottom Line: The Marketing of Higher Education* (Cambridge, Mass.: Harvard University Press, 2003), pp. 80–85.

37. Transcripts of the Millennial Evening of October 12, 1999, are available on several Internet sites. See, for example, "Millennium Evening at the White House: Informatics Meets Genomics," December 22, 2003, www.rand.org/scitech/stpi/ourfuture/Rosetta/millennium.html#top (accessed July 2005).

38. See [U.K.] Department of Trade and Industry, Office of Science and Technology, "Excellence and Opportunity: A Science and Innovation Policy for the 21st Century," chap. 4, available at www.ost.gov.uk/enterprise/dtiwhite/ (accessed June 2005).

39. Dan O'Neill, personal communication with the author.

40. For a partisan version of the firing, see John Creed, "Fairbanks Daily News-Miner Demonstration Draws Large, Sign-Carrying Crowd Supporting Fired Writers," April 19, 2002, www.nonukesnorth.net/Creedlongversion.htm; for O'Neill's collected columns on Poker Flats, see "Dan O'Neill's Columns," www.nonukesnorth.net/ONeillscolumns.htm (accessed July 2005).

EIGHT: The Disposable Faculty

1. "Okay, We Give Up," editorial, *Scientific American*, April 2005, p. 10.

2. See the Web sites of the American Association for the Advancement of Science (www.aaas.org) and the Union of Concerned Scientists (www.ucsusa.org).

3. American Association of Higher Education (AAHE) information sheet, "The New Pathways II: Academic Careers for a New Century from Inquiry to Practice" (n.d.).

4. I noted in chapter 7 that conservative criticism of the humanities and social sciences curriculum absolved science from accusations of political bias for the very reason that facts speak for themselves. Creationists have not given science a pass, however.

5. Louis Menand, *The Metaphysical Club: A Story of Ideas in America* (New York: Farrar, Straus and Giroux, 2001), p. 431.

6. Ibid., p. 432.

7. Menand suggests that Dewey played a major part in writing the declaration, but Jordan Kurland of AAUP's Committee A reports that Dewey had little to do with writing the statement. Its main author was Frank A. Fetter (economics, Princeton), with Lovejoy contributing substantially. It was, after all, a committee report. The other signatories to it were among the most important thinkers of their time. The full list is available with the text of the Declaration in AAUP, *Policy Documents & Reports*, ed. B. Robert Kreiser, 9th ed. (Washington, D.C.: The Association, 2001), pp. 291–301. This statement is also available online at www.aaup.org/statements/Redbook/1940stat.htm (accessed August 2005).

8. The phrase belongs to Holmes; see Menand, *The Metaphysical Club*, p. 431. Holmes's decisions helped ally the courts with the concept of academic freedom.

9. AAUP, *Policy Documents & Reports*, p. 297.

10. Walter Metzger, "The First Investigation," *AAUP Bulletin* 47 (1961): 206, 208.

11. Thomas S. Kuhn cites Lovejoy's book as one of the major influences on his own thinking in *The Structure of Scientific Revolutions* (2nd ed. [Chicago: University of Chicago Press, 1970])—a study that has itself been immensely significant in our contemporary understanding of the forms of perception on which science has been constructed.

12. Menand, *The Metaphysical Club*, p. 298.

13. AAUP, *Policy Documents & Reports*, p. 295.

14. Ibid., p. 294.

15. Ibid., pp. 300–301.

16. Ibid., pp. 3–7.

17. The AAUP's collection *Policy Documents & Reports*, also known as the "Redbook," contains the first tenure statement and its revisions as well as numerous other statements of principle. It has become an essential manual for personnel and ethical practices in higher education, and is often quoted verbatim in the contracts for faculty appointments.

18. A useful account of court findings can be found in Erwin Chemerinsky's "Is Tenure Necessary to Protect Academic Freedom?" *American Behavioral Scientist* 41 (1988): 638–51.

19. AAUP, "1940 Statement of Principles on Academic Freedom and Tenure with 1970 Interpretive Comments," in *Policy Documents & Reports*, pp. 3–7; see also www.aaup.org/statements/Redbook/1940stat.htm (accessed March 2006).

20. The Harvard Project on Faculty Appointments convened a panel on academic freedom and freedom of the press in 1998. The findings were not published, but my perception as a participant was that individual journalists had little protection compared with the protections for faculty. See also David M. Rabban's remarks at the 2000 AAUP Annual Meeting as reported in "Annual Meeting Explores Intellectual Freedom," *Academe*, September–October 2000, p. 17.

21. Ernest L. Boyer, *Scholarship Reconsidered: Priorities of the Professoriate* (Princeton: Carnegie Foundation for the Advancement of Teaching, 1990), pp. 78–80.

22. Ibid., pp. 65–66.

23. Charles E. Glassick, Mary Taylor Huber, and Gene I. Maeroff, in *Scholarship Assessed: Evaluation of the Professoriate* (San Francisco: Jossey-Bass, 1997), cite research that shows that faculty and administrators blame one another for failure to reward teaching (pp. 51–53).

24. R. Eugene Rice, "Making a Place for the New American Scholar," Working Paper Series, Inquiry #1 (Washington, D.C.: AAHE, 1996), pp. 10–11; this paper is hereafter cited parenthetically in the text. The fourteen papers from the series are now available as a set from Stylus Publishing (1998).

25. Rice further discusses some of his findings, and those of his colleague Ann E. Austin, in the New Pathways publication *Heeding New Voices: Academic Careers for a New Generation*, ed. Rice, Austin, and Mary Deane Sorcinelli (Sterling, Va.: Stylus Publishing, 2000).

26. The word *contingent* is now the preferred designation for non-tenure-track and part-time faculty. According to the AAUP's most recent policy statement on the matter, "the term calls attention to the tenuous relationship between academic institutions and the part- and full-time non-tenure-track faculty members who teach in them." See AAUP, "Policy Statement: Contingent Appointments and the Academic Profession," November 9, 2003, www.aaup.org/statements/SpchState/Statements/contingent.htm (accessed August 2005).

27. Emerson's 1837 essay "The American Scholar" is widely available; see, for example, the *American Transcendental Web*, www.vcu.edu/engweb/transcendentalism/authors/emerson/essays/amscholar.html (accessed August 2005).

28. "New Pathways: Faculty Careers and Employment in the 21st Century: A Preliminary Statement for Consideration by Colleagues," March 7, 1997 (flyer).

29. J. Peter Byrne, "Inquiry 5: Academic Freedom without Tenure?" Working Paper Series (Washington, D.C.: AAHE, 1997), p. 15.

30. Ibid., p. 10.

31. Ibid., p. 16.

32. Peter Byrne, "Constitutional Academic Freedom in Scholarship and in Court," *Chronicle of Higher Education*, January 5, 2001, B13.

33. AAUP, *Policy Documents & Reports*, p. 300.

34. David W. Breneman, "Alternatives to Tenure for the Next Generation of Academics," Working Paper Series, Inquiry #14 (Washington, D.C.: AAHE, 1997), pp. 1–2; this paper is hereafter cited parenthetically in this section of the text.

35. Judith M. Gappa and David W. Leslie, *The Invisible Faculty: Improving the Status of Part-Timers in Higher Education* (San Francisco: Jossey-Bass, 1993); Leslie and Gappa, "Two Faculties or One? The Conundrum of Part-Timers in a Bifurcated Workforce," Working Paper Series, Inquiry #6 (Washington, D.C.: AAHE, 1997).

36. AAUP, "Policy Statement: Contingent Appointments and the Academic Profession."

37. Coalition on the Academic Workforce home page, "About CAW," www.academicworkforce.org/about/index.cfm (accessed August 2005).

38. Breneman, "Alternatives to Tenure," p. 13.

39. Henry Rosovsky, "Some Thoughts about University Governance," in *Gover-*

nance in Higher Education: The University in a State of Flux, ed. Werner Z. Hirsch and Luc E. Weber (London: Economica, 2001), p. 101.

40. This Web page, www.studentsforacademicfreedom.org (accessed August 2005), presents all the major documents in the movement—including the main statements against its aims and methods.

41. Azar Nafisi, *Reading Lolita in Tehran: A Memoir in Books* (New York: Random House, 2004), p. 193.

42. AAUP, "Academic Bill of Rights," December 2003, www.aaup.org/statements/ SpchState/Statements/billofrights.htm (accessed August 2005).

N I N E : Staging a Comeback

1. Bill Readings, *The University in Ruins* (Cambridge, Mass.: Harvard University Press, 1996), p. 129. I cannot quote from Readings's work without recording my personal sense of loss at his untimely death in 1994.

2. Martin Finkelstein, "The Morphing of the American Academic Profession," *Liberal Education,* Fall 2003, pp. 6–15; quotation, p. 14.

3. Paul Lauter, "From Adelphi to Enron," *Academe,* November–December 2002, pp. 28–32.

4. Advertisement for Adelphi, quoted in Al Ries and Laura Ries, *The Fall of Advertising and the Rise of PR* (New York: HarperBusiness, 2002), pp. 142–43.

5. See Aldelphi University's "Fact Sheet 2004–05," www.adelphi.edu/about/facts .php (accessed March 2006).

6. AAUP, "Policy Statement: Contingent Appointments and the Academic Profession," November 9, 2003, www.aaup.org/statements/SpchState/Statements/contingent .htm (accessed September 2005). See Gary R. Matthews, "Contract Issues Continue to Percolate and Brew," *WMU AAUP Advocate,* October 2002, pp. 1–3; Piper Fogg, "Widening the Tenure Track," *Chronicle of Higher Education,* January 3, 2003, A8; and Article 20 of the WMU AAUP contract, www.wmich.edu/aaup/contract/2002_2005_ Contract.pdf (accessed March 2006).

7. Ariel L. H. Anderson, "From Your Contract Administrator," *WMU AAUP Advocate,* September 2002, p. 3.

8. Western Michigan's 2005–2008 contract is available online, at the AAUP chapter's Web site; see www.wmich.edu/aaup/news/index.php (accessed August 2005).

9. Limitations of academic freedom because of religious aims are accepted under AAUP's 1940 statement on tenure so long as they are clearly expressed at the time of hiring. See AAUP, "1940 Statement of Principles on Academic Freedom and Tenure with 1970 Interpretive Comments," August 2004, www.aaup.org/statements/Redbook/ 1940stat.htm (accessed March 2006).

10. David A. Hoekema, "Academic Freedom at a Pervasively Protestant Place (alternative alliteration: a Curiously Calvinist College)," presentation at "Academic Freedom at Religiously Affiliated Institutions," conference sponsored by the Association of American University Professors, Chicago, October 24–26, 1997, www.calvin.edu/admin/ provost/pubs/aaup.htm (accessed August 2005).

11. "An Open Letter to the President of the United States of America, George W. Bush," *Detroit News,* May 20, 2005; available at www.commondreams.org/views05/ 0520-27.htm (accessed March 2006).

Index